PHILOSOPHY AND
THE HISTORICAL UNDERSTANDING

PHILOSOPHY AND THE HISTORICAL UNDERSTANDING

W. B. GALLIE

Second Edition

SCHOCKEN BOOKS · NEW YORK

To Menna Gallie

CONTENTS

Drum, da gehäuft sind rings
Die Gipfel der Zeit,
Und die Liebsten nahe wohnen, ermattend auf
Getrenntesten Bergen,
So gib unschuldig Wasser,
O Fittiche gib uns, treuesten Sinns
Hinüberzugehn und wiederzukehren.

Hölderlin, *Patmos*

PREFACE TO THE FIRST EDITION

IN this book I have attempted a new approach to two central and closely connected problems in the philosophy of history. In my first five chapters I have tried to give an intelligible account of the kind of understanding that is commonly ascribed to historians and is commonly contrasted with the understanding that is achieved in the natural sciences. Then, in the light of this account, I try in the remaining five chapters to show the relevance of historical considerations to political life, to the practice of science and, in more detail, to the practice and problems of philosophy.

What is new in my account of historical understanding is the emphasis that I have put on the idea of narrative. I have tried to analyse what it means to follow a narrative and have argued that whatever understanding and whatever explanations a work of history contains must be assessed in relation to the narrative from which they arise and whose development they subserve. What is new in my account of philosophical methods and problems is the claim that, when we regard them from an historical point of view, we can fully appreciate their intellectual importance without denying or trying to cover up the fact that, whilst philosophical methods have long been in a more or less continuous state of revolution, the central problems of philosophy survive successive revolutions with surprisingly little change. In particular, I have tried to show that certain philosophical ideas can fulfil their proper philosophical function only so long as they continue to be the subjects of apparently endless philosophical conflicts and debates.

An abridged version of Chapters 2 to 5 has appeared in *History and Theory*, Vol. III, No. 2, 1963; and some passages of Chapters 7 and 8 are taken from articles which I have published in *Philosophy* (Vol. XXIV, No. 9, 1949), in *The Philosophical Quarterly* (Vol. 6, No. 23, 1956), in the *Aristotelian Society*

PREFACE

Proceedings (NS, Vol. LVI, 1956) and in the *British Journal for the Philosophy of Science* (Vol. VIII, No. 30, 1957). I thank the editors concerned for permission to reprint these materials.

I also wish to thank Mr W. W. Bartley for some useful criticisms; and I cannot adequately express my debt to Ann Greer for the inexhaustible patience which she has shown in helping to prepare my manuscript for publication.

W.B.G.

The Queen's University of Belfast

PREFACE TO THE SECOND EDITION

THE writing of this book was an essay in revivalism. I wanted to breathe new life into a way of philosophising which had shot up vigourously around the turn of the last century, only to be ploughed under and forgotten among the rapidly succeeding waves of philosophical fashion. The central idea of that movement, of which Windelband and Rickert and later Croce and Collingwood were the main spokesmen, was that the way we understand history is basically the same as that in which we understand all purposive thought and action, and radically unlike the way in which we understand natural phenomena as instances of some scientific law or theory. More specifically, the writers just mentioned affirmed that in history we understand *particular* thoughts and actions in respect to their aptness or un-aptness for their particular contexts, so that in history to understand *what* happened is also to understand *why* it happened; and they succeeded in drawing out some interesting implications from this central insight. But none of them found for his thesis a sufficiently clear-cut and arresting starting-point from which to shake the entrenched presuppositions of the dominant empiricist epistemology of our age. And none of them succeeded in conveying the characteristically philosophical importance of his thesis, viz., its relevance to the whole range of human knowledge. The result is that their writings have been taken to be of primarily methodological concern, and so peripheral to the main issues of philosophy.

I have tried in this book to make good these two failures of the Windelband-Collingwood school. In the first place I have tried to supply their thesis with what I believe to be its proper starting-point, the concept of a story, regarded as a form of human understanding *sui generis* and as the basis of all historical thought and knowledge. To begin with the latter point: Although there are obviously many different

1

forms of historiography, it seems to me no less obvious that narrative history is the basic form. The question whether such-and-such materials or techniques or interpretations or explanations are historical in character is ultimately decided by asking Do they contribute, however indirectly, towards the description and substantiation of something that is *worth narrating*, something that is *worth following through* stage by stage to a known or at least vaguely adumbrated conclusion? I have expressed this claim by saying, in terminology adapted from Professor Popper's philosophy of science, that, as in the sciences there is always a theory, so in history there is always a story—or at least the presumption or hope of a story. And, to pursue the analogy a little, just as an investigation becomes scientific only as a result of critical dissatisfaction with received theories and the consequent desire to find an agreed method for testing and selecting among these, so an investigation becomes history only when critical minds are impelled to devise tests for the vague and often inconsistent claims to truth which most traditional stories contain. But, of course (to show the limitation of the analogy), whereas in the sciences a phenomenon is selected for study as a promising starting-point for the discovery of more comprehensive and systematic explanations and theories, an incident or action cries out for historical investigation primarily because it is memorable, story-worthy, and because it embodies one of those failures or achievements, opportunities lost or taken, which we want to know about, to understand in the most intimate relation to its total context, either for its own sake or because of its continuity or comparability with our own concerns.

These claims, however, evidently depend upon how we answer the questions What makes an action story-worthy?, What is a story?, and What does it mean to follow a story? I have worked out my answers to these questions in Chapter 2, but it may be useful to restate my answer to the first of them here. To be story-worthy, an action must be in a broad sense an adventure. Its circumstances and occasion must contain notable elements of surprise, accident, and the unforeseeable. In other words, it is non-routine and so cannot be judged for aptness or un-aptness, for merited success or failure, by general criteria derived from previous similar instances. It can be understood only as a venture, as an attack on a new problem or an attempted adaptation to the unforeseen. As such, it requires us to follow it through on its own terms, viz., in terms of the purposes and values that prompt it, the calculations that direct it, the resolution or inspiration that sustains it. This means that every such action has to be read by its overt manifestations. Such reading may be tentative or dubious and is always liable to contain a greater or lesser amount of error. Nevertheless, story-worthy actions, in the sense here explained, play a most important part in revealing and establishing the over-all quality of the individuals to whom we ascribe them. Routine and habitual actions may occupy ninety-nine point nine per cent of life; but non-routine ventures, story-worthy actions, supply an essential test of the moral and intellectual vitality underlying our habits and routines. They occasion the breaks in the seemingly steadfast continuity of a life, they disclose the flaws in a character, or, as may be, they confirm an impression of unfailing initiative and vigour. Small wonder that individuals, families, institutions, and nations build their memories and histories around story-worthy events!

From this account of what makes actions story-worthy, it is fairly easy to derive an account of what makes a story, and of what it means to follow a story, and I have done my best to answer these questions in Chapter 2. But even if it were ideally elucidated, the concept of a story would not provide a complete answer to the question What is history? or even provide the one and only really important clue to the correct answer to that question. What I do claim for my own answer, however, is that it helps us to see much more precisely why historical understanding must differ in kind from the understanding that is the goal of the sciences. History is, of course, always much more than story: all history contains elements of interpretation, generalisation, reflective discussion, and explanation, some but by no means all of which I have touched on in my attempt to apply the concept of a story to the problems of historical understanding. Whether or how far I have succeeded in this task, to which the first half of this book is devoted, and whether the concept of a story is equal to the job I have assigned to it, I will not try to decide here. I will say only that, on the whole, the first half of the book has been well received by historians and has enjoyed a better reception from philosophers than has the second half. I therefore feel reasonably confident that I have done something to revive interest in the main philosophical claim of the Windelband-Collingwood school.

There is, however, one grave gap in the earlier chapters of this book that I must mention. For purposes of exposition I have naturally tended to work with instances of historical understanding in which individuals or groups or successions of individuals play a predominant part, as opposed to instances in which what we understand is an institution, technique, or doctrine, or any mass phenomenon, whether static or changing; and I have gone so far as to urge that the act of following (and especially of following story-worthy events) is always directed primarily onto individuals. Now set against this is the clear fact that in a good deal of cultural history—histories of the arts and the sciences and of technologies and all 'pre-history'—the required story-worthy individuals are not to be found. In Chapter 4 I have tried to meet this difficulty by my doctrine of 'dummy variables', i.e., X's whose identity we have no means or hope of establishing; and I have no wish to go back upon what I have written on this topic. Nevertheless, it remains true that our historical interest is sometimes directed to the development or decline of such abstractions as a style of composing, building, or fighting, a method of government, a legal system, or even a mass movement of peoples, *quite irrespective* of the individuals who sustained or failed to sustain them. Or, to urge the point in more positive fashion, do we not sometimes want to follow the course of such an abstraction for its own sake, conceived, so to speak, as a *persona* on the historical scene, or at least as a set of communicable skills and habits of thought having life possibilities quite as story-worthy as those of any individual artist or lawgiver or man of action? Here we are faced with the Nominalist/Realist dilemma, as it applies to historical understanding, in a much clearer and more pressing form than I have recognised and discussed in Chapter 4; and the issue is certainly not one that can be decided by *a priori* considerations. There are areas of human thought in which progress depends upon our readiness to reify our abstractions, e.g., in mathematics; and there are areas in which our readiness to do so leads to nothing but sophistry and absurdity, e.g., in 'faculty' physics and psychology; and again there are areas, such as that under consideration, where the right course is very far from clear and where it will not be attained without a great deal of further investigation and debate. Nor is the issue here merely one of philosophical concern. The question of the relevance of historical considerations to the social sciences, and consequently of the proper methods and aims of these sciences, is clearly bound up with it. In these sciences, is the historical approach, with its emphasis upon story-worthy events, in some way privileged? Is the understanding of an institution 'from within'—which always also means from the standpoint of its past—to be preferred in principle to the kind of understanding afforded by comparative methods and causal analysis? Some of the ablest and most penetrating of my critics, in particular Professor Ernest Gellner, have made me recognise how much is yet required to be done with questions such as these before the task I have set myself in the first half of my book can be regarded as complete.

This gap in my development of the concept of a story has entailed a further disadvantage. It accounts for some of the difficulties critics have had over the last four chapters of my book. Some have complained that these are a mere miscellany of essays on different aspects of philosophy, linked only by the vague historicist claims that are voiced in the course of them. In fact, these chapters provide the second leg of my attempt to rescue and revive the teachings of the Windelband-Collingwood school, by showing their relevance to the whole range of human knowledge. It seemed to me that this might be done at a single stroke by asking whether and in what way historical considerations, interpreted in the light of my earlier chapters, apply to the key concepts of philosophy. For these would appear to provide the least probable or plausible test case for the thesis in question (if we exclude the purely formal concepts of mathematics) and should therefore, on falsificationist principles, be considered first and be counted as crucial. But this procedure would no doubt have been more easily appreciated if it had been preceded by a general argument affirming the continuity that runs from our understanding of particular historic actions and incidents *via* our understanding of political, legal, or religious institutions and of the beliefs on which these institutions depend, to our appreciation of the most general philosophical concepts which these beliefs themselves embody. In brief, it would have been wiser to defend the necessity of a historical approach across this whole spectrum of topics before testing out that claim on its ostensibly least plausible instance. And this would of course have required, as a first step, the filling of the gap discussed in the preceding paragraph.

Despite these difficulties, the basic aim of my last four chapters can be explained easily enough. Almost all great philosophies have revolved around the point of intersection of two lines of speculation: the one seeking to relate subject to object, or mind to the world, and the other seeking to relate what is changing and contingent to what is timeless and necessary. Thus, all classic epistemologies have tried to explain the possibility of knowledge either by equating what is knowable with what is unchanging (e.g., the Parmenidean One, the Platonic forms, the Cartesian simple natures) or else by restricting knowledge and indeed all genuine thought within necessarily fixed limits (e.g., Kantian *a priori* categories or the alleged over-all requirement of public language). And of course the latter claim commonly carries the implication that the constantly changing and expanding empirical content which such restrictions allow is no concern of philosophy, whereas the fixed conceptual framework, which is enshrined in and imposed by the categories of thought or of language, is the proper study of philosophers. The trouble with this classic doctrine in all its forms is its neglect of history. It neglects the fact that large sections of our con-

6

ceptual framework have a perfectly well-known history—in some cases a highly dramatic and explosive one in which changes in what is conceptual and changes in what is empirical are not easily held apart but are continually overlapping and reinforcing one another. And it neglects the fact that history, conceived as a form of understanding, has a proper concern with every other field and form of knowledge and understanding. As a result of neglecting these facts, philosophers are in the main curiously blind to the impression their activity presents to any historical-minded observer.

On the one hand, philosophers, more than any other type of investigator, persistently work at what appear to be the same unchanging problems. On the other hand, although these problems appear not only to be unchanging but to admit of rational or even necessary solutions, yet the history of philosophy presents them as the centres of unending conflicts and debates, punctuated briefly from time to time by claims that a revolution has taken place and that philosophical problems will now be speedily wound up—after which things go on again very much as before. This picture is not presented in irony or in cruel mockery of philosophy. On the contrary, I have claimed that the never-ending debates over the central concepts of philosophy provide a clue to their special nature (which I call their essential contestedness) and to their peculiar function, which is to ensure intellectual vitality across the whole spectrum of human knowledge. An essential feature of philosophical concepts, as opposed to both empirical and purely formal concepts, is that their criteria *must* always be in dispute. This is so for two main reasons. First, as has often been recognised, every philosophical concept has surprisingly wide, if often rightly neglected, bearings upon other areas of human life and thought. How a particular philosophical concept is interpreted or how and why it is criticised and rejected will have some effect, however slight, upon how all other philosophical concepts are interpreted and applied. This makes philosophical concepts peculiarly susceptible to change or at least to challenge in respect of their proper interpretations and defences. But second, and with closer relevance to my historicist thesis, philosophical concepts are never as simple and stable as the Plato-Descartes tradition has claimed. Collingwood showed real insight when he wrote that their structure displays 'not the simplicity and calm that characterise the subject-matter of mathematics but the intricacy and restlessness that characterise the subject-matter, say, of constitutional or legal history.' Consider, for example, those concepts that express the great divisions of human activity: art, science, philosophy itself, production, force, organisation, law, etc. It takes only a little reflection upon their histories to see that their respective domaïns are far from fixed and final: that they are continually threatened by encroachments from without and that their persistence, far from being necessary, is at best a matter of a temporary equilibrium within an inherently unstable situation. At the same time, the particular form or interpretation a philosophical concept happens to enjoy is no less liable to be contested from within—by rival forms and interpretations, akin to rival branches of a single historic dynasty, which resurrect old claims to recognition by means of old arguments suitably refurbished for the times.

In my account of essentially contested concepts I have offered a model in which considerations such as these are systematised and so admit of systematic criticism. I have exemplified my model in a variety of favourable instances, and I have argued that with some modification it can be used to illuminate the key concepts of moral philosophy and of metaphysics. This leaves much to be done in the way of more careful demarcation as well as of critical testing of my claims. But already, I would maintain, my model has the merit of having awakened interest in the following line of thought: In order to fulfil the function that I ascribe to essential contestedness, a concept must be understood historically, as a phase in an inherited and unending intellectual task. At the same time, this insistence upon historical context and perspective need not involve relativism, at least in any logically and morally objectionable form. For the arguments in and through which an essentially contested concept lives are genuine arguments. In the history of their conflicting interpretations genuine, rational conversions and illuminations take place, although in ways that are limited by the inheritance from the past and that never preclude the possibility, and indeed the necessity, of future debate. On this score I believe that I have carried a little further one of the main intentions and endeavours of the Windelband-Collingwood school; and for this reason more than any other I hope that my book will continue to make its way.

W. B. GALLIE

Peterhouse, Cambridge.
January, 1968

PHILOSOPHY AND
THE HISTORICAL UNDERSTANDING

Chapter 1

CRITICAL PHILOSOPHY OF HISTORY

To Hegel the philosophy of history meant the philosophical history of the world: a presentation of the known facts of human history designed to bring into clear relief the 'immanent reason' which, according to him, those facts exist to express. Alternatively we could say that Hegel in his philosophy of history seeks to disclose a rational purposive pattern in human history as a whole. Something like this aim can be found in Hegel's great predecessor Vico; and something like it persists in the Marxists' doctrine of an inescapable order in the succession of types of human society. But, when thus conceived, philosophy of history has generally been repudiated with scorn by historians in our Western tradition; and it is, no doubt, the main cause of that distrust of anything bearing the name 'philosophy of history' which British historians in particular constantly betray even if they do not express it in words. This distrust is unfortunate. For not only do the aims, standards and methods of history form a proper subject for philosophical discussion, there has in fact grown up over the past century a considerable literature devoted to such discussion, a literature which M. Raymond Aron has aptly entitled 'critical philosophy of history'.

The starting-point of the present study is the claim, common to almost all critical philosophers of history, that historical study aims at a kind of understanding quite different from that which is characteristic of the natural sciences. I sympathise with this claim, but I find most previous expositions of it distressingly weak and unpersuasive. In the first place, with hardly an exception, they persistently confuse delineations and analyses of historical understanding – or, if it be preferred, the task of marking it off from the kind of understanding that is achieved in the sciences – with the problem of its vindication, with the question of how historical theses are or should be tested, of how the subjective bias of particular writers should be overcome, and so on. It is with the first of these tasks alone that we shall here be concerned; and by considering it in isolation from the problem of vindication we shall see the more clearly how scrappy and ineffective previous work upon it has been. But more particularly, I find it astonishing that no critical philosopher of history has as yet offered us a clear account of what it is to follow or to construct an historical narrative. And yet such an account is plainly essential to any successful answers to more complicated questions regarding either the nature or the vindication of historical thinking. The effects of this omission are as great as those that we might expect if in philosophies of science we were to find no discussion of measurement or of controlled observation.

There are, of course, explanations and even excuses for these failures and omissions. Critical philosophy of history has suffered from having to take over terminologies, logical apparatuses, accepted groupings of problems and methods of approach, from a philosophical tradition which, since its beginnings in ancient Greece, has been almost exclusively concerned with our knowledge of universal truths, truths that can be arranged in a system and are known to hold irrespective of any peculiarities of time and place. From the point of view of this tradition the historian's claim to understand particular situations seems either trivial or else delusive: either it is the mere application of already known laws to particular cases, or else – if it is a claim to understand *what is particular* about particular cases – it is directed on to what is, in the nature of things, un-understandable. This slick criticism is, as I shall show, ill-founded; nevertheless few critical philosophers of history have faced up to it with any confidence, and those who have done so have commonly made a poor dialectical showing against the spokesmen of successive philosophical establishments.

But if critical philosophy of history has been unfortunate in its general inheritance, its immediate inheritance, from the great movement of German idealism, has exercised an even more baneful effect upon its development. Like all philosophical movements, German idealism was highly complex in character and admits of many different interpretations; but certainly it was, among other things, a rearguard action fought against the confident and popularly persuasive claims of the prophets of the new natural sciences. It gave expression to the anxieties of all those who saw traditional forms of knowledge threatened by (to employ a much favoured metaphor) rising tides of atheism, materialism, relativism and other evil things which seemed to result from taking the natural sciences at their face value. Hence the main task of German idealism was to justify, as being equal if not superior in certainty and importance to the natural sciences, the kinds of knowledge that are embodied in religion, in morality, in law and custom, and incidentally in history. Now leaving to one side the question of the validity of the justifications offered, and the question whether such justifications are in principle either necessary or possible, it is evident that they must depend on a prior task, that of description and demarcation. It has first to be made clear in what ways knowledge of the kinds that are to be justified differ from the knowledge which has been accumulated so impressively and so rapidly by the observational and experimental methods of natural science. Critical philosophers of history have certainly recognised the necessity of this prior task; but they have constantly confused it with their attempts to justify, in Kantian fashion, history as a general form of knowledge. Hence the sketchiness, the lack of thoroughness and incisiveness of their analyses of historical understanding, and hence in particular the surprising fact that none of them to date has worked out a careful account of what it is to follow, or to construct, an historical narrative.

These are very severe as well as sweeping charges to bring against a distinguished succession of thinkers. Certainly they are not brought in a spirit of ingratitude: and indeed probably the best way to substantiate them is by running quickly over the four or five really important contributions to critical philosophy of history that have been made to date. I mean those of Cournot,

Dilthey, Rickert, Collingwood, and finally a number of studies by contemporary Anglo-Saxon philosophers on the nature of historical explanation.

That Cournot[1] should have failed to put the question 'What is it, what does it mean, to follow an historical narrative?' is understandable: his contribution to the critical philosophy of history was essentially an oblique one, a penetrating side-glance from one whose main interests were in very different fields. He maintains that there are in the natural world absolute contingencies, sheer theoretically unexplainable juxtapositions and collisions, including in particular collisions of human wills. The primary task of history, distinguishing it from all forms of scientific thought, is to display such contingent happenings in their mutual intrusiveness. Nevertheless there is a sense in which the terms of history are explainable enough, in which they can still be regarded from the scientific point of view. For these terms belong in all cases to causal series which in themselves are regular and intelligible: it is only the combinations, the coincidences of these series that are essentially contingent. Cournot gives as an example a game of chess, in which the successive decisions of each player are no doubt theoretically explainable in terms of his psychology, but in which nevertheless these decisions 'give rise to a multitude of accidental encounters when crossing those of his opponent'.[2] There is, however, a second and peculiarly historical sense in which the game as a whole may be said to admit of understanding: namely, the way in which, to a chess-expert's (or chess-historian's) eye, the individual moves of either player can be seen to fall under certain dominant phases or aspects of the game – to exemplify the master's characteristic strategy or the beginner's progressive beguilement. But understanding of this kind, with its obvious affinities to artistic appreciation, is something very different from explanation in the theoretical or scientific sense.

Cournot introduces these important ideas with an impressive ease and confidence. But he gives us not the slightest hint of how they are to be exemplified in the commonplace experience of following an historical narrative. No doubt this could be done, and I shall attempt to do it in later chapters: but we can get no aid or guidance in this task from Cournot's writings.

By contrast, Dilthey[3] was a thinker dedicated to critical philosophy of history. No man has ever seen so many possibilities for philosophical exploration, from the point of view of critical philosophy of history, as Dilthey did. The trouble with him, as his critics have commonly complained, is that he could seldom express these possibilities clearly because he was incapable of explaining clearly his own critically historicist standpoint. Nevertheless, through his successive efforts, Dilthey did succeed in bequeathing one immensely important insight to his successors. The connections between events with which history is concerned are, he constantly tells us, of a much more intimate kind than those investigated or established by the natural sciences: they are connections – often by overt physical actions – between phases of psychic life: for instance, between feeling and expression, between sign and communication, between gesture and action, between act and general purpose or policy. Every such term of psychical life gets its meaning from the way it contributes to a larger intelligible whole; and historical understanding consists in the appreciation and articulation of live and intelligible wholes. In other words, for Dilthey meaning is the supreme category in historical thinking. But it is also the supreme category in all thinking about man – in all 'human studies', the philosophy of man, the philosophy of culture, literary and artistic criticism and appreciation, and in what Dilthey quaintly called 'real psychology' – as opposed to analytical and laboratory psychologies of which he had a poor opinion. And this brings us to a difficulty which all serious readers of Dilthey must have experienced: it is often impossible to decide when he is referring to the ways in which we understand particular human actions and when to the ways in which we reflect about human action in general. Now if anything could have clarified Dilthey's thinking on this issue it would have been a straightforward discussion of what an historical narrative is, and what it means to follow one. But Dilthey never offers us anything of the kind. No sooner does he set himself to discuss what historical thinking is than he is distracted by the question of the justifiability of historical judgments; and he endeavours to settle this question by pointing to the inherent historicity of all thinking, indeed of every characteristic action of that 'historical being, Man'. And in this intellectual whirlpool sink many brilliant insights into the nature of history and the nature of philosophy.

Similar remarks apply to Rickert,[4] whose writings develop an important idea which originated with the German romantics and was later taken over by the great Max Weber. The principle of selection that governs historical thought and writing is of an entirely different sort from that employed in the natural sciences. The scientist finds certain data relevant to his problem because of a connection which he believes to hold universally between certain general properties of those data. The historian, on the other hand, selects his data because of his interest in some individual person or institution or nation; so that his data may include any event, no matter how rare or bizarre, which helps him to understand that particular individual. Alternatively we can say: the historian's selection is guided by his idea of what was of value – of interest and importance – both *to* and *about* the individual that he is studying; so that his principle of selection is the individual conceived as the centre of a network of values, and not, as in the case of the sciences, with some universal law conceived as the explanation of any and every event of such and such definite description.

This is an important claim. But can it be made good? Rickert, a careful academic thinker, made a useful start by exemplifying and qualifying it in relation to different divisions and subdivisions of historical and scientific writing. But he never carried his analyses far enough. His real concern was with the seemingly more exciting question: have we any good reasons for thinking that the selections, the directions of interest, of historians of any particular age or circle are valid or even significant for other ages than his own? Rickert toiled to settle this question once for all in a kind of Kantian, transcendental fashion, regardless of the fact that historians have their own methods for dealing with the issue of relativism (methods which he would have done well to study) and of the fact that no sane person needs a transcendental proof to assure him of the truth of many historical descriptions and of the soundness of many historical judgments. Humourlessly absorbed in the task of hitching history to its transcendental star, Rickert failed to elaborate his account of historical selection in terms of our everyday experience of following and accepting historical narratives.

This kind of criticism, his admirers may feel, cannot justly be levelled at R. G. Collingwood, whose book *The Idea of History*[5] certainly has the merit of reflecting its author's own experience both as a reader and as a writer of history. Indeed, in a number of places Collingwood might seem to be giving us (although in his own somewhat different terminology) exactly the kind of account that we are seeking. But on closer inspection we shall find that Collingwood's account, so far from meeting our demand, has the effect of throwing doubt upon its propriety. Simply to follow a narrative is something altogether too passive to have a place in Collingwood's intensely activist account of historical thinking.

Basically Collingwood wants to assert two things. First, that thinking can be historical only if it is *real* thinking, by which he means only if it is in the nature of problem-solving. Secondly, that thinking can be historical only if it is the re-thinking of the thoughts of – resolving the problems that once faced – some other rational being. Collingwood regards these two propositions as very intimately related: each, for him, requires the other. Thus, on the one hand, he maintains that I can solve an historical problem only when I succeed in re-thinking some other man's – say Plato's or Napoleon's – thought; and, on the other hand, I can only do this or at least can only know that I have done this correctly, when the thought which (in re-thinking it) I attribute to Plato or Napoleon has the effect of solving the problem, in either Platonic or Napoleonic history, from which my original puzzlement, and hence my need to think historically, arose. In other words, successful (or the appearance or the sensation of successful) problem-solving is taken as a sign of the reality, the re-lived-ness, of the thoughts which the historian ascribes to his subject.

This doctrine of Collingwood's has been criticised chiefly on the ground that it offers yet another intuitionist theory of truth, i.e. a theory which rests upon some entirely subjective criterion of truth, in this case the feeling or sensation of successful problem-solving. And there can be no doubt that it does offend on this score. But equally it offends on a second score which has a more direct bearing upon our present inquiry. For Collingwood's account appears to neglect one of the most obvious facts about the general context in which the need for fresh historical thinking, the need for problem-solving history, commonly arises. This context is, of course, the narratives which the historian inherits from his predecessors or sources and which it is both natural and inevitable for him to regard – in a first provisional attitude – as witnesses of truth from a certain limited point of view. He must first adopt this attitude, whatever his final judgment may be, if he is to know, if he is to be able to follow, what his predecessors' narratives amount to. Now to follow is to think – to connect, to appreciate continuities, to feel the forward-movement, and so on: and following, in this sense, is an essential element in, or basis for, other more complicated forms of historical thinking. But Collingwood, with his detestation of all 'authorities', not only neglects but appears to deny the existence of this obvious fact. How is this blindness on his part to be explained?

Largely because his critical philosophy of history is inspired by too much reformist zeal. His readers will recall Collingwood's scorn of 'scissors and paste historians', by which he meant historians whose work is not inspired, as is that of an archaeologist, by the desire to solve particular problems arising from the discovery of new evidence. Collingwood, quite rightly, wanted historians to be regarded as discoverers, as contributors to human knowledge and culture, of at least as great importance and originality as physicists and biologists. But oddly enough, despite his passion to prove the autonomy of historical work and thought – as against the old-fashioned positivistic view which saw in history nothing but log-keeping plus the application of relevant scientific laws – Collingwood *does* tend to assimilate historical thinking too much to scientific research and discovery. No doubt this was because his own main experience of historical work, in late Roman history based largely on archaeological evidence, was very untypical: it is the kind of history in which the materials, the clues, are relatively limited, and in which the kind of thinking most required is indeed not unlike that of, say the diagnostician. This certainly would explain Collingwood's disregard of the basic experience of following a narrative, and his consequent failure to appreciate types of thinking other than problem-solving which an adequate analysis of that basic experience would have helped him to discern.

Lastly a few remarks on some recent studies on the subject of historical explanation.[6] These studies are, broadly speaking, so many exercises in applied logic: their starting-point is always the general idea of explanation, and they tend to present historical explanations as deviant or degenerate cases of other logically more perfect models. Not that the writers under consideration are guilty of any crude positivistic or scientismic bias against historical styles of thinking. On the contrary, whilst pointing out the various 'oddities' or weaknesses that we find in historical explanations, they are willing to admit that practising historians have no doubt every excuse, perhaps every good reason, for using the kinds of explanation or semi-explanation that they do. They recognise that general laws, explanations and hypotheses cannot be the primary object of the historian's attention, and that he is interested in them only in so far as they help him to tighten up his narrative, to see how the jigsaw pieces fit, to eliminate seeming discontinuities, incredible surprises and so on. Such admissions are all to the good; yet in making them our contemporary analysts leave us, and leave the weight of their argument, resting entirely upon our familiarity-bred, intuitive, unanalysed and indeed undiscussed notion of what an historical narrative is and of its resemblances and differences to other basic forms of communication. Inevitably, therefore, these writers have so far contributed more to the general philosophy of logic, to which they have added an interesting annexe, than to the foundations of the critical philosophy of history.

One suggestion of positive value has, however, emerged from a number of these studies. This is that not all explanations need be of the applicative Rule/Case/Result pattern made familiar by logical and methodological textbooks. What an explanation is, or can be or ought to be, depends in any given case, upon its context and upon the character of the inquiry in which it occurs. It is a natural inference from this that the kinds of explanation which are required to elucidate an historical narrative may be very different from those required to co-ordinate a set of observation-statements in science. But again, with a very few exceptions, recent philosophers have little or nothing to tell us about what these other possible forms of explanation are like. A notable exception to this rule is Professor William Dray, whose conception of rational explanations points to one way in which historical explanations fulfil a special function in relation to historical narratives. Professor Popper provides another exception in one part of his work: in a few paragraphs towards the end of his *The Poverty of Historicism* he has introduced the important idea of 'situational logic' and has suggested a number of ways in which this idea might be developed in the critical philosophy of history.[7] I shall return to these suggestions in Chapter 5.

So much in vindication of my charge against previous critical philosophers of history. But now I must add that their failure to get off on the right foot is not philosophically so culpable as my curt summaries of their main contributions may have suggested. For the idea of an historical narrative, although it is logically prior to almost all the questions with which critical philosophers of history have struggled, is itself very far from simple or easy to grasp. On the contrary, its complexity is of a kind that is likely to irritate and repel minds nursed and exercised on relatively safe, long-cultivated philosophical topics. To approach it is rather like looking for one's bearings in a fairly familiar country, but from a new viewpoint from which many well-known features reappear, but in new relations, as if in the wrong order, certainly not according to the book. This difficulty is a result of that bias in our philosophical tradition, from Plato to the present day, in favour of theoretical knowledge, i.e. knowledge admitting of universal statements and of being set out in systematic form. Given the accepted terminologies and characteristic presumptions of that tradition, it is virtually impossible to describe convincingly the most basic and familiar things that historians and readers of history are always doing – but doing without bothering to analyse or to justify what they are doing. Because of this difficulty I shall approach the question of what an historical narrative is, and what it means to follow such a narrative, indirectly; and making use of a time-honoured scientific device, I shall replace my original questions, to begin with, by the logically much simpler and more general questions, 'What is a story?' and 'What does it mean to follow a story?'

By concentrating first upon these simpler issues, I can set aside all questions about the verification of historical judgments and hypotheses, and about the so-called relativity of historical knowledge – questions by which, as we have seen, discussions of historical understanding have so often been bedevilled. Of course, it is a most important fact about historical narratives, and about following them as historical narratives, that we believe they rest on evidence or could be supported on every main point by evidence of some kind. But one may admit this and yet insist that while we are trying to describe and demarcate historical understanding as such we should not get entangled either with discussions of the general problem of truth or with discussions of the kinds of evidence, and of the different ways of using evidence, that historians tend to favour. These questions are obviously of the first importance in other contexts; but to the initial anatomy of the historical understanding they have almost nothing to contribute.

Chapter 2

WHAT IS A STORY?

WHAT is a story? And what does it mean to follow a story? At the commonsense level we might answer:

1. Every story describes a sequence of actions and experiences of a number of people, real or imaginary. These people are usually presented in some characteristic human situation, and are then shown either changing it or reacting to changes which affect that situation from outside. As these changes and the characters' reactions to them accumulate, they commonly reveal hitherto hidden aspects of the original situation and of the characters: they also give rise to a predicament, calling for urgent thought and action from one or more of the main characters. The predicament is usually sustained and developed in various ways that bring out its significance for the main characters. Whether or not the main characters respond successfully to the predicament, their response to it, and the effects of their response upon the other people concerned, brings the story to within sight of its conclusion.

2. Following a story is, at one level, a matter of understanding words, sentences, paragraphs, set out in order. But at a much more important level it means to understand the successive actions and thoughts and feelings of certain described characters with a peculiar directness, and to be pulled forward by this development almost against our will: we commonly appreciate, without needing to articulate to ourselves, many of the reasons and motives and interests upon which the story's development up towards its climax depends. It is only when things become complicated and difficult – when in fact it is no longer possible to *follow* them – that we require an explicit explanation of what the characters are doing and why. But the more skilful the story-teller, the rarer will be the intrusion of

such explicit explanations. Ideally, a story should be self-explanatory, even when following the story as a whole requires us to correct (in the light of later developments) the natural and in a sense appropriate ways in which we first followed and accepted its earlier stages. An equally important facet of the experience is that we follow – or, we might better say, are pulled along by – the characters of the story, as if they were real individuals. It goes without saying, however, that these characters must first be presented and described in general terms, so that we can know the kind of people that they are. Thus we both recognise them as types and are interested in them as individuals; but it is in the latter spirit that we follow their actions.

It might be objected that this idea of story is too vague to admit of useful general discussion, and that one could find exceptions to all my suggested generalisations – most obviously in those stories, from Tristram Shandy to shaggy dog stories, whose point depends on breaking the usual rules or patterns of story-telling. But these exceptions prove the existence of some rules which are commonly, if not strictly or universally, exemplified in stories. And it is these rules – or rather some philosophically illuminating facets of them – that I am going to discuss. The above provisional and, as far as possible, philo-sophically non-committal answers may therefore be usefully borne in mind as a rough sketch-map of the area that we shall be discussing, although in fact I shall work with only a few of the phrases which they contain, in particular 'following', 'interest' and 'conclusion'.

To begin with the last of these. What kind of conclusion does a story arrive at? My first main contention is the truism or near-truism that the conclusion of a story is essentially a different kind of conclusion from that which is synonymous with 'statement proved' or 'result deduced or predicted'. The conclusion of any worthwhile story is not something that can be deduced or predicted, nor even something that can be seen at a later stage to have been theoretically or ideally predictable on the basis of what had been revealed at some earlier stage. A story always contains some surprises: as a rule it makes use of coincidences, unforeseeable recognitions and revelations, and other fortuitous, happy or unhappy, events. Admittedly, these events should never offend our sense of what is possible, or even of what is acceptable, in the circumstances supposed. Nevertheless the conclusion of a good story–a conclusion which we wait for eagerly–is not something that could have been or should have been foreseen.

The relevant implications of this point can be introduced by means of the following considerations. First, we can imagine almost any good story being presented, and probably ruined, as either a cautionary tale or as the illustration of a moral homily. Let us consider the latter more extreme case. In the homily the persons and early incidents of the story will be introduced somewhat in the manner of instantial or factual premisses from which, in conjunction with appropriate wise saws and moral principles, the conclusion of the story–the exemplification of the appropriate moral lesson – can be deduced. But in this process the conclusion will, of course, have lost all its virtue *as the conclusion of a story*. Inevitably it will have become a foregone conclusion, possibly to be assimilated with moral profit, but certainly not to be awaited with eagerness and excitement. Clearly, therefore, the sense of 'following'–following *to* a conclusion–that applies to stories is of an altogether different kind from the sense of following an argument so that we see that its conclusion *follows*.

Secondly, it is worth recalling that we sometimes compare people, especially children, in respect of their capacities to follow stories–with more or less quickness, comprehensiveness and insight. Now different levels of skill in this respect presumably depend in part upon having had the right kind of training and experience. But what sort of training and experience would here be relevant? Training in 'guessing the end' of story after story? Surely not. We can, to be sure, imagine a game–'guessing the end of the story'–being used, no doubt for good educational reasons, in the teaching of young children. And presumably in becoming skilful at guessing the ends of different stories, a child would be displaying (and

cultivating) a certain generalising power: he would be developing a kind of knowledge of human nature–as revealed in the
kinds of story that he has come across to date. But the crucial
sign that a child is good at following stories is that he can follow
developments or *volte-faces* of a kind that he and his fellows
have never met before and that other children (more restricted
by their experience of more nearly foreseeable conclusions in
other stories) just cannot 'get' or 'take'. Good 'end-guessers', in
the game supposed, would not necessarily be 'good followers',
though they might well be, and *vice versa*. Just as in real life good
prophets are not necessarily good historians, and *vice versa*.

While stressing this point we can perfectly well admit that
there are many developments in every story which can be
predicted: i.e. routine developments such as are easily telescoped into a single phrase, since they can almost be taken for
granted; or developments which, although materially important
for the story's result, are so obviously foreseeable that they
cannot contribute in any way to its dramatic value. We can go
further, and admit that often, in reading or listening to a story,
we may have a powerful presentiment about its conclusions.
But such presentiments, in story-reading as in real life, are very
seldom predictions in the sense of conclusions drawn from
explicit evidence. The truth is rather that the whole style and
set-up of the story often makes it clear from the outset that its
conclusion is bound to take either of two forms: either the lovers
will or will not be reunited: the lost child will or will not be
rescued: and so on. Indeed, it may well be that the author
intends that we shall feel from early on that some particular
love-story cannot end in any normal happiness. We feel this
about Clyn Yeobright and Eustacia, or about Meaulnes and
Yvonne de Galais, even before they meet. Yet we follow their
story with no less interest, eager to have our presentiment
specified and articulated, rather than to have it verified.

We can go still further and admit that sometimes, while
following a story, we can foresee pretty clearly, on the evidence
provided by the course of the story so far, that its conclusion

must take one of a number of specifiable alternative forms. Here indeed is prediction, if of a rather weak kind. But when this happens, what do we do? If we are wise–and if the story is indeed worth following–we shall not let this predictive insight prevent us from following the story further and from enjoying the incidental, subordinate surprises that it may still have to give us. So that even when we follow a story to a conclusion that we have predicted, this predictability, so far from being the essential factor, is rather something that we have to keep from spoiling the characteristic experience.

In general, the possibility of prediction figures in stories very much as it does in most of our thinking about everyday life. There is a dominant sense of alternative possibilities: events in train are felt to admit of different possible outcomes–particularly those events that count, that evoke praise or blame, that deserve to be recorded, that could be the pivot of a good story. But side by side with this there is the recognition that many events, or aspects of events, are predictable either exactly or approximately. But, although recognised, this predictable aspect of life is, so to speak, recessive or in shadow. It is in contrast to the generally recognised realm of predictable uniformities that the unpredictable developments of a story stand out, as worth making a story of, and as worth following.

We should notice here that perhaps of greater importance for stories than the predictability relation between events is the converse relation which enables us to see, not indeed that some earlier event necessitated a later one, but that a later event required, as its necessary condition, some earlier one. More simply, almost every incident in a story requires, as a necessary condition of its intelligibility, its acceptability, some indication of the kind of event or context which occasioned or evoked it, or, at the very least, made it possible. This relation, rather than the predictability of certain events given the occurrence of others, is the main bond of logical continuity in any story. In particular this relation obtains and plays an evidently crucial role, whenever clues laid down early in a story are made use of later to establish guilt or identity or what not, and indeed whenever an important revelation, by speech or deed, is evoked

by some earlier information or question or command. In these
cases what happens is intelligible, we see how and in a sense see
why it happened: but it is not necessarily (and indeed not
usually) predictable. And on this score the logical texture, the
ground of the intelligibility, of stories matches exactly with that
of everyday life.

What I have claimed with regard to the conclusion of any
story – that in the typical case we come to it, wait for it, follow
the story through and up to it as something unpredictable yet
in its own way intelligible and acceptable – seems to me to be
equally true of every main interim outcome, every main pivot
or watershed, in any story. Whenever we accept an 'And so it
turned out that . . .' we are accepting something in exactly
the same sense that we will accept the story's conclusion when
we come to it. We could therefore, if we wished, speak of
following a story through a sequence of interim conclusions to a
final conclusion.

We can confirm this by recalling the kinds of criticism of a
story that we make or hear made on other than purely aesthetic
grounds. For instance, its conclusion is said to be far-fetched,
ill-prepared, obviously manufactured, unconvincing, and so on.
But criticisms such as these could for the most part be just as
applicable to any defective link or pivotal scene, any main halt
or watershed in the development of a story. From the point of
view of intelligibility and acceptability, or in respect of the way
that it makes the story followable, every main interim outcome
in a story is thus on all fours with the actual conclusion.

Further confirmation of this point can be got by noticing a
kind of ambiguity in the idea of the conclusion of a story. We
apply the idea of a conclusion, in this connection, sometimes
with aesthetic considerations uppermost in our minds, whereas
at other times what we have chiefly in mind is the kind of
understanding that we reach at the end of a story. From the
former point of view the conclusion of a story is the point at
which it ought to stop, to obtain its optimum artistic effect:
from the latter point of view it is the point at which we accept
that last 'And so it turned out that . . .' with which our under-

standing of the action is completed. Usually, indeed, these two ways of regarding or assessing a story's conclusion coincide: the right place for a story to stop is the place at which fullest understanding of what happened in it has been achieved. But there is no absolute necessity about this coincidence. There are cases in which our final understanding–certain final revelations perhaps–are of too violent or overwhelming or ecstatic a nature to provide an aesthetically suitable stopping-place. So we have the well-known devices of the subdued ending in minor key or the epilogue. In other cases the final moment of understanding is of a kind that defies verbal description: it has been left *beyond* the story's concluding sentence. It would be banal to describe the eventual happiness of Tom Jones and his Sophia: while the last lonelinesses of condemned or dying men is, by both logical and psychological necessity, indescribable. These considerations help us to appreciate that, from a logical point of view, the final point at which we accept an 'And so it turned out that . . .' is of the same general character as all the previous points at which we accept or have followed what has happened so far in the story.

Yet there is something else to be said about the conclusion of a story. There is something special about it, distinguishing it from all other incidents, halts, outcomes, watersheds that we pass on the way to it. Without being predicted, and often without being even vaguely foreseen, the conclusion of a story nevertheless guides our interest almost from the start. Admittedly, when we are first introduced to the main characters of a story and begin, so to speak, to live in them and with them, we are willing to go with them, to follow them, in almost any direction. They interest us, and all we ask is 'What will happen to them now?' and 'What will happen to them next?' But very soon these questions are replaced by one that expresses a much more serious concern, namely: 'How will things turn out for them *in the end*?' Our hopes and wishes have become involved in their imaginary fortunes. We must hear whether it went well or ill for them in the end – in whatever sense of end applies to their story. Thus the conclusion of a story is the main focus of our interest before we know what that conclusion is going to be. And it is chiefly in terms of the conclusion—eagerly awaited as we read forward and accepted at the story's end— that we feel and appreciate the unity of a story. Its other episodes and incidents will, of course, have contributed to that unity; indeed, they will have prepared for and contributed to the acceptability of the conclusion. But there is a sense, to be examined in detail later, in which the influence of the conclusion is here predominant.

Putting together the main points in our discussion so far, we thus reach the idea of following a story towards its conclusion through a sequence of incidents and outcomes which are, from the standpoint of reader and audience, acceptable yet unpredictable. Now in any worthwhile story this unpredictability is not something entirely subjective to the audience—a function of their slow-wittedness or the result of artful tricks of concealment played by the narrator. It would be a poor story whose surprising dénouement depended simply upon the author's holding back certain crucial facts until the very last moment. In all good stories the factor of contingency matches that which we feel to be part and parcel of daily life. For example the author brings two very strong personalities face to face: how they will react to one another is anyone's guess. Yet we find ourselves accepting the author's account, however much it may at first surprise us, and (if he knows his business) we shall find it progressively more acceptable as the story advances, no matter how many further unpredictable twists and turns its development may involve. Or again some outlandish disaster—or windfall—strikes a character in a story. Our feeling is that anything might happen—he might go off in any direction. Yet here again, not only do we follow in the direction which the story-teller indicates, no matter how surprising it may be, but we find, as we look back from the story's later stages or its conclusion, that this direction was all the time entirely in character.

These are the familiar unquestionable facts of the experience of following a story. We follow a story through or across contingencies—accidents, coincidences, unpredictable events of all kinds; yet the story's general direction and continuous advance towards its final conclusion somehow succeed in rendering these contingencies acceptable. Yet to traditional philosophical ways of thinking there is something paradoxical about the juxtaposition of the terms: contingent and acceptable. Contingencies, our philosophical tradition teaches, are things that we no doubt have to accept, like so many knocks on the chin, willy-nilly: but this does not mean that they are, or ever can be, intellectually acceptable. By definition, what is contingent is not under our intellectual command: it is the unexpected blow that gets under our intellectual defences. But only that which is, or which can be brought under our intellectual command, so that it conforms to our anticipatory (or in some cases timeless) classificatory systems, is intellectually acceptable. Somehow or other, therefore (or so traditional ways of thinking suggest), we must transform this appearance of 'acceptable contingencies' into something more intellectually respectable.

This recommendation rests on a presupposition about human knowledge which goes back to Plato and Aristotle and has been accepted, although with very different feelings, by almost all Western philosophers ever since. To challenge it, even to seek to modify it a little, may therefore seem the height of audacity or even of impudence. But as it stands (as we noticed in our first chapter) this view has the effect of ham-stringing any attempt to describe what is peculiar to historical thinking: its attempt to understand, and its success in understanding, particular actions. Yet historical thought and knowledge exist, and are something of far greater solidity, of far more unquestionable worth and necessity to human life than even the most deeply entrenched of philosophical principles or prejudices.

In order to correct the prejudice now under discussion I want to consider it in one of the most extreme – indeed one of the most blatant and therefore philosophically most useful – forms that has ever been given to it: namely, Mach's principle of economy of thought in the sciences. According to Mach the sole point of possessing general knowledge is that it enables us to act purposefully and masterfully in anticipating and forestalling future or distant events. Our possession of scientific principles and formulae means that we need no longer slavishly contrive to observe natural events in all their multifarious immensity. Like absentee landlords we can extract all that we want from what actually happens by applying the relevant scientific generalisations, and adjusting our desires accordingly. Or, to use less colourful language, to understand a particular case always amounts to being able to anticipate or forestall, indeed in a sense to *neglect* the particular case in question, because, through our understanding of the type or kind which it exemplifies, we know all that there is to be known about it already.

Mach's principle does not, in fact, explain all uses of generalisations in science. It is quite common in science for a generalisation to be used to enable us to observe and to judge certain particular events more carefully, more appreciatively, than would be possible without the direction which that generalisation provides. (Examples are the use of a new classificatory system to sharpen discriminating observations in botany, or the use of certain features of a theoretical model to assist the observation and interpretation of the photographic results of physical experiments.) Nevertheless, Mach's principle gives a usefully exaggerated expression to the widespread philosophical belief that to understand a thing is, in a sense, to command it—to have its development, so to speak, under one's hand, so that it can't bolt off with one, or, more simply and more generally, spring any real surprises. It is as a corrective of this widespread belief that an adequate account of what it is to follow a story, or an historical narrative, is of general philosophical importance: since following, in this sense, provides the most striking case of our use in thought of generalisations, not to command or forestall events, but to find them intellectually acceptable *after all*—i.e. after all the shock and the surprise that their coming may well at first have caused us.

It would be possible to elaborate this criticism of Mach's principle, and of the general view of thought and knowledge which lies behind it, by discussing the kinds of account of following a story to which they would inevitably lead. Briefly, there would seem to be two main possibilities, if the idea of a story developing through successive acceptable contingencies is to be ruled out. First, the idea of absolute contingency might be removed from our account: what we take to be contingencies, as we follow a story, must then be explained as developments that we could, or should ideally, have been able to predict. This means that following a story must be a kind of inductive exercise—perhaps presented a little unfairly by the story-teller, perhaps performed not very intelligently by his audience—but aimed at eliciting from successively presented bits of evidence, better and better or progressively more exact forecasts of what is to come. In fine, a kind of guessing-game such as we imagined earlier in this chapter. But the conclusive objection to such an account is, quite simply, that following is not identical with forecasting or anticipating, even although the two processes may sometimes coincide or assist one another. This is perhaps clearest in the simple contrast between following a track and anticipating how a track will go in the light of observations made while following it to date. Secondly, we might try to exclude the factor of intellectual acceptability. The experience of following a story would then be reduced to a pre-intellectual process of logging or registering successive imaginary incidents—possibly possessing a vaguely recognised unity in virtue of some over-all pattern quality or because of strong associational links, as seems to be the case with dreams. On this account all interpretative, inferential, judicative and appreciative factors must be considered as unnecessary adjuncts to the bare, basic act or attitude of following. The obvious objection to this is that following a story is *a* form of understanding—and indeed *the* form of understanding that is appropriate to stories: witness the fact that we commonly speak of understanding a story *better*, say on a second reading, after having had time to reflect upon it, or after having some of its obscurer incidents explained. And this is something which the second proposed account of following simply cannot allow.

Rather than pursue here such conceivable essays in misunderstanding, I shall proceed to my own account of how certain contingencies which play a crucial role in a story's development can be entirely acceptable. And here by 'acceptable' I mean much more than that a number of contingencies may be logically compatible. What I have in mind is this. The category of contingency has usually been discussed, both by those who accept it as ultimate and by those who regard it as ideally dispensable, in relation to the category of law or sufficient reason. In other words, contingencies are commonly regarded as facts which either are or appear to be recalcitrant to scientific ordering and explanation. But when our interest is focused on the particular development or story of some individual, rather than on that story's explanation, then the contingencies or accidents that figure in it can be regarded in quite a different way and give rise to the question: Why are certain contingencies acceptable in relation to that story whereas others are not? To answer this in terms of our standard 'static' idea of compatibility, holding between general terms or descriptions, is not sufficient, since the acceptability of the different contingent events that are described in a particular story is something that has to be gradually recognised and constantly assessed and reassessed as the story proceeds. Alternatively we could say, a story is understood or followed on the basis of (a) certain general traits that are ascribed to its characters, settings etc., and (b) certain chances or contingencies that befall its characters. These latter help to shape the story's development in one particular way: but other contingencies, or combinations of contingencies, while logically compatible with one another, would have made – not a story at all but a sequence of accidents that led us nowhere, that added up to nothing, that signified or told us nothing. Hence the question 'What makes certain contingencies acceptable in a particular story?' is virtually equivalent to the question 'What makes a particular story followable?' and is best answered by an analysis of what it means to follow a story.

But before embarking on this task, I shall take what may seem like yet another step backwards. The question 'What does it mean to follow a story?' was introduced as a simplifying device to help us to understand what it means to follow an historical narrative. But now, to help with our understanding of following a story, I want to use a still simpler model, that of following a game of chance and skill. This device has many advantages, but they all stem from the facts, first, that it is easier to imagine different spectators, at different levels of knowledge and intelligence, watching a game, and second, that the spectators follow a game by observing it directly, so that all difficulties about words and the ways they come between us and what we follow by means of them are eliminated.

Imagine, then, a group of people watching a cricket match. They range from a youngster whose grasp of the rules and whose knowledge of the players is slight, through a gradation of better and better informed enthusiasts, to a figure whom we will call the local expert. Not only is he a complete master of the rules of the game and of its tactics, he is also fully conversant with the relative strengths and weaknesses of the two opposing teams, the oddities of the local pitch and outfield, the effects of likely changes in the weather and so on. We can imagine that all our enthusiasts will follow the game, ball by ball, over by over, with equal interest and enthusiasm. Nevertheless, according to their levels of technical knowledge, judgment and experience, different members of the group will follow some moves with far more understanding than the majority, whilst some moves (say of captaincy or of batting or bowling tactics) will be fully appreciated only by the local expert and noticed perhaps by only a few others. Quite possibly, therefore, the expert will point these moves out to his younger friends. He may explain, e.g., what the captain is up to when he sets an unusual field or makes a surprising declaration. But he will do this only on the assumption that his younger friends have *failed* to follow what is happening. In explaining the captain's moves the expert will, roughly speaking, be bringing them under certain relevant generalisations or principles of captaincy, which his younger friends have not yet come across or whose appropriateness is not immediately obvious in the present situation. After assimilating and appreciating the expert's explanation, these younger spectators will be in a position to follow again, or certainly to follow more fully, the progress of the game.

The need of explanation in this sense shows that following a

game always admits of degrees of fulness or depth of understanding. The spectators, like the audience in a theatre or those
listening to a story, are all expected to be able to follow in a
sufficient degree. But some will follow more fully than others,
and there is not–and could not conceivably be–any criterion
for deciding when a story or any kind of performance has been
completely or perfectly or ideally followed. We should also
notice that the kinds of difficulty which call for explanation are
not to be identified with improbabilities or with apparent
exceptions to the rules. On the contrary, once they are
explained, they are usually seen to have been the natural thing
to do or to be clear examples of some general rule; whereas the
most improbable turns of fortune in the game, say the succession
of lucky lusty strokes by which the last man in carries his side to
victory, will be followed without difficulty, despite its freakish
improbability, by the cheering crowd.

Next let us suppose that, before the game begins, the local
expert has expressed his opinion about its result. Naturally as
the game goes forward, he will notice some of the grounds of his
prediction proved wrong, whilst others will be confirmed; for
the game is bound to be full of minor surprises, even if its broad
course corresponds with his prediction. But such confirmation
or refutation of his initial opinions will not in the least affect the
eagerness with which he continues to follow the play. Finally,
in contrast to our cricket enthusiasts, let us imagine a rather
seedy individual whose only interest in the game is due to a bet
which he laid on the result, after overhearing the expert's view
of what the result will be. From the point of view of the game
and of following the game he is a sheer outsider; but from
another point of view, that of the principle of the economy of
thought, he is the one truly rational character in our story. He
obtains what is for him the only really important information
about the game by a fairly reliable method, and he is able to
act on it–and no doubt also to employ himself profitably in the
meantime–without troubling himself with the game and its
development, its frustrations, its freakish turns of fortune, its
inevitable, irritating lack of complete intelligibility. Apart from
the fact that his motives are low and that he obtains his informa-

tion on authority he might be taken to represent Mach's ideal of the theoretical scientist. At least he serves to underline the fundamental difference between those who use any number of different generalisations in order to follow a game as closely and fully as possible, and those who would use such generalisations simply to predict some important selected fact about its result.

The experience of the spectators, just described, repeats a number of general features which, we have claimed, are also essential to the experience of following a story. Two of these features are exemplified with particular clarity in the experiences of our spectators. First, there is the matter of the minimum or basic qualification for following a game at all; and arising from this the question of how further experience and practice, and more particularly the comments and explanations we receive from others, can help us to improve that basic capacity. Secondly there is the point that it is not the most striking contingencies—the utter surprises, the sharp breaches of continuity—that call for explanation, but certain of the game's more complicated and obscure, yet perfectly regular and proper developments. Beginner and expert alike follow the game across the most unimaginable contingencies without the slightest sense of difficulty. They may wonder, they may whistle at the second hat-trick or the succession of dropped catches: but these are things which are not only followed without difficulty, they are followed and felt as the living heart of the game.

What, then, are the minimum prerequisites for following a game of chance and skill? Philosophers, when they discuss games and our capacity to take part in them, usually place great emphasis on knowledge of the rules. Yet it would be quite possible for someone (perhaps especially for a philosopher) to have a complete mastery of the rules of cricket and yet, in a perfectly real sense, to have no idea what the game is like, what it is like to play it or why it is worth playing or watching, etc. And conversely, children, when learning to play cricket or any other game, don't begin by mastering the rules. They begin by learning to perform certain acts—hitting or bowling or catching or stopping the ball—within a complex round of acts which they accept as a whole, as a kind of ritual in which they take part. The rules are gradually recognised, and eventually explained, as part of what always happens (e.g. at this point the umpire raises his hand and you walk out) not as the logical *sine qua non* of certain actions being counted as part of the game of cricket. Moreover, it is quite possible for a boy to play cricket well – certainly to be 'really playing it' – and yet to be ignorant of certain rules, e.g. those relating to overthrows or to stopping play for bad light and so on. Granted, therefore, that certain special preparation, including special knowledge, is needed if we are to follow a game, this cannot be equated simply with knowledge of the rules.

What following a game presupposes is, rather than a knowledge of the rules, some sense of the point and purpose of the game, of what makes it 'go', of what makes it move towards its climax, of what counts most from the point of view of the pleasure of playing it and so on. Stated more precisely, what is required is a much more-than-legal appreciation of such concepts as: winning or losing (or drawing or tie-ing or abandoning) a game; playing a good or worth-while (as opposed to a flat or farcical or bad-tempered) game; and then a whole range of concepts that serve to suggest the contingencies to which the game is so subject, e.g. the luck of the toss, the advantages of pitch and weather, the different types of accident in the run of the play, strokes of luck and 'jinxes' that can dominate a player or a team, and so on; and a corresponding battery of ideas about the ways in which players and captains try to minimise the dominion of chance – by concentration, forethought, encouragement, sustained team-spirit, variations in tactics, etc. Ability to apply these and similar concepts is essential if one is to follow a game of cricket as cricket, not simply as an English Saturday afternoon ritual performed in accordance with the rules printed in *Wisden's Almanac*, or as an out-of-door all-male ballet.

Of all these concepts that of either winning or losing – to extract this crucial pair of opposites from the other more complicated possible results – plays a paramount role. Unless we know its more-than-legal meaning, we cannot begin to follow a game, as a game, at all. Not only do we always follow a game with its result as the guide and goal of our attention: we usually follow it with definite hopes and wishes that one side, our side, will win. This shows us how, in following a game, we are all the time truly looking forwards, future-wards towards its result, but yet in a way that has nothing necessarily to do with prediction of its result. Following a game is a teleologically guided form of attention, with the peculiarity that the end towards which it is guided is essentially open: it could always be either victory or defeat. It is within this teleological framework that we note certain continuities in respect of the play, captains' tactics, etc.: and these recognised continuities, together with other reasonable expectations and presumptions, influence the way in which we recognise and feel and watch for the game's developments towards its still undecided end. Conversely, it would be impossible to follow a game, to have one's attention kept drawn towards its undecided conclusion, unless the game had shown a certain amount of continuity—of shape and character and quality—in its development to date. A game with absolutely no shape, no point, no spirit to it simply could not be followed, even if its result could be read in clear figures in the score-book and every describable step in it had been in conformity with the rules.

The normal situation, however, is that in which the formally required yet always quite open result is felt to be well worth watching for. And an essential part of this situation is that, just because the result is entirely open, so there are indefinite numbers of ways open, by which it may be reached. In other words, there is almost no limit to the contingencies that may intrude into and completely revolutionise the game's development. To be sure, the contingencies must not lead to an infringement of the rules or preclude further followable, worth-while development. For instance, a freak hailstorm in a June afternoon, a succession of hat-tricks, a century by the worst batsman in the side—such surprises are entirely acceptable from the point of view of following the game through to its conclusion. But an earthquake which broke up the pitch: a rebellion by one side against an umpire's decision: a crazy policy of entirely 'negative' bowling and fielding aimed at preventing the opposing side from ever losing a wicket–unpredictables such as these would certainly wreck the game and render it unfollowable because not worth following.

Here, in terms of what it means to follow a game, we have an indication of how certain contingencies can (whilst others cannot) be perfectly acceptable. We can 'take' the most surprising incidents, take them–not just 'on the chin' but 'into consideration', we can weave them into our advancing picture of the game advancing to its still-to-be-decided result. We can do this, so long as the contingencies in question do not preclude the possibility of further, continuous and acceptable, advance. We weave the oddest contingencies, more or less perceptively, more or less correctly, into our picture of the game's progress so far; and we are always ready for–often indeed are hoping for– some still odder turn of fortune to set in from now, and to force us to alter drastically our picture of how the play has gone.

Now let us return to the analogy between this experience and the experience of following a story. Certainly the analogy is not perfect. For one thing, there is nothing in the relation between story-teller and listener that corresponds at all closely to the rules of a game. On the other hand, there are commonly accepted conventions that to some extent limit possible developments in a story of this or that particular *genre*. And there are vague standards of an author's good faith: he must not mislead our natural expectations too far, although he may, of course, lead us quite a way up the garden. Secondly it must be admitted that the main forms of possible endings to stories are nothing like so clearly articulated as are victory, defeat, draw, tie and game abandoned. To be sure, once we have passed from the *mise en scène*, our interest in a story is dominated by the idea of the conclusion, of how it will turn out for the characters who have won our sympathetic attention. (And incidentally our interest in any *mise en scène*, no matter how prolonged and elaborate, always includes the natural presumption that something dramatic, something followable and worth following, will come out of all this.) Nevertheless, the great variety of possible forms of conclusion to any story endows it with a freedom of development such as we do not find in any game. Thus we commonly get the impression that some (as it will turn out) relatively minor character is going to be of dominant interest, only to find him or her giving way to someone bigger or better. Or think how, in the fairy-tale of Cinderella, our interest moves on from the question, How will she get to the ball? to the question, How will the prince ever find her?

These differences, however, leave unaffected the all-important analogy between the ways in which, in following a game and in following a story, we accept contingency after contingency as so many openings up of yet other possible routes towards the required although as yet undisclosed conclusion. In the case of a story, where there are no definite rules to help to decide what contingencies can be accepted into it, it is up to the writer to vindicate his acceptance of a given contingency in terms of the subsequent, sufficiently continuous, development of his story. It is worth considering how he succeeds in doing this.

Let us go back to our example of a character suddenly faced with a quite unparalleled, hope-shattering disaster. What will he do? Our first feeling is—he might do anything, his course is unpredictable, for the whole framework of his life and his hopes has been wrenched away from him. But the exigencies of living require that he picks up some of the bits of his old life in some of his old ways; that he resumes some parts of the pattern of his former self. Only parts of that former self, however, since we are assuming that it has suffered a severe maiming or distortion. But in the rest of the story we shall get accustomed to actions, words and thoughts which are characteristic of his new, maimed or distorted, or perhaps also deepened, self. This will be accepted as the logical ground of his later characteristic actions, as his old self was of his earlier actions. The unforeseeable disaster, the extreme of contingency, has the effect at first of creating a complete discontinuity, a kind of logical void: there is loss of old bearings, old values, old continuities and predictabilities in conduct. But later it is seen to have allowed the emergence of the new, the altered character displaying its own, new or modified, continuities and predictabilities. And through this difference, or in terms of the effect of the disaster upon the hero's reaction and character, we find that we have accepted it: we have understood what it meant for that man to meet that utterly unforeseeable disaster, whether it be the remediable loss of a Gabriel Oak or the irremediable one of an Oedipus.

The intrusion of such a contingency into a story means a discontinuity in our understanding of its main characters. But whereas for a scientist a revealed discontinuity usually suggests some failure on his part, or on the part of his principles and methods and theories, to account for that aspect of nature which he is studying, for the man who follows a story a discontinuity may mean, irrespective of any change or correction of his theoretical apparatus, the promise of additional insights into the stuff a particular character is made of, into the range of action and adaptation which that character can command. Only, the man who follows a story must be prepared to wait for this promise of further insight to mature. And this helps us to vindicate the intellectual indispensability of the act of following, even when it seems most passive. In following a story through such a contingency as we have discussed we must wait—must wait and see—if we are to know what it amounted to. Of course, we have to wait and see in order to know what happens in the end. But being prepared to wait and see, being actively ready to see during one's waiting, is the essential prerequisite of ever understanding what such and such contingencies, whether disasters or windfalls, added up to, in terms of one particular developing whole, viz. one man's life, in the end. What is contingent, e.g. coincidental or unpredictable, is of course, *per se* unintelligible. But in relation to a man's life, or to a particular theme in a man's life, it can be understood as having contributed to a particular, acceptable and accepted, conclusion.

We can perhaps make this point clearer by using it to correct Aristotle's dictum that characters exist for the sake of the story and not stories for the sake of the characters they contain. From one point of view Aristotle is right. Characters are introduced and described in the first instance, in easily recognised terms, in routine or characteristic situations, so that we know roughly the kind of people whose actions we shall be following; and the purpose of such routine introductions is that the story-teller can then proceed to show us his characters in peculiar unpredictable collisions and entanglements and predicaments. Thus the characters do seem to exist for the sake of the story. On the other hand, Aristotle's dictum calls for correction, in so far as it suggests that our knowledge of and interest in people is confined to their routine or easily recognised and appreciated traits. The truth is that our knowledge or understanding of people, in any worth-while sense, is shown when we succeed in following changes in their habits of thought, or in following unexpected developments in their motives and purposes. But this is just the kind of understanding that is typically called for when we follow a character's reactions through a sequence of largely unpredictable collisions, entanglements and predicaments in a story.

To sum up this part of our discussion. At any stage in a story we are following it because our interest is pulled forward by the presumption that its result is to be one of a few roughly specifiable kinds. The hero will either win or lose – be it his girl or his glory: he will be rescued – either by his own cunning or because of the compassion of his guard, and so on. In every case what is presumed is a strong disjunction: this or that or the other, not both or all. But the disjunction is not something predicted on the basis of the incidents narrated so far and of certain general truths about human nature. Rather it is presumed because our sympathies with the chief character or characters of the story – sympathies which the story-teller has been at pains to evoke sometimes through the very title of his story – demand that the story shall end in one of such and such possible ways. If the hero is a prisoner, then the story must end either with an escape or a heroic death: that or some vaguer presumption guides our following, our forward-looking interest, though precisely how the ending is to be achieved we have as yet no idea.

In the early stages of a story, then, or at least once the main characters and their circumstances are sufficiently established, we are ready for almost anything to happen: we are willing to follow them in almost any direction. Contingencies, the strangest combinations or successions of events, can be accepted provided that they do not patently prevent the story from advancing towards some appropriate outcome, and do not destroy too many of the continuities, too many of the dependencies of later upon earlier events, that we have recognised so far. The logical mesh of the connections between key incidents always remains loose, however: no matter how confidently and clearly we may have followed and interpreted and accepted a certain character or action, there is always the side-thought that this interpretation may have to be corrected or supplemented in the light of later developments. We should also recall here that the processes of following and interpreting and accepting can take place at very different levels of understanding and of sophistication. Every member of a family circle may be listening to the story: but no two of them follow or interpret it in exactly the same way, and no one of them can be said to have followed it perfectly or ideally or completely.

No doubt, as a story progresses, its connecting threads, especially the dependence of later upon earlier incidents, tend to become tighter, less mistakable, less questionable. This is partly a matter of the convention and of the story-teller's good faith: certain drastic *volte-faces* in character and conduct, which might be acceptable early on in a story, would be a kind of insult to the reader if they were brought in at the end. But our disinclination to accept such developments has a more objective basis than this. The more the story-teller has told us about each of his characters, the greater the number of continuities in their interests and motives that he has helped and encouraged us to recognise, the closer the threads of the action have been drawn together, by so much the narrower does the scope for entirely new, hitherto unsuggested developments become. But whilst this tightening up of the plot is a familiar part of what we experience in following a story, it must not distract us from more important and distinctive features of that experience. In following a story we must always keep our minds open and receptive to new possibilities of development, new hints, clues and leads, up to the very last line: besides exercising our intelligence in making routine predictions or seeing complicated but definite lines of continuity, we must be ready constantly to reassemble and reassess different possible relevances, links, dependences, still unexplained juxtapositions. Indeed, there is probably no better way of suggesting the general structure of the act of following a story than to recall the kind of intelligence, the kind of person, who excels in following (and perhaps also in creating) stories, and by contrasting this kind of intelligence with that which excels in systematic studies but is slow or insensitive in appreciating stories or histories of any subtlety or complexity. To deny that intelligence of a high order can be displayed in progressively assembling and discarding suggestions, leads, evidences, without being able to fit these into standard *cadres*, is simply to show ignorance of the kind of intelligence that alone can achieve historical understanding and indeed any worth-while understanding of our fellows.

I want now to return to the question of the basic or minimal capacities required for following any story. And we can usefully pose this question in terms of one of our earlier examples. Why presume that a story that begins by describing a brave prisoner longing for his home must, almost certainly, lead up to, or be drawn on to, an account of his escape, or, failing that, of his death trying to escape, or at least to some equally acceptable conclusion? The natural answer is: once our sympathies for the prisoner have been powerfully evoked, any flat or feeble conclusion, e.g. that he settled down to a hopeless acceptance of his condition, would seem like a hoax: the story-teller wouldn't be playing fair. But what lies behind this conventional presumption? Some accepted, inductively established truth about how brave men behave in captivity? Not at all. A story-teller, although his genre may demand plausibility and even verisimilitude, is not a popular illustrator of established or alleged statistical truths. His job is to present his characters, usually to be sure in plausible fashion, in situations which are calculated to call out our interest; and this interest is always ultimately based–if we excuse a few types of sophisticated trick-story–on our strongest, most elemental feelings of sympathy with and antipathy for our fellows. It is worth noticing that, once embarked on a good story, we cannot properly be said to choose to follow it. It would be better to say that we are pulled along by it, and pulled at by a far more compelling part of our human make-up than our intellectual presumptions and expectations. We read (or hear) that the lovers are parted, that the child is lost in the forest, and we must hear more about them, we could almost cry out like children 'What happened to them next?' However disguised such basic directing feelings may become in the case of more sophisticated stories, they are always there. If they were not, if we were not following the to us irresistibly compelling thoughts and actions and feelings of other human beings, we simply wouldn't be following a story. This means that there is something arbitrary, something due to the peculiar set and structure of our basic interhuman feelings, involved in the following of any and every story. Or, in other words, following, in the sense that concerns us, cannot be regarded as a purely intellectual operation, definable by reference to a specific task or problem, as is, for instance, following a mechanism, or following a geographical or geological feature on a map, or a biological form through a succession of variations. For this reason also it is impossible to delimit the relationship of 'followability' between one episode and another within any definite logical boundaries, save those of blatant logical or causal impossibility. Still less is it possible to equate what is *directly* followable, in contrast to what requires justification or explanation in a narrative, with the use of any specific grammatical forms, e.g. simple indicative sentences.

To all this it may be objected: No doubt the initial enlistment of our sympathies and the orientation of our interests in the characters of a story depends upon the arbitrary make-up of our all-too-human natures. But how a story develops and the adequacy and persuasiveness–and hence a large part of the interest–of its development are clearly matters for intellectual appreciation and judgment. To follow a story means, in the main, to follow the thoughts and the intentions of its main characters: and to follow in this sense is certainly not a matter of being pushed and pulled by our basic human sympathies and antipathies: it is something, rather, that calls for the exercise of keen intelligence in the appreciation of the relevant possibilities of action and the cool application of our general knowledge of human nature.

But this objection can be countered as follows. First it is evident that to follow a human being's trains of thought and action–especially through a sequence of varied and unpredictable incidents–is something very different from following their *rationale*, such as he (or another) might give in justification of what he had come to think or of what he had done. Sometimes, to be sure, following a story includes following, with proper excitement and admiration, the ingenuity, the judiciousness, the imperturbability of some character's thoughts and deeds: but it may equally well include following his or her vacillations, inconsistencies, failures of nerve and purpose. In general the capacity to follow, in the sense that concerns us, is not confined to continuous and consistent processes: it includes (and we have seen that it is essential that it should include) the capacity to follow events across discontinuities, contingencies, unpredictabilities of certain kinds. But exactly what discontinuities we are willing to accept or able to follow depends partly upon the set or orientation of our sympathy for some particular character as established so far, and partly upon the intrinsic nature of the kind of sympathy that has been established. To take an example. In Book V of *Tess of the D'Urbervilles*, Tess, having wisely and courageously decided to seek out her parents-in-law, quite suddenly and inexplicably loses her courage when she comes in sight of their house. The ability to follow, to accept this quite illogical weakness on her part, is essential if we are to follow at all adequately the rest of her story. And it is, of course, an essential part of following and accepting her weakness that it in no way affects the sympathetic feelings which she inspires.

This point has an important bearing upon the main conclusion of any story, and to a lesser extent upon the main halts or interim conclusions that it contains. The main conclusion is not simply the goal of our following and understanding; it must also be, from the point of view of our emotional response, some kind of culmination. It may be a culmination of love, or of rescue, or of heroic achievement, of progressive disillusion, or of suffering or of horror, or of a series of grimly or delightfully farcical events. But culmination of some kind there must be, if there is to be a story. More simply, unless we were in some degree emotionally involved in a story, the point, nay the very existence of its climax would escape us.

Does this imply that, in order to follow a story, our point of view must all the time be that of the agent—or, more likely, that of a succession of different agents—as opposed to that of a detached observer? Certainly we can all recall moments when in imagination we *were* the hero of the story, when our own feelings and those that we imagined him to have were quite indistinguishable. But there are other moments in almost every good story when the exact opposite seems to hold: moments in which our feelings are heightened to the limit precisely because we imagine ourselves watching, forced to observe the hero in some torturing predicament or facing irrevocable disaster; in which our desire to cry out is due to the fact that we are, irremediably, the detached inactive observer. It is not, therefore, any subordination of the observer's standpoint to that of the agent, but rather an unusually rapid movement and interplay between the two standpoints that characterises our appreciation of a story's development. A little reflection on how we first come to follow stories at all will help to make this point clear.

It is worth remarking, to begin with, that a story is always told in the first or third, never in the second, person. This means: we never try, so to speak, to hypnotise a child into imagining a story in which he himself takes a leading role. On the other hand, children clearly respond to stories, and in a sense live them, in the medium of their own native energies and emotions; and by the age-old art of tones and pauses and stresses the simplest adult narrator gradually extends the range of

feelings with which a young child can realise or animate the
incidents that befall the (spoken) 'I' or the described 'he' or
'she' or 'they' of the stories that are fed into him. Thus, stories
are one of the main means by which a child is taught to 'have
feelings' in characteristically human ways: that is, feelings for
and with other human beings and for himself *as* a human being.
He draws on his own raw emotional responses to realise, for his
own imaginative satisfaction, the characters in his favourite
stories: but equally, when he begins to think of his own feelings
and those of other people in real life, he will do this largely
through the medium of trappings, postures, attitudes, gestures
and words that he draws from those story-characters that he has
delighted to imagine. Hence imagination is far better described
as anticipation of life than as imitation of it.

The result is that in all our thinking about people, whether
in real life or in stories, the attitude of the agent and the attitude
of the observer are in constant and rapid interplay. Of course,
we can point to examples in which one attitude is predominant.
But in general it is true that I learn to conduct myself effectively
and humanely on the basis of how I observe and describe to
myself the actions and manners of others; whilst, in thinking
about other people, I inevitably emphasise those aspects of their
conduct and character which my own native powers of sympathy and tendencies to action have enabled me to realise.
More simply, can we think of other people effectively only so far
as they interest us; and in this respect our most serious historical
and practical judgments on our fellows show a clear affinity
to our experience of the first stories we ever listened to.[1]

A final important point arises from combining the two main
theses that have been defended in this chapter: namely, that the
crucial developments in any story are essentially contingent,
and second, that the act of following such developments depends
upon their human interest, their power to enlist certain
peculiarly human feelings. We have already contrasted the
crucial contingent developments of a story with other features
of it which are accepted, or perhaps taken for granted, as
routine, predictable, reliable. We should now also notice that

the individual characters who are at the focus of our attention are usually presented over against other characters or groups of characters who are accepted, or taken for granted, as background, as attendants, often as not anonymous, the people who just happened to be there. Thus, to combine these two further points in one example, let the story be about the little girl lost in the forest, in which the most fearsome or wonderful things happen to her. Yet everything else about the setting of the story—her father and his occupation, her mother and her motherly words of warning, the reasons for the little girl's outing, the way time flies, etc.—is all entirely to order. It is within the altogether acceptable framework that things worth telling begin to happen.

Now we naturally say that a story is about the contingencies, the exciting and surprising events, not about their regular background; and about the hero and heroine, not about the anonymous figures who surround them. Nevertheless the background persons or events commonly stand in what have been called 'internal' relations to the foreground persons and events: the latter simply could not be what they are presented as being without the former. The king cannot be king without his subjects and his domain, the belle of the ball requires her anonymous beaux, and a number of comparative wall-flowers as well. These background figures and factors will often as not be suggested in a story, through the feelings and reactions of the main characters in the course of their predicaments and adventures: if they are explicitly mentioned, it will usually be in a line or a phrase or two, perhaps repeated in the course of the story. (Think of the anonymous hosts, loyal but war-weary, that made Agamemnon and Achilles the war-lords that they were, or of the unnamed servants in the home of the Prodigal Son.) And it is no doubt for this reason that we would naturally say that the story is not about them, that they are background characters and nothing more. But because certain characters or events enter a story chiefly through the medium of the hero's habitual beliefs and assumptions and actions, this does not mean that they do not make a real and indeed a vital contribution to the story. Public opinion, a local or family prejudice or tradition, often play a crucial role in the development of a story, and these are things which, by definition, *anyone* from the locality or the family or the society in question can represent: in a sense the more anonymous their expression the more effective the suggestion of their force. Moreover, how a character visibly stands to those around him—whether his dependants or equals—powerfully affects the way we interpret and evaluate his actions and sufferings. The eclipse of a great leader is a very different affair from the eclipse of a matinée idol; the temptations of a good public-spirited man are worth telling, those of a shallow egoist are not. Again, in some stories at least, the more or less anonymous background figures and factors are shown undergoing a most dramatic change of role, in a manner which, while no doubt suggesting conformity to higher or more general laws, has most dramatic and unusually disconcerting effects on the foreground characters. But here we reach an occasional feature of stories whose significance becomes clear only when we turn to histories.

Chapter 3

WHAT IS HISTORY?

COMMON usage contains, and commonsense reflection will readily admit, two distinct but connected ambiguities in the word 'history'. First, 'history' can be used to stand either for a well-known genus of researches and writings, and in this sense historical results usually take the form of historical books: or else 'history' can be used to stand for the objects of these researches and writings, i.e. for what actually happened or what men actually did at certain particular times and places: in this sense historical results are ultimately the world we wake up to every morning. This ambiguity may occasionally give rise to misunderstandings or force us to employ laboured periphrases to avoid misunderstandings; but in itself it is neither dangerous nor otherwise of great significance. For peoples and individuals who have left no records or interpretable evidence of their existence can never be studied by historians and in that case can hardly be said to possess historical interest. Works of history are in this way comparable to our several personal responsibilities: in either case we are limited to such past actions as have been recorded or remembered, or as can be inferred and recognised on the basis of partial records or memories.

Nevertheless, this first ambiguity in the word 'history' has one important consequence which is not immediately obvious (and perhaps not easily acceptable) to common sense. Thus, certain past events, which for whatever reason lie beyond the range of historical study, have certainly exercised momentous effects on the later–partially recorded, historically studyable–developments of mankind. The events that lie back of the origin of language, of the family, of law and government are obvious examples. Now these events might conceivably be reconstructed anyhow in schematic outline, by biological or psychological theorists, working from evidence that is appropriate to their methods and theories. And such reconstructions might, conceivably, profoundly affect our ways of thinking about all human beings and human societies. But would we regard them as history? I do not think so. For presumably these hypothetical reconstructions would deal with changes in human life that were not subject to conscious purpose and control. And it is certainly part of our idea of history that it shall deal with human actions, efforts and purposes which we can recognise as akin to our own. Hence the supposed biological or psychological reconstructions would at best supply part of the naturalistic background of history, along with many other biological, geological and astronomical descriptions. The lesson to be drawn from these considerations can be expressed in two ways. Negatively, they force us to concede that not all knowledge of the human past is history. Positively, they force us to recognise that there is no history of human beings or societies that cannot and do not, in an extended sense of the phrase, *speak* to us: that do not belong with us in a single—no matter how fragmentary—communication system. Thus there is no single study or method of study of the human past *per se*. To be studied as history, a set of past human actions must be felt by members of some human group to belong to *its* past, and to be intelligible and worth understanding from the point of view of *its* present interests. This is part of what is meant by the oft-quoted, though to my mind singularly infelicitous dictum, that all history is contemporary history.

The second ambiguity in the word 'history' is of greater importance. It can be expressed by asking: Is 'history' simply a general or common name that we apply to all the immense number and wide variety of types of historical writings—a supposition which leaves open and undecided whether there is any essential connection, no matter how indirect, between all works of history? Or, alternatively, is every separate work of every admitted type and style of historical writing in some way a contribution to History, conceived—no matter how vaguely—as some kind of whole?—a conception which is perhaps most easily recognised or rendered plausible by reflecting on what we mean by such phrases as 'historical sense' or 'historical culture' as applied either to individuals or groups or generations. The practical importance of this question will be the greater, the further the proliferation of types of historical research and writing proceeds, and the higher the claims made for history, whether as a particular branch of human knowledge or as a general method of obtaining knowledge and understanding in other branches. Thus suppose it were claimed—as I think it would be reasonable to claim—that their idea of human history contributes as much to the world outlook of contemporary thinking men as does any body of philosophical doctrines or scientific theorems, then it would be of the first importance to decide whether 'history' can properly be said to stand for some kind of whole or unity, and if so of what kind.

On this issue the respective responses of historians and of philosophers have been amusingly in character. Historians, here as elsewhere, show an almost pathological disinclination to commit themselves to any general statements about their work, its aims, subject-matter and methods; but on the whole, both by occasional precept and general practice, they give the impression of wanting—perhaps not unreasonably—to have things both ways. On the one hand they are agreed, anyhow as a matter of general practice, in maintaining what we may call the tenet of historical liberalism: it is permissible for every historian to work not only at the topic or problem or period of his choice, but to approach his chosen subject from whatever angle and with whatever predominant interest seems good to him. Adherence to this tenet does not imply that any approach to a given topic is likely to be as fruitful or as illuminating as any other: but what it does imply is that no approaches or avenues, no styles or methods even, are excluded in advance or *a priori*. On the other hand, historians are equally at one, in both precept and practice, in their insistence on the 'interconnectedness of events', and on the need of synoptic mastery of a period or epoch if one is to contribute genuinely to the interpretation of even a minor corner or facet of it. By common agreement the man who tries to isolate a particular event or episode with a view to covering it completely and finally, as its faithful miniaturist, is just not an historian. Historical understanding of any event involves seeing it in relation to other events that are at once its context and its condition; and to the range and variety of these other events no limit can be set in advance, on either *a priori* or empirical grounds. Sense of context thus moves insensibly in the direction of sense of the whole. But what sort of whole?

The inadequacy of the historian's apparently two-faced position on this issue can best be shown if we think of sense of context and pursuit of the interconnectedness of events as leading to the recurrent historians' dream of a World or Universal history. The idea of such histories, of which Ranke's may be taken as the classic example, is that they shall succeed in connecting up all the main historic themes that can be expected to be of interest to any intelligent reader of the age. The achievements of particular nations, religions and cultures will, of course, dominate certain sections of the work: but only in so far as they served for a period as torch-carriers for the civilisation that is now common to 'us all', which to Ranke meant common to all intelligent and educated citizens of any of the great nation-states of Europe and of North America. But, alas, every such would-be-Universal history, like every narrower history, must be told with certain pre-selected interests to the fore: e.g. for Ranke those of nineteenth-century national civilisations. Even in his day this selectiveness showed a certain lack of sociological imagination; today it would be simply unthinkable. Yet, in fairness, some selection of viewpoint must be made if history is to be written at all. We can appreciate this by putting the question: What sort of Universal history will be of equal interest to equally intelligent readers from all over the world of today—i.e. for readers selected from Borneo to Massachusetts, from Oxford to Novosibirsk, from Tokyo to Brasilia? The truth is that, as a purely theoretical supposition, the number of possible Universal histories is as great as the number of possible histories of narrower, e.g. of national, compass. And thus the historian's most strenuous pursuit of the interconnectedness of events is inevitably hamstrung by his adherence to the tenet of historical liberalism. The whole, towards which he seems pledged to expand his interpretative vision, must always escape him, and might well seem, to the unsympathetic outsider, to be a delusive will-o'-the-wisp.

This brings us to the philosophers of history who, on the present issue, show none of the experienced caginess, none of the sensitive deviousness, of the historians. The philosophers here have spoken out in bold, clear tones. Unfortunately they have spoken in completely opposite senses, and, with one notable exception, have shown little appreciation of the dilemma that here faces historical thinking. On the one side we have those 'pre-critical' philosophers of history who claim to disclose a single direction or cyclical pattern in all historical events, and claim further that it is in the light of this direction or pattern that all real, or at least all characteristic historical understanding is achieved. These philosophers of history have, as we have seen, aroused the sharpest suspicion, sometimes the quite outspoken detestation of practising historians; and recently they have been subjected to such a systematic and relentless lambasting from Professor Popper that further discussion of them here would be superfluous. No one has ever in truth descried a single unmistakably dominant pattern in all human history; and no practising historian has ever explained or illuminated the events of a particular period or epoch solely or even mainly by exhibiting them as instances of such a pattern. Admittedly the ablest of these pre-critical philosophers of history, Vico and Marx, have exercised immensely powerful influences on later historians. But these influences (where they were for good) are quite independent of Vico's cyclical and Marx's apocalyptically dialectical world-pictures. The originality of Vico lay in his appreciation of hitherto neglected sources of historical information and insight; that of Marx in his bold delineation of certain important long-term trends and in his systematic, even if entirely inadequate, attempt to provide an explanation of why these trends had persisted.

But have later critical philosophers of history done nothing to illuminate or resolve this conflict between the tenet of historical liberalism and that pursuit of interconnectedness which seems to be endemic in historical thinking? Regretfully we must answer that, with the exception of Collingwood, they have shown themselves virtually unaware of the second term in this conflict—no doubt because of the efforts they put out to obtain recognition, and to prevent misunderstanding, of its first term. Thus Rickert and Weber were remarkably effective exponents and defenders of the tenet of historical liberalism. Weber, in particular, pushed its claims to the extreme limit and demonstrated brilliantly (and to common sense astonishingly) that complete freedom of approach to historical problems is compatible with the acceptance of publicly admitted tests and standards of objectivity. Unfortunately Weber combined this thesis with another of quite different character, viz., that since the historical world admits of many different approaches and evaluations, we must regard it as meaningless and valueless as a whole. Our account of the one historical world effectively rebuts this thesis, without claiming to establish the contrary thesis that the historical world *must* admit of a single scheme of evaluation and interpretation.

It is one of the great merits of R. G. Collingwood, as a philosopher of history, that he constantly shows his awareness of—or at least sensitivity to—our problem, and that in one place he comes near to indicating a satisfactory answer to it. In an important section of *The Idea of History*[1] Collingwood asks: How does a work of history differ from a work of fiction? In answering this, he takes it for granted that the historian's work and the novelist's have something important in common. Each, he says, seeks to construct a 'coherent picture' (we should prefer to say, to construct a 'followable narrative'). But evidently the historian is under the further obligation that he must make his 'picture' as true as possible: it must be an account of things that really happened. This requirement is then specified as follows.

 1. The historian's picture must be located in space and time.

 2. 'All history must be consistent with itself. Purely imaginary worlds cannot clash and need not agree; each is a world to itself. But there is only one historical world, and everything in it must stand in some relation to everything else. . . .'

3. The historian's picture 'stands in a peculiar relation to something called evidence'.

Collingwood's own chief concern was with the third–and through it with the first–of these three conditions. But it is condition (2) that is relevant to our present discussion: in particular the juxtaposition in it of the requirement of consistency in all history (i.e. between as well as within different historical works) and of the idea of the 'one historical world'.

As it stands, however, condition (2) could be interpreted in a number of different ways. First, quite simply, the one-ness of the one historical world might be taken to be a necessary consequence of its forming part of the one (real) spatio-temporal world. On this view the one historical world would be an intuitable, or at least imaginable, quasi-substantial whole, viz. that very thin slice of space-time within which human beings have lived and achieved things in characteristically human fashion. Now all these actual human achievements must have been causally or ontologically compatible. Therefore, it could be argued, all true accounts of any selected parts or aspects of them must be logically compatible or consistent. Hence the one historical world is the ground of the requirement of consistency as between different histories.

But, as we have already seen, in considering the first obvious ambiguity of the word 'history', nothing but confusion can result from equating the idea of history with the idea of the total human past. We need only add here that our ignorance of where the past limit of the proposed slice of space-time should be set, and of the nature and order of importance of the main events that fall within it, is terrifying in its immensity. Hence the one historical world, if conceived as a quasi-substantial whole, would, in fact, give us no grounds for accepting, and *a fortiori* no guidance in applying, the rule that all history must be consistent with itself.

Suppose, however, that this crudely substantialist view of the one historical world were qualified as follows. The one historical world, it might be said, refers to the sum of recognisable and recordable human actions which happen to be known by historians. Thus the rule that all history must be consistent with itself would come simply to this: no description or explanation of past human actions can be accepted if it is inconsistent with other currently accepted descriptions or explanations of other known historical events. This seems reasonable enough. But suppose we ask ourselves how this rule of consistency is to be, or can be, observed in practice. Different histories, we must remember, have been written by authors who, although contemporaries, knew nothing of each other's work or indeed of the subject-matter of each other's work: for example, Greek historians and Chinese annalists of the fifth century B.C. And, although in much lesser degree, this sort of thing is always bound to happen. No historian can ever be certain that he has consulted and kept in mind all the works of history, and *a fortiori* all the possible pieces of evidence, that might conceivably have some relevance to, and therefore might conceivably show some inconsistency with, his own account of his own chosen topic. Again, there are historical topics between which it is quite impossible to be certain what should count as inconsistencies. Is it conceivable that Caesar's account of one of his campaigns in Gaul is inconsistent in some respect with a military description in some mediaeval chronicle or for that matter in some work of modern European history? At first blush, we might be tempted to say, no–unless either of the later writers included in his account some gratuitous and unorthodox references to Caesar's campaign. Then on reflection we might agree that there could be inconsistencies between the three in respect of certain geographical details. But can we be quite sure about this? Can we be sure that the three writers, of such very different dates, were referring to the same physical details? Can we be sure that the physical features that they might severally name and describe have not, over the centuries, altered their relative positions? And so on.

In the face of these difficulties I feel that Collingwood's account needs to be amended in two closely connected ways. First, the relation between the one historical world and the requirement of consistency as between different histories is not that of ground and consequent, as Collingwood's statement of condition (2) suggests, but rather that of mutual entailment between two distinct yet necessarily connected notions. Second, the idea of the one historical world must be given an interpretation which frees it from the confusions which result from regarding it as a quasi-substantial whole—as a slice, or even any selection of known parts or aspects of a slice, of physical space-time. The one historical world, I should like to suggest, is an intellectual ideal or device which is essential for the practice of history as we know it; but its location, if it must be given one, is in the heads, because in the hopes of historians. To speak more exactly: the one historical world is an idea without any definite descriptive content, indeed it is not an empirical idea at all. It is comparable, rather, with a Kantian ideal of reason (as regulatively employed); only, whereas Kant proposed his ideals of reason as principles guiding and encouraging all theoretical science, in particular the search for universal physical laws, the idea of the one historical world serves to guide research into the particular sequences and developments of human actions during a (very roughly) indicatable stretch of time and range of places. The required one-ness exists in the readiness of historians to look for and learn about the relatedness of incidents, persons, movements, periods which at first sight, or to traditional belief, have no mutual relevance whatsoever. This claim may sound paradoxical, and suspiciously 'idealistic'. But it can easily be rendered convincing if we consider a question which Collingwood, oddly enough, nowhere raises: namely, what are the necessary antecedents of the practice of historical thinking and writing as we know it? Or, more simply, from where do histories come into being?

All history presupposes, and ultimately rests upon, an amalgam of memories—personal, family or folk memories—and of commonly accepted legends and myths—religious, tribal or national—backed up by a certain amount of visible evidence; a ruined fort or temple, the remains of an irrigation system, a ceremonial drinking cup, a folded papyrus or what have you. But, as a result of what more positive causes or influences, can we imagine history arising from this necessary pre- or sub-historical amalgam? There seems to be only one possible answer: namely, when a man of that adventurous and restless turn of mind, which we today tend to associate with scientific endeavour, begins to feel an acute dissatisfaction with his own family's or nation's received account of certain happenings, because of its blatant inconsistency with the account of the same happenings that is accepted unquestioningly by the people from beyond the mountain or from the offshore islands. And this dissatisfaction, which is essential to the beginnings of history, remains essential, in some degree, at every further stage of its development. An historian in whatever field starts from a received account–no matter how fragmentary or naïve –which he sees to be inadequate in certain ways, chiefly on the score of its inconsistency with other accepted historical descriptions and conclusions. Hence the requirement that different histories shall be mutually consistent can be regarded as a logician's formal statement of an intellectual demand which, for all that we commonly express it in negative terms, is of truly positive, truly creative character. This is to the effect that the historian shall not be tied to his received national or tribal or religious legends: that, although his prime concern is with the past of his group, the group with which he identifies himself in writing, yet he must combine this concern with a constant struggle against parochial-mindedness; that in developing any part of his own proper theme he must take into account all other treatments of it and all evidence that bears upon it, no matter how indirectly or how surprisingly or embarrassingly. In working in accordance with this demand, which is the positive side of the requirement of consistency within all history, the historian, no matter if unwittingly, is at once inspired by and contributing to the idea, and the reality, of the one historical world.

When we construe it in this way, we can readily grant that the idea of the one historical world contains more than merely descriptive content, more than any description or reference to any past actions or achievements of mankind. But is it plausible to maintain, as we have done, that it contains no descriptive content whatsoever? Well, if it did, what would the content be? Certainly it would not be the same for historians (or their readers) of different civilisations, or even of different nations in one and the same civilisation. Here, too, we may usefully recall, as an extreme case, those past ages in which two different groups of historians, Greek and Chinese, wrote in entire ignorance not only of each other's work but of the worlds that they were separately describing. Yet certainly, had the required information been available to them, Herodotus and any Chinese annalist of the fifth century B.C. would have taken it into account. In this extreme instance, therefore, we have two groups of historians, with every member of either group sensitive in some degree to the idea of the one historical world; yet this idea must possess two totally distinct descriptive contents, if it is to have any at all! Or again, let us consider the naïve belief, which certain notable historians have entertained, that a kind of composite history of a long period or a far-reaching historical topic could be collated out of the sum of all the best monographs dealing with any particular aspect of it. Now generalise—and parody—this belief a little, and we reach the more than naïve belief that the one historical world could be represented, say, by the contents of the latest editions of the Cambridge Ancient and of the Cambridge Modern Histories plus a few more series of the same general character. But the suggestion that the one historical world, or that that endless interconnectedness of events which historians strive to unravel with such passion, could be enshrined—if only for a decade – in a few such series, has only to be mentioned for its absurdity to answer our question for us. The one historical world is not a synopsis nor a formula nor a blue-print nor a symbolic picture of the endless interconnectedness of events. The one historical world is a demand laid upon the conscience, a challenge set to the passion, of any and every historian.

So we come back to our dilemma. The historian is committed to the search for interconnectedness and is thus drawn on by an ideal demand that expresses his ideal of the whole, of the one historical world. But at the same time, because of the inevitable selectiveness of all historical thinking, it is impossible that he should ever reach, that he could ever have come perceptibly nearer to that ideal goal. Now, however, we have seen that this seeming paradox is equivalent to a fact that is virtually a commonplace: namely, that the one-ness of the one historical world depends upon, and is indeed a function of, the degree of real community of thought and knowledge that exists among historians at any given time. Indeed, in an ideal community of historians, every member of which would be fully alive to the relevance of all his colleagues' works to his own, we might find a semi-substantial (but still inter-cerebral) form for the one historical world. But then we remember that the members of such a community must be men. And that reminds us that in a year's or a week's or an hour's time their ideal condition of mutual understanding and co-operation may be shattered by the march of human events. Separation, ignorance, bias, provincialism are always poised, ready to return; and have therefore to be recognised and resisted by the historical conscience in every generation.

Of course, it can be objected to this idealistic-sounding account of the one historical world that there would be no possibility of a communion of thought and knowledge, of methods and standards, among historians unless *in fact* a great many past actions of men had been interconnected or mutually relevant even if in the most indirect ways; and that historians commonly and rightly think of themselves as trying to reveal the nature and degree of that interconnectedness. Taken in itself, there is nothing objectionable in this way of describing the situation. The danger about it is that it can lead people to assume that history is the human past, that the one historical world is a substantial slice of the one spatio-temporal world, or a quasi-substantial whole of combinable bits of historical knowledge. But history is not just past human actions, nor just those past human actions that happen to be known by men of a later generation. It is our name for the study of any past human action in so far as it is understood through its interconnectedness with other actions which a particular community or generation regards as of special interest to *them*. In other words 'our' history is whatever past actions our historians have succeeded in making intelligible to us, whoever 'we' happen to be.

This correction of the second of the three conditions to

which, according to Collingwood, a narrative must conform if it is to be history and not fiction, has led us to a point from which we can see a fourth condition, neglected by Collingwood, but quite as important for his purpose as the three which he considers. In an easily illustrated sense of the word 'public', historical narratives stand in contrast to fiction because both the received materials out of which they are formed and the final use to which they are submitted give them an emphatically public character. Ultimately the historian draws or receives his material from the memories, stories and legends and records of the people or civilisation for which he is writing his history. Similarly, to be sure, a novelist or poet may receive his materials from national or personal memory or myth or record. But the novelist or poet will not attempt to improve upon his received material in the way that the historian does, viz. by deriving from them a truer or intellectually more acceptable version of some part or aspect of the human past. Hence, whilst a thorough knowledge of the previous literature of one's subject and an appreciation of the main conflicts and convergences of judgment which it displays is a prerequisite of any serious historical work, no comparable obligation is laid upon the poet or novelist in respect of earlier poetic treatment of his subject, whether that subject be mythical–an Orestes, a Don Juan or a Wandering Jew–or historical–a Jesus, a Jeanne d'Arc, or a Lincoln. When successive poets or novelists or playwrights give us their Jesus or their Jeanne (and *a fortiori* when they give us their Orestes or Don Juan) they do not claim to be contributing to, to be getting us nearer to, the finally acceptable, fully interconnected truths about their respective subjects. What the poet gives us is something which we prize for an entirely different reason from that which makes us search for and prize successive approximations to public truth. The poet gives us something of his own, a new slant or re-action or comment that is particularly pertinent to his own age, or else the affirmation of some universal value which he finds instanced or symbolised in his hero's or heroine's fate. The poet of Jesus or Jeanne or Lincoln may thus be giving us something of incomparable value, but he is not sustaining and improving and revising, in the historian's way, a people's conception of some crucial character or episode in its actual past.

By emphasising the public character of the historian's materials and finished work–by assimilating him, if you will, to the community's curator of its inherited relics and records, charged with the duty of explaining, from the standpoint of his own generation, their significance and value–we can correct two widely held but equally inadequate views of the historian's essential task. On the one hand a number of textbooks of historical methodology have presented the ideal historian as a mixture of police-inspector concerned with fakes and forgeries and pedantic schoolmaster concerned more with identifiable mistakes than with potential informativeness in his received material. A good (or a 'scientific') historian, on this view, can be conceived in entirely negative terms: his main job is to unmask past falsehoods, errors and superstitions–especially when these relate to the Middle Ages and have been passed down by monkish hands. On the other hand, we have Collingwood's scornful attack upon historians of 'scissors and paste'[2] who commit the (to him) unforgivable sin of treating parts of their predecessors' work as authoritative–as though in any well-developed field of knowledge we do not have to accept most of our beliefs on some kind of authority or other. By emphasising the public character of the historian's task, we can correct both these extreme, and alike extremely one-sided views, whilst at the same time admitting what they have sought to emphasise– that historical thinking includes a continuous task of criticism and revision of received materials on the one hand, and of original conjecture and hypothesis for the improved interpretation of such materials on the other.

* * * * *

We are now in a better position to consider the relevance to historical understanding of those essential features of narrative, and of the following of narrative, which we discussed in Chapter 2. Following a story, we saw, is a teleologically guided form of attention. We are pulled along by our sympathies towards a

promised yet always open conclusion, across any number of
contingent, surprising events, but always on the understanding
that these will not divert us hopelessly from the vaguely
promised end. Can this analysis of story help us to articulate
what is peculiar to historical understanding? I believe that it
can. But evidently this claim presupposes an answer to two
prior questions. First, is an element of story or narrative
essential to all history? And secondly, assuming that our answer
to this first question is Yes, then what is the place and function
of narrative *vis-à-vis* other features or aspects of works of history,
e.g. the discussions, analyses and explanations that they
contain?

We must bear in mind that an immense variety of literary
productions and contributions—books, articles, discussion notes
etc., in which are expressed thoughts of the most varied forms,
styles and intentions—are today bracketed under the rubric
History. So true is this that any sane essay in the methodology
of history would probably have to begin from an examination of
the principles of historical bibliography. But for our broad
purposes, I think it fair to take it for granted that a great deal of
historical literature is ancillary to or parasitic upon history of a
more central and substantial kind. As examples of ancillary
history I have in mind not only the production of lists, accounts,
diary jottings, etc., as evidence for or against some general
accepted conclusion as to some historical matter of fact, but the
kind of book or article which sets itself the modest purpose of
filling in the background to certain major and already deeply
studied events, and again the ever-increasing amount of
discussion between leading historians as to the proper or most
profitable line of approach to and interpretation of different
topics and periods. It seems to me quite clear and certain that
historical contributions and discussions of these kinds are
ancillary to the kind of history that interests us all *most*
(historians themselves included): namely histories which treat
of some major achievement or failure of men living and working
together, in societies or nations or any other lastingly organised
groups. Examples are the unification or disintegration of an
empire; the rise or fall of a party; some crucial invention—or

what held back its discovery for decades or perhaps centuries; the achievement of some great legal or moral reform; the dissemination of some religious or philosophical idea; the origin, flowering and decline of a great artistic style. Conning over the most famous works of history, one can easily find titles to match these general headings.

But can such central and admittedly most important works of history be considered as primarily narratives, as narratives before all else, i.e. as stories although subject, of course, to the four conditions which we have considered above? Do we not rather find that in them all manner of elements and aspects of story have been excised or flattened out; so that in place of dramatic and heroic national or religious myth we are being offered a highly complicated yet rationally explained and acceptable unfolding of this or that society or institution or idea or creed? This is obviously true of the kind of history that is intended to de-bunk earlier traditional accounts. But is it not largely true of all serious histories? Are they not so many fights against the parochialism and the crude personification which seem to be endemic in our everyday thinking about our past and present affairs? The causes which serious historians attribute are in the main massive and impersonal, but for that reason perhaps more easily calculable, than the personal motives and intentions by which we commonly explain human actions: they may be terrifying, they may often act with a fearful justice, but seldom with that dramatic rightness and clear poetic justice which is characteristic of stories. History offends against both romance and simplicity: typically its accounts of important events are more complicated and yet more natural than our traditional stories or our all-too-human expectations would have led us to believe.

All this may be granted, and still it can be maintained that narrative is the form which expresses what is basic to and characteristic of historical understanding. Granted that every genuine work of history is also a work of reason, of judgment, of hypotheses, of explanation: nevertheless every genuine work of history displays two features which strongly support the claim that history is a species of the genus Story. To appreciate, and in a proper sense to use, a book or a chapter of history means to read it through; to follow it through; to follow it in the light of its promised or adumbrated outcome through a succession of contingencies, and not simply to be interested in what resulted or could be inferred as due to result from certain initial conditions. Both the natural and the social sciences are particularly and properly interested in results in this sense, since it is their logically required and predicted results that prove their laws and hypotheses right or wrong. The systematic sciences do not aim at giving us a followable account of what actually happened in any natural or social process: what they offer us is idealisations or simplified models of the sorts of thing that should have happened, if their currently accepted laws and theories are to be trusted, and from which further testable deductions can be made. But history, like all stories and all imaginative literature, is as much a journey as an arrival, as much an approach as a result. Again, every genuine work of history is read in this way because its subject-matter is felt to be worth following–through contingencies, accidents, setbacks, and all the multifarious details of its development. And what does this mean if not that its subject-matter is of compelling human interest, that we must hear more and more fully and accurately what these people really did and failed to do, even if the story of their achievements and failures has to be told in mainly abstract terms that are oddly remote from the lost feelings and gestures and acts of the actual participants?

But against these defences of our claim that history is essentially story, a second objection can be pressed. Can it seriously be maintained that all works of history–of history of the kind that interests us all *most*–display the kind of unity that is characteristic of story? Do we in all cases follow them as wholes, as complex unities of human action and reaction developing, through no matter how many complications and delays, to some kind of culmination, to some long-awaited, to some promised or adumbrated conclusion? Is it not obvious that most histories do not centre and emanate from particular individuals and groups of individuals, but rather run through successive groups and generations of individuals, dropping them with complete indifference once they have served their part in a development about whose total character and eventual significance they may have remained ignorant or indifferent? More simply, are not the subjects of most history books too large to allow them to be treated as stories? Either they cover too long a period–histories of England, say, or of the Papacy or of human technology; or else they deal with so many different peoples or other groups–as in histories of wars and alliances and so on; or else they deal with such abstract features of some relatively short-term period, that appreciation of individual effort and aim is almost impossible, e.g. histories of Allied plans and policies regarding coal or merchant shipping in the last World War.

If taken in one way, this objection is easily met. Many serious and important historical works are not real unities. We could say of them, as Ranke said harshly of his own first book: all this is still histories, it is not yet history. And the obvious inference would be that such books, despite the important materials and the valuable individual judgments and descriptions that they contain, must be considered failures: failures, that is, from the point of view of presenting as a followable unity the great theme which they sought to bring to life in a single work.

But this way of meeting the above objection misses what is really important in it: namely its challenge to us to vindicate the claim that every successful work of history (of the kind that interests us all *most*) must be followable, as a unity, in the way that a story is. For this purpose two considerations from the side of story are, I think, particularly pertinent. First, many of the world's greatest and most moving stories are, so to speak, trans-personal in exactly the way that the objection mentions. Think of the Orestes cycle, for example, with its theme of recurrent interfamily guilt and revenge, or the story that runs from Abraham through Isaac and Jacob to Joseph. Some themes require not simply a group of dramatically opposed characters, but a succession, perhaps generation after generation, of characters who are related at every stage by the gradual working out of a great unifying idea. But secondly, we may recall from our discussion in Chapter 2 that the conclusion of any story can be regarded either from the aesthetic standpoint or from the standpoint of understanding the story's development, and that our judgments about the conclusion of a given story may well differ according to which of these two standpoints we are adopting. Thus the event which we would all count as the conclusion of the story, inasmuch as it serves as the focus and goal of our interest, may not in fact occupy the last chapter or paragraph of the story: there may be an epilogue, or the final act may be left entirely untold. We can now go further than this and add that, when we reach what we would naturally take to be a story's conclusion from the point of view of understanding its development, we may quite possibly find the story-teller intervening to tell us that this seeming conclusion is merely an interim halt, a re-starting place for further developments within a larger narrative whole. This is what happens in effect in those multi-sequelled popular novels that theoretically might go on for ever. But something rather like it is found in a form of serious literature, lying half-way between story and history, namely the saga. A saga is not simply a succession of stories, most of them believed to be true, and linked together by the fact that the heroes of the successive stories were ancestors of the original audience, and that the stories are usually set out in chrono-logical order. There is also usually an overlap of certain dominant interests from one part to the next. There is always unfinished business—if only the business of keeping the peace in the next generation—waiting to be taken up in the next book of the saga.

Now it might be suggested that the kind of unity that we find in successful works of history shows a partial analogy both with the kind of unity which is characteristic of saga and with that which is illustrated in, e.g., the tales of Orestes and of Jacob. All history is, like saga, basically a narrative of events in which human thought and action play a predominant part. But most historical themes tend to run beyond the interests, plans, lives and works of any one group or generation of men. History, as we have remarked, seems to run past individuals, using them perhaps for a little while and dropping them without any compunction when once their usefulness is exhausted. On the other hand, we know, to quote Marx, that men make history: history is made up of human actions within the world and of nothing else. Both these aspects of life are perfectly conveyed by the great sagas. But equally all history—at least all history of the kind that interests us all—expresses and is in a way de-limited by the influence of what Ranke quaintly called 'the ideas', meaning by this such dominant trends as can give shape to the aims and actions of successive generations, and which we can see mounting to some kind of culmination. It would not be difficult to obtain general agreement as to the 'ideas' that find expression in, for example, *The Peloponesian War*, *The Annals*, *The Decline and Fall of the Roman Empire*, *The Papacy*, and *The Waning of the Middle Ages*. The outstanding question is whether appreciation of such 'ideas' can somehow be brought under, or brought into organic connection with, the act of following a narrative.

A trend or tendency is something that we see gradually disclosed through a succession of events; it is something that belongs to the events which we are following and no others; it is, so to speak, a pattern-quality of those particular events. It would thus seem that our appreciation of any historical trend must depend upon, or be a resultant of, our following a particular narrative, a narrative of events which happen to be arranged in such a way that, roughly speaking, they move in some easily described relation to some fixed point of reference. To be sure our appreciation of any such trend is in its way a kind of intellectual feat: it requires us to stand back a little and reflect upon the progress of the narrative that we have been reading. But this is just as true of many of the subtler indications of motive or influence which a complex narrative may contain. Again, a trend may, of course, admit of explanation in terms of laws which hold universally of the kinds of ingredient elements which enter into it. But in itself, and simply as a recognised pattern-quality of a succession of events, a trend is neither a law nor a manifest instance of any law. It is something recognised in and through the development of this particular set of events. And when these events are of a kind that make up or can be expressed as a story, then it seems reasonable to regard the trend itself as an aspect or facet of the story in question, and not as an explanatory factor that has been dragged into the narrative, so to speak, from outside. On these grounds it could be maintained that what Ranke called 'the ideas' can perfectly well be accommodated under the notion of narrative.

What, then, does the word 'history' mean? We have seen that it stands for a wide family or syndrome of researches and writings, the key members of which always contain narratives of past human actions. These narratives are followable or intelligible in the same general way that all stories are. Of course, to be historical a narrative must rest upon evidence, i.e. it must deal with events that can be shown to have actually happened at roughly assignable dates and places. A historical narrative, furthermore, will usually succeed in making its subject-matter more intelligible to its readers (who are usually presumed to have some vague acquaintance with it) by showing its interconnections with other relevant historical evidences and results. These characteristics of history are commonplace enough, and agreement with regard to them does little to illuminate the kind of understanding which works of history communicate. Nevertheless, this preliminary review of the relationship between story and history was necessary before we could ask how the salient characteristics of story, as disclosed by our discussion in Chapter 2, can be applied to the special case of history. In turning to this question we shall be facing the main problems of the historical understanding.

Chapter 4

THE HISTORICAL UNDERSTANDING

I

THE characteristic situation of the historian when he settles into the research that will grow into a book is that he knows broadly how his narrative and general treatment of his subject will go, but that, once he is immersed in the relevant materials, there is almost no limit to the surprises that they may hold in store for him. What was first conceived as an introductory chapter may become the bulk of his work: a proposed epilogue may swell to such proportions that it reduces all that went before it to the status of a *mise en scène*, or the whole shape of his narrative may be changed because he recognises that some long-unquestioned 'truth' rests on surprisingly little direct evidence, or that some allegedly necessary interpretation of events is really quite unplausible once national or sectarian bias is set aside. Or again a historian may, in the course of studying some seemingly isolated topic, say in military history, become progressively more and more impressed with the relevance to it of a whole range of evidence and of general considerations which had never previously won his close attention – evidence derived from economic or social or religious history, for example. Nevertheless it remains true that, from the moment an historian first conceives his task, he conceives it as a certain kind of story, with a roughly descried track of development towards a main conclusion. If it is true that in the physical sciences there is always a theory, it is no less true that in historical research there is always a story. In the former case there is always a provisional theory which guides experimental researches, even though these will lead to its replacement; in the latter case there is always an initial or provisional story that acts as guiding thread to the successive assessments, interpretations and criticisms which lead the historian to his final judgment as to what the story really was, or as to what actually happened.

This characteristic situation of the historian is to some extent matched by that of his readers; and the nearer to being ideally prepared and intelligent his readers are, the more perfect the matching becomes. Typically, the reader of a work of history will know the broad course of the events which it covers and something of their consequences for later history. No matter how remote from here and now the events described may be, he must at least know (or believe) that they led ultimately into one of those main streams of history whose waves are still beating the shores of today and tomorrow. This initial appreciation directs and sustains his interest as he reads: but it is compatible with his receiving any number of jolts to his previous beliefs or natural expectations as to what 'ought to happen' at this or that point in the narrative. To read a genuine work of history intelligently is thus to receive a lesson in liberation from in-born prejudices and provincial brashnesses. But in the experience of reading, one's critical powers are not called out only against one's former self. An essential part of accepting an historian's analyses and judgments is that one shall be ready to question, to probe and to criticise them: how else can one come genuinely to accept them for what they are – as one man's serious contribution, on the evidence available to him, to the ideally acceptable account of the events in question?

There are, to be sure, exceptions to this general position; for example, records and memoirs of explorations and adventures in parts of the world which were – anyhow to the book's first readers – hitherto entirely unknown. Imagine the state of mind of the first readers of certain chapters of Raleigh's or Dampier's or Bougainville's accounts of their voyages. What they read and followed must have had for them all the glorious improbability of a boy's adventure-book. The only obvious links with familiar, commonly accepted facts were that the expedition left some known port in accordance with governmental orders at such a date and returned to another so many years later. But, oddly enough, this kind of exception only serves to substantiate, to bring out the general validity, of our account of the characteristic situation of the historian and his readers. It is fatally easy, in reading, e.g., the Tahiti chapters of Bougainville's narrative, to slip from reading them historically into reading them as a sheer story: the scenes are so brilliant, the incidents so compelling, the passions involved so inevitable and yet so unheard of, the whole story bathed in a freshness such as we associate with dream or imagination, but which here is due to a kind of irresponsibility that attached to the circumstances—which were such as could obtain once only and never again. To read such pages as history is difficult, because this means reading them as a narrative that is accepted as broadly true on the grounds of the evidence supplied and of the apparent correctness of its explanations and their coherence with the rest of our relevant historical knowledge. Let the critical, doubting, questioning, assessing attitude of mind lapse—or rise—into the sheer joy of following an absorbing narrative, and the historical mind has passed into the land of story, and is heading hard towards the land of dreams.

The same point can be made in connection with the 'sensation of pastness', the experience of touching right back to a past lived reality, which it is perhaps natural to expect in reading any work of history. We should notice, first of all, however, that successful expression of this sensation is by no means the peculiar privilege of historians. The poet, the novelist, the essayist are every bit as capable of conveying it. But further, when the historian does succeed in giving us the sensation of pastness, how does he do it? By a prolonged, detailed, pageant-like reproduction of some vanished scene? No. He is much more likely to suggest a living—or rather a having-been-lived—past, by, to quote Huizinga, 'a line from a document or chronicle, by a print, by a few notes of an old song'.[1] But such means as these only serve to set off the real job of persuasion, the job of convincing the reader that this and only this can be the true interpretation of some campaign or revolt or reform, that thus and only thus can things have really happened in certain towns, on certain roads, in certain rooms, which is the historian's way of making the past give out its secrets, and of preparing us to receive the back-taste of its vanished life.

Thus from a number of points of view we can see how the intellectual, i.e. the strenuous, the critical, the technical elements in any historical work feed into and give properly historical form to that initial interest, that eagerness to travel all the way to the achievement of a promised conclusion which is the common basis of both history and story. The nature of these intellectual elements will be made clearer by our discussion of the factors of 'human interest' and of 'contingency' in historical narratives.

II

A work of history, we have claimed, can move forward to its goal through the actions of an indefinite number of groups or generations of individuals, so long as its characteristic unity grows out of, and is appreciated as emanating from, the actions of these individuals. But does this mean that what carries us forward in reading a work of history is always, basically, that interest in human beings and their doings which compels our attention in the case of stories? This appears to have been the view of Ranke, who required of every historian

> a real affection for this human race in all its manifold variety.
> . . . If he feels this affection for the living being as such, he will
> enjoy seeing how man has perennially contrived to live . . . he
> will readily follow the development of his nature under such diverse
> conditions, his institutions and his morals, the sequence of events and
> the development of major enterprises–all this he will try to follow
> *without any purpose beyond the pleasure in individual life itself* [2] [our
> italics].

In fact, Ranke combined this requirement with a repeated insistence upon the peculiar unity displayed by different historical themes and periods, as well as by a life-long adherence to the idea of Universal History. This, however, does not prevent Ranke from serving as an exemplar of the thesis that I shall defend: namely, that to think historically, or to exercise historical understanding, always means, or at least includes as a predominant element, the appreciation of certain human aims, choices, valuations, efforts, deeds–things that are to be attributed exclusively to individual men, whether acting on their own or (more likely) in concert, whether acting on their own personal behalf or (more likely) as representatives of their group or cause or nation.

This view is, I think, attractive to common sense. Unfortunately, however, it has not won, either from historians or from philosophers, the kind of exposition and defence which it deserves. Those who have accepted it have either been content with its intuitive persuasiveness, or else have identified it with the much more extreme 'Nominalist' view that general propositions—statements that evidently cannot be said to be about known individuals—have no place in history, unless as the major premisses of explanations of particular events. Now writers of history differ enormously in their habits of thought and tricks of style. But can one conceive a work of political history, say, which does not contain a number of sentences having for their subject such phrases as 'the government's policy', 'the progress of reform', 'the condition of the working-classes', 'the growth of the opposition', 'the constitution', 'the general level of education', and so on? Phrases such as these do not, on the face of it, refer to identifiable actions of identifiable individuals. Yet they stand for something: let us say, without committing ourselves as to how exactly our words should be interpreted, that they stand for 'institutional facts'. But now, it seems perfectly reasonable to maintain that we understand such facts, that we follow changes and developments in them, in a way that is quite different from that in which we follow the thoughts and feelings and actions of individuals. Thus, we would naturally say that we *notice* a general shift or trend in the direction of legislation over a certain period, but that we *understand* and *appreciate* the motives that inspired the reformers and the arguments by which they advanced their cause. If, then, these differences in usage do point to a distinction in the facts—in the ways we follow trends on the one hand and motives and reasons on the other—who is to decide, and on what sort of grounds could it possibly be decided, whether the following of general trends or the following of individual motives and reasons is of greater importance in history?

There are a number of ways in which this question could be decided. Suppose, for instance, that the following of general trends could be shown, despite appearances to the contrary, to be logically reducible to, or totally explainable in terms of, the following of individual thoughts and actions. Or, a milder possibility, suppose the following of trends could be shown to presuppose or logically to require the following of a number of individual thoughts and actions. Then, on either of these suppositions, it would be obvious which sort of following is of greater importance in history. But suppose again that the exact opposite of our last suggestion could be shown to be true, and that the following of individual thoughts and actions could be shown to presuppose, logically, the power to follow trends or general types of change in certain institutional facts: then equally our question about the nature of historical understanding would apparently be answered. Interest in individual actions and thoughts and decisions would then be subordinate to interest in general social–e.g. political, economic, sociological, psychological–truths. This last may seem a very far-fetched suggestion. But, in fact, a number of important considerations appear to support it. I propose, therefore, to set out these two extremely opposed theses, which for convenience I shall call Nominalism and Realism respectively, with regard to historical understanding. Neither of them is, in fact, wholly acceptable. But their dramatic opposition provides a framework within which we can sort out what is at stake in the claim that human interest is as essential a factor in the following of histories as in the following of stories.

First, then, to outline the two positions for the purposes of our present discussion. The Nominalist bases his case on the truism that only individual things, including persons, exist. In particular it is only in the thoughts, beliefs, actions, etc., of individual men and women that institutions, doctrines, etc., can be said to exist. Hence all talk about these institutional facts is a kind of intellectual shorthand: for instance, to talk of a change of doctrine is to talk, summarily, about the ways in which certain individuals changed their ways of thinking; to talk of the growth of a nation is to talk, summarily, of the fact that a lot more people began habitually to obey and to pay taxes to a common ruler or government.

The Realist accepts the Nominalist's main premiss, but strenuously denies his conclusion. Every characteristically human action–performed, to be sure, by some individual man and woman–involves a tacit reference to other actions, and not simply to such other actions as actually have taken or will take place. To talk, to think, to promise, to trade, even to fight (in characteristically human fashion) is to engage in an activity whose procedure requires reference to what *any* persons subject to certain conditions or answering to a certain description would do or can be expected to do. In other words, characteristic human actions are performed and interpreted as expressions of generally accepted institutions, beliefs, routines and norms, quite as much as of personal feelings and dispositions. But further, these real (although abstract) entities have histories; and historians can trace out these histories and can render them followable even when the names and separate individualities of all concerned in them are entirely lost. How then can history owe its interest, the power by which it draws us, to our desire to hear more of what individual people did?

It is easy to see what each side in this debate is hitting at. The Nominalist gains our approval in so far as he attacks that tendency to reify–and sometimes indeed to deify–abstractions, which is one of the last infirmities of the human mind. The Realist (as we have described him) is most obviously right when he attacks the view that history is merely one damned thing – or king – after another, and undercuts the brash presumption that human action means simply the sum of the acts that are ascribed, in the legal or the physical sense, to different individuals. But how, and to what extent, can either side meet and criticisms of the other, or account for the more obvious truths that support the other's case?

Let us begin again with the Nominalist. He will, of course, concede that historical narratives abound in abstract-sounding phrases that stand for what we have called 'institutional facts'. He must, therefore, first of all explain why historians choose or are forced to adopt types of literary expression which so successfully disguise the true, i.e. the purely individual, character of historical facts. Certain lines of explanation readily suggest themselves. Most obviously, phrases like 'the nation', 'public opinion', 'the state of industry', etc., are sometimes used simply to cover or summarise the actions (which could be described in detail) of individuals (who could, in fact, be named). But why, assuming that he has the names and the details, does the historian prefer to work with these common or abstract nouns? Is he constrained simply by stylistic reasons or the need to save space and time? Clearly there are other factors that affect him. In particular it would detract from the effectiveness of his narrative to detail and specify again and again such and such actions of this, that and the other individual, if, as is often the case, all that the development of his chosen topic requires is a single general reference to one common feature of the actions or agents in question. (This consideration of course leaves open the possibility that these details may figure most usefully in some other historical work, on some closely connected topic.) Evidently, then, the historian's use of abstractions is, among other things, an indication of the selective character of historical interest. The simplest way to select is, of course, to ignore: a more satisfactory way is to highlight certain individuals or incidents and to treat others as background, so that, like all objects at a distance, their detailed features are lost or blurred and only certain of their abstract properties stand out clearly.

A second reason why an historian will sometimes prefer abstract to concrete description is this. He is explaining, e.g., a government's action as a matter of necessity or as a matter of course: it is what any government would have had to do in the circumstances. In this kind of case it would be quite unfitting to dwell on the special thoughts and feelings of the individuals who joined in taking it, for they did not take it in their individual capacities as Mr Smith, Mr Jones and Mr Robinson, etc., but in their roles of supreme and jointly responsible executives. Thirdly, for what we may call explanatory purposes, an historian may decide to present certain individuals simply as instances of an 'ideal type' whose defining traits suffice to explain, or enable us to infer, what the relevant actions of the individuals in question must have been. Yet, as Weber has shown by both precept and practice, we can perfectly well make use of 'ideal types' in this way and still adhere, for the purposes of interpretation and testing, to a most stringent Nominalism. Fourthly, a somewhat more complicated reason. When historians write of, e.g., 'mounting opposition' to a monarch or government, or of 'widespread discontent' or 'economic instability' in a particular society, they are sometimes filling up a sheer gap in their knowledge by what might be called a dummy variable. A genuine variable, e.g. the usual x in an algebraic problem, is one whose value can be determined by judicious manipulations of and inferences from its given relations to other quantities. What I call a dummy variable is one whose value depends upon the chance of a relevant piece of evidence turning up to determine it: and in the meantime the dummy keeps up the continuity of the narrative by filling the place of whoever in fact constituted the mounting opposition or was responsible for the discontent or the economic instability. This device is by no means despicable, although it is liable to misinterpretation; its main importance is that it expresses the historian's resolve to come as near to the actual, individual facts as his present information will allow. It is his way, or the technically respectable way, of asserting that someone was doing something highly relevant to his narrative, but unfortunately he knows neither who nor what.

Now let us see how the Realist meets the Nominalist claim that, quite obviously, history's main concern is with particular actions of individual men, and that, but for certain misleading literary forms and expressions, no one would ever have doubted this. In the first place, we have the Realist's retort that every characteristically human action – the sort of individual action that comes to be described in histories – involves a tacit reference to some general social or institutional fact: i.e. to what any person, answering to a given description, would do or think with regard to the action in question. For example, if A is to insult B, it is not enough that A should use certain words or gestures and that B should thereupon feel pain or anger. The action and reaction must be connected to – and by – the general fact that any normal third party C would expect B, quite irrespective of the rights or wrongs of the case, to react to A's words in a characteristic way, and would expect A to expect this to be the result of his words. And further, let a fourth party D be a relative or close associate of B, then anyone (C) would expect D to react much as B does, or at any rate to react on B's side or in defence of B. Or again, to take an example beloved of C. S. Peirce: if A is to give an object Z to B, it is not enough that A shall part with Z and B take it up. If A throws his date-stone (Z) out of the window and B looks up and receives it in his eye, A hasn't given his date-stone to B. For an act of giving to take place, it is necessary that A shall regard Z as from now on B's property in all respects, and shall take reasonable steps, as and when necessary, to see that other people shall so regard it. Without society and its institutions, without the organisation and expectation of certain attitudes within society, we should have no gifts and no insults.

But this account of the 'institutional reference' of individual actions leaves open the question: how do we come to understand and to accept the general institutional facts which an understanding of individual actions requires? The answer seems to be perfectly straightforward. Broadly speaking, we learn to appreciate social and institutional uniformities as we do any other general facts about nature: we learn to pick out recurrent patterns and only in the light of what is socially familiar and expected–and approved or disapproved–do we begin to appreciate the special intention or purpose or other property of this or that individual action. On this score it is important to emphasise the truism–which our interest in historical understanding might incline us to ignore–that in many of our dealings with human beings we are not interested in them *as individuals* at all. This is clearest, perhaps, whenever a human situation approximates to a biological situation. When desperately hungry we feel desire for food–almost any food; and similarly, after enforced solitude, with our desire for human company. Then, think of the countless cases in everyday life when our attention is occupied with getting hold of any porter–or policeman or doctor or perhaps clergyman–to assist us with the job or problem on hand. And what is true of these obvious practical interests is no less true of many of our most sophisticated intellectual interests in human beings: witness the use of random sampling in social researches into the responses or habits of a given sub-class or cross-section of a human population. Or again, we can recall to what an extent our feelings towards individuals whom we come to know and treat as individuals were first influenced by the groups or institutions which they represent. The fugitive, the foreigner, the professional soldier, the member of a religious order, the businessman, the artist–how enormously our reactions to an individual are likely to be coloured and directed by the fact that he belongs to one or other of these groups!

So much for the Realist's account of the meaning and possibility of our understanding of characteristically human actions. We can now apply this account to support his main claim with regard to our actual historical knowledge of such actions. The Realist can perfectly well agree with the Nominalist that institutions have to be served and doctrines have to be accepted by individual men. Yet in many cases we know little or nothing of who these individuals men were, or how many there were or how they stood to each other. Our records are all too often full of gaps, and yet across these gaps we can see or infer lines of development or decline, bifurcations or coalescences of certain institutions, styles or doctrines. The evidence may afford us a real grasp of the institution's history, but the individuals who made and manned it are not only anonymous, they are totally undescribable and indistinguishable. So why pretend that the history of the institution in question is basically about *them*? Now it has been claimed on the Nominalist's behalf that in this kind of situation any reference to individuals consists in the use of 'dummy variables', i.e. of somewhat noncommittal descriptions for which real individuals (or descriptions of individuals) may with luck some day be substituted. But the Nominalist should remember that even dummies are not nothings. If X is to stand for whoever it was that opposed or organised opposition to a certain government, X must be thought of as possessing, or must have attributed to him, a number of characteristics over and above that of being an opponent. Now how are these further characteristics selected or inferred? Surely on the basis of all the known institutional facts of the case and of all other relevant social and political knowledge–about the kinds of men who tend to oppose or to organise opposition, about the kinds of situation in which opposition flourishes, the kinds of opposition which no government can tolerate, and so on. In fine, the honest use of a dummy variable presupposes a great deal of general knowledge about how political institutions tick, and it amounts to selecting from our stock of general knowledge a number of features which suffice to give elementary cohesion to the dummy so that it can indeed stand for or seem to suggest 'whoever it was that did oppose the government'. The historian's use of 'dummy variables', therefore, proves the exact opposite of what the Nominalist claims. The historian's inferences and references to 'person or persons unknown' simply *are* his uses of his relevant general knowledge of political societies, which thus evidently predominates in his historical thinking. Historical understanding therefore is not focused on individual kings–or chaps–but on those changes in a given society which can be seen to make sense in the light of our general knowledge of how institutions work, of what can and what cannot be done by means of them.

The question now before us is not to decide between the Nominalist and the Realist theses, but to assess the relative values of their mutual criticisms and counters and retorts, and, if possible, to combine whatever is of value in them. In general, I would say: the Nominalist thesis contains the truer (though still an imperfect) indication of the aims of historical thinking; but, paradoxically enough, the Realist thesis contributes much more to any acceptable account of how these aims come to be realised. More explicitly, the historian's primary task is to provide a followable (and on the evidence an acceptable) account of such social changes as are of characteristically human interest because they depend upon the ideas, choices, plans, efforts, successes and failures of individual men and women. But in order to provide such accounts, the historian must draw on all manner of general knowledge about life in society, from traditional truisms to the theorems and abstract models of the social sciences. Again, the Nominalist is right when he claims that the truth of his main contention could hardly have been doubted had not historians adopted certain conventions of language and tricks of style. But in attempting to explain away all the abstract descriptions that we find in history as so many literary tropes and conveniences, the Nominalist goes too far. In particular, Nominalists persistently ignore the fact that, although all historic acts are performed by individual men (whether acting singly or co-ordinating their actions in groups is hardly material), yet most historic acts are of a kind that no individual would or could have performed except in his general role of, e.g., citizen or Frenchman or capitalist or cook or socialist or slave. And it must also be conceded to the Realist that the historian's—and our own— understanding of what it means to fill any of these roles is not to be equated with knowledge of certain agents' actual past behaviour or expectation of their behaviour in certain specified future situations. It includes knowledge of how anyone would be expected to behave in a certain kind of situation, whether that situation ever did, or indeed could, exist in fact.

But, while conceding all this to the Realist, we must draw back from his conclusion that therefore history's primary concern is with such social changes as can be seen to conform to our general knowledge of how societies tick. For this would be to equate historical understanding with the noting of such facts as confirm our general accepted beliefs and hypotheses about human societies: i.e. to read or to write history would be to notice or to produce checks on these beliefs and hypotheses. And it is obvious that this equation is inadmissible. It entirely misrepresents the character and function of historical narrative: which is to enable us to follow the actual course of certain events to a known conclusion, for the sake of the events themselves and their direct human interest, quite apart from whatever exemplification of scientific truths or accepted truisms they may afford. There is a basic difference, in direction of interest, between docketing a succession of descriptions as so many exemplifications of–or so many exceptions to–certain general laws, and noticing that these descriptions, which we accept as contributions to an unfolding narrative, happen to conform to certain general accepted laws. This difference in orientation of interest was admirably expressed by Huizinga, when he wrote: 'The sociologist and the psychologist are concerned mainly with whether the facts of a case conform to a system of ideas; for the historian this conformity is of little or no importance–indeed the term "case" does not belong in history at all.'[3] This, we may add, is true–and for the purposes of the present discussion decisively true–even where an action of some individual or group of individuals has actually been prepared, rehearsed or otherwise contrived *as a case*, i.e. as a perfect and predictable sample of a given kind of behaviour. That the three hundred should have died as Spartans were always trained to die; that a Marxist should contrive to speak or act in strict conformity with Marxist principles; that individuals by the thousand should voluntarily submerge their individualities in some common cause–these are facts of the greatest human interest, facts to be followed for their human interest even although they should unfold with an almost machine-like predictability.

Indeed, we could go further than this and say, in an effort to accommodate Realist insights within a basically Nominalist or individualist philosophy, that the crucial moments in any great historical work consist in indications of how this or that individual or group of individuals adopted or sustained or dropped or failed in certain institutional roles. In such moments we see and feel the true growing-points–or dying-points–of history. In between such crucial moments we are usually content with general summary statements, couched in institutional terms. That the king's peace continued to be kept, that the bureaucracy grew more complicated and less efficient, that the depression went on unchecked–these are facts that we are willing to accept in their broad anonymity until some historic, story-worthy act breaks in to alter their course. Such an act or moment of origination within an institutional development is usually and rightly identified with some individual or group of individuals. For historic individuals are not simply those whose capacity and ambition to take on important roles excite our attention; they hold and deepen our attention by making us wonder what changes they will impose on the roles they have taken up. Will the cap or the mask or the mantle or the mitre fit? And will it ever be quite the same again, suited to the same kind of purpose, in the same kind of society as before? We read on, our appreciation of such long-term institutional questions quickened by our interest in an enthralling human story.

Before leaving the problem of human interest in history, I must mention briefly one simple-seeming but unsatisfactory solution to it. This would maintain that whilst we do follow a great many works of history, of a traditional kind, because of their human interest—because of the dramas of human motive and choice and effort and invention which they disclose—yet, in the case of more sophisticated works, especially of economic and social history, the importance of such human interest is reduced more and more, sometimes indeed to vanishing-point. There would therefore be no one answer to our question, but at least two, with no doubt a host of intermediaries, according to the kind of history that is being discussed. This sounds plausible and sensible, but in fact it represents a fundamentally mistaken view of, for example, economic history and social history. These are every bit as much history, and every bit as much distinct from systematic sociology and economics, as political and military history are. It is, of course, true that in describing and explaining very pervasive forms of social change, the historian cannot easily pin his narrative to the decisions and actions of a few well-known men. In most economic systems, for example, there is no simple chain of command down which orders and actions flowed; there is rather a continuous network of influences and adjustments comprising countless individuals whose peculiar motives and characters it would be quite pointless to describe, since what mattered about them was that there were so many of them behaving in the same, or at least in characteristically adjusted–or sometimes characteristically con-flicting–ways. Hence the massive anonymity of the greatest achievements which economic history has to record, and hence, when not presented by a master, its apparent lack of human interest, its apparent overlap with sociological or economic studies. But let us recall in this connection an acknowledged masterpiece of economic and social history: Pirenne's *Economic and Social History of Western Europe*. Several chapters of this book come near to the paradoxical ideal of a history written without the use of proper names; and most of the proper names that it mentions belong to figures, great no doubt in the fields of politics, but peripheral to its main economic theme. Yet how frequently and how persuasively does Pirenne suggest to us the individual qualities of mind that must have been responsible for the economic development that his story unfolds: initiative, courage, desperation, sense of the main chance, flair for leaping on the bandwaggon, whether displayed by a Lincoln-shire peasant or a Flanders merchant or a Scandinavian navigator linking western European trade with the Black and the Caspian seas! Pirenne's book is, no doubt, generally prized for its brilliant correction of a number of long-standing prejudices and errors regarding mediaeval economic institu-tions, but few works of history convey better the truth of the dictum that it is men who make history. To understand what happened in a given economic epoch we must certainly appre-ciate first what possibilities of expansion it actually contained: but those limits once grasped, our understanding of what was accomplished must be in terms of the choices and deeds, even if largely conjectured, of individual men, even if their names have usually been forgotten.

* * * * *

The conclusion that we have reached regarding human interest in history points to the answer to our outstanding question: namely, are the main events in any historical narrative–those upon which interest is most sharply focused and upon which the broad development of the narrative is hinged–always presented as contingencies, as essentially unpredictable although acceptable stages in a followable, historically intelligible whole? Here we have an issue upon which it might seem impossible to find, or to help to articulate, a generally received opinion. For are not historians evidently divided upon it, and divided with metaphysical and moral as well as with ideological passion? Again, we are likely to meet the objection that there is no single answer on this issue that holds good of all history, from the most primitive to the most sophisticated. No doubt primitive histories tend to turn on contingencies much in the way that stories do. But is this the case–is it at all obviously the case–with the best, and (as some would say) with the most scientific, modern histories?

I want as far as possible to avoid being caught up in the metaphysical and ideological conflicts that here raise their heads. If the Realist/Nominalist dichotomy proved too sharp and narrow to provide an answer to the question of human interest in history, it is unlikely that discussion of the Free Will controversy, with all its moralistic nuances and logical subtleties, will aid us here. Certainly the problem of contingency in history has to date been retarded and confused by those who have equated it with the problem of the responsibility or the inevitability of the actions with which history is concerned. We can clear up the question about the historian's right or need to praise or blame without going into any metaphysical depths or logical niceties. A good historian must, evidently, be a man through whose writings the moral standards of his age or circle speak out clearly: this is essential to the unity of his work. And it also means that he will sometimes show–and will indeed sometimes inevitably express–his admiration of certain actions, his loathing of others. A good historian, however, must also possess the unusual (and at least partly the moral) gift of appreciating the moral standards of ages and circles other than his own: this is essential to his understanding of how and why men have acted as they did. And it means that he will often forgo expressions of blame, and perhaps of admiration also, in which intellectually and morally less sophisticated people might well indulge. There is, then, very often a genuine question about whether a particular historian has blamed too much or forgiven too much on some particular score: but such questions fall within the scope of historical judgment itself, and the historian's answers to them stand in no need of either metaphysical or ideological sanctions. And in any case such questions, although sometimes fascinating, are never of paramount interest in history. It is no more the primary job of the historian to allot praise and blame among the individuals and groups and societies that he describes than it is the novelist's job to indicate how he would praise or blame the characters whom he has created.

Let us therefore fix our attention entirely upon two salient, and at first sight logically opposed, features of historical understanding: first that our basic attitude is that of following the historian's narrative—in the same broad sense in which we follow a game or story—across all manner of real-life contingencies and surprises to its broadly fore-known conclusion; and secondly that we are quite prepared to have any incident on the road to that conclusion explained to us, or justified, not simply by the production of appropriate evidence, but by all manner of general considerations and arguments. Now we are naturally tempted to equate these latter with explanations of a particular kind, viz. that in which, on the basis of certain antecedent or initial conditions and of certain general laws, we can deduce that such and such an event had to happen. And if this equation is justified, then, whenever an historian has successfully explained an incident in his narrative—and there can be no incident which he might not conceivably feel called upon to explain—then, *eo ipso*, he has eliminated the alleged element of contingency from his narrative.

But this account of explanation ignores entirely that function of explanation which we have already seen to be specially relevant to narrative. Let us recall our example of the spectators watching a game of cricket. In that example the expert's explanations consisted in supplying his less experienced friends with a number of requisite generalisations which helped them to follow the game at points where its development had baffled them, where they were, in fact, failing to follow it. His explanations put them in the position of being able to say: 'So that was a perfectly intelligible move after all'; they enabled his friends to follow again, for all that, of course, the now followable move was in no wise necessitated by the current state of the game and might well have consequences which would surprise all the spectators. Applying generalisations so as to be able to follow a developing performance or game or story or history is thus basically different from applying them with a view to deducing, and in particular predicting, some future event. The latter use of generalisations enables us to anticipate and even to dispense with observation: the whole purpose of the former is to render possible, or to set in motion again, certain kinds of 'progressive observation'. The former admits what the latter precludes, that the event to which the generalisation is applied and which it explains might have happened otherwise: the whole point of explanations of this kind being that the event can now be followed as part of a still developing whole to which it belongs.

But our retort, in its turn, is palpably incomplete and fails to do justice to the claims that we commonly find made for explanations in history. It may be sufficient, for the purpose of following a game or a story, that we should obtain that amount of explanation which enables us to go on following–with pleasure or with unimpaired credulity. But the job of the historian is to see that we shall follow and appreciate the events that he narrates, with an *optimum* understanding (on the evidence available), and with the fullest possible sense of their intelligibility (and hence acceptability also). The above retort presents explanations in history as a kind of necessary evil: as something that is needed only to keep the narrative from lapsing into obscurity or apparent incoherence. But in history, as much as in science, explanations have a positive role: not only do they enable the historian to classify and clarify and endorse facts which at first seem puzzling or improbable, they help him to enlarge his vision of the context and potential relevance of particular actions and episodes. In fact, the quest for explanations is a main cause of the 'outward drive' of historical interests –away from contemporary and parochial happenings to a larger, more complete and more complex presentation of the surrounding whole.

All this may be granted; and we shall see in our next chapter some of the ways in which explanations in history fulfil this positive role. But this does not necessarily mean that the elimination of all contingency–or the quest of general laws that will have the effect of explaining away all apparent contingencies–is a primary aim for the historian as it is for the physicist. The latter, we may agree, accepts any number of contingent (or at least unexplained) facts within the world in which he performs his particular observations and experiments: but he accepts such contingencies only because he believes that they will have no marked effect on the particular result, or on that particular aspect of certain physical changes, which he is concerned to explain. In so far as uncontrolled, contingent factors enter into any carefully designed experimental situation, the scientist believes either that they will 'cancel each other out' or else that they will ultimately be themselves explainable by means of general laws. Or again consider the contingent facts which Newton had to accept in working out his demonstration of the inverse square law. These included, in particular, the number of the planets and their distances from the sun. How and why these are what they are, Newton's laws are, of course, not competent to explain. But the natural assumption of physicists is that with the aid of other data and additional physical laws or hypotheses these contingent facts could be–and no doubt some day will be–explained in a manner that coheres with Newton's, and with all other established physical laws. Now the question is whether an historian, in accepting certain unexplained combinations or turns of events and using them as part of his explanation of certain other events, necessarily believes that these odd combinations and developments must themselves be explainable with the aid of certain further general laws, and so on to infinity. Does he always believe this? *Must* he always believe this? Is it an essential part of his craft and calling as an historian to believe in the deducibility of any and every human historical event from certain general laws and certain earlier existing conditions, and to proceed in the light of this belief in all his characteristic ponderings and researches? It seems to me perfectly certain that it is not.

To begin by giving two quite general reasons in support of this answer. The first amounts to recalling and emphasising the pervasiveness, the variety, and, so to speak, the extreme nature of many of the contingencies which we all admit to have been crucial pivots of history. Think of the convergence of the different kinds of causal lines that met at Sarajevo in 1914 or in the successful seizure of power by the Bolsheviks three years later. Can anyone seriously maintain, as he traces even a few of these lines backwards, that they evidently belong to–that they must be conceived as belonging to–a single, comprehensible causal system? Or, to give a more homely example, think of the track of King William III's horse and the underground track of the mole whose burrowings overthrew horse and monarch? Is one committed by the task and calling of history to maintaining that this coincidence must exemplify, or be believed to exemplify, a single comprehensive causal system, from which could be deduced, in the particular circumstances then obtaining, every relevant thought, feeling, movement and effect of man and mount and mole? The truth of the matter surely is that historians accept such contingent combinations of facts, and make use of them in their explanations of further facts, quite as happily and naturally as they make use of plans and purposes, calculations and intentions, in explaining how this or that situation turned out in the way that it did. Along with the calculable or foreseeable or logically appraisable factors entering into an explanation, there are also commonly so many contingencies–this or that unforeseeable insight or decision, this or that unpredictable coincidence.

But to argue in this manner is simply to call attention to the more extreme and arresting instances of a truth which we have already sufficiently elaborated in our discussion of human interest in history, namely that there is a clear and indispensable distinction between studies in which our predominant interest is to increase the range and accuracy of our generalisations and studies in which our predominant interest is in how things actually went, actually developed, in teaching some already broadly known result. Now it seems to me quite clear that the distinction between these two types of study is equivalent to the distinction between studies in which contingencies are unimportant either because they cancel each other out or for some other reason, and studies in which, as in history, certain contingencies are seized upon because they help us to see how other things actually worked out the way they did. Conceivably two studies of these two different kinds might result in the acceptance of an identical conclusion regarding some sequence of events: e.g. application of a developed sociology of power may some day enable us to deduce some particular result which we today accept as the conclusion of a highly complex and in places surprising narrative. But the difference in the two ways of reaching such a common result is of immense importance. Certainly we have no reason for suspecting that one of them must be practically redundant. As we shall see later, the different characteristic uses of historical and of scientific understanding are equally indispensable to the general conduct of life.

I want now to reinforce this thesis by a succession of arguments which will, I hope, have a positive appeal to historians, since they are based upon some of the most obvious lessons of the history of historiography. This shows us that historians, despite their generally suspicious aversion to examining their own methods and presuppositions and prejudices, have nevertheless at different times banded themselves together under certain slogans which indicate roughly what they have believed to be of paramount importance in the treatment of any historical problem or period. I choose three such slogans: the primacy of foreign policy; conflict as the key to history; and technological progress—or failure to progress—as the key to history. Personally I would not claim that any one of these is an ideal slogan for the inspiration of historical work and thought. But I do suggest that, because of the very great influence which each has exercised, each of them must have something in it, must point to something that is of significance to historical understanding. If then each of these slogans, and of the attitudes which it serves to express, can be shown to require not only that historians must accept contingent facts in their narrative but must treat them as crucial to their narrative, then we have, I think, the makings of a strong empirical argument in defence of contingency as a predominant feature in history.

THE PRIMACY OF FOREIGN POLICY. This thesis is commonly attributed to Ranke, and in particular to his treatment of European history between 1492 and 1789. Roughly, the thesis is this. The nation-state system dominated European history, and consequently world history, during the period in question. That system arose in different countries from partially different causes, but the most important common cause, operating in all cases, was the characteristic interaction of nation-state with nation-state. Nascent sixteenth-century Spain exercised paramount influence on renascent France and Italy, and the same is broadly true of the mutual relations of Spain and England, and of France, Italy and Germany in the sixteenth and seventeenth centuries.

A *locus classicus* of this view is Ranke's preface and introduction to his *Histories of the Latin and Teutonic Nations*. This book deals with the external relations of the four central European nations, France, Spain, Italy and Germany, between the years 1494 and 1514. Those years afford a most striking example of the thesis to be discussed, since not only were they filled by the most intense and continuous international conflicts and combinations: these conflicts and combinations were between powers that were in the process of *becoming*—or fatally failing to become—characteristic nation-states for the first time. In this kind of situation the predominant part played by contingencies is unmistakable.

Any nation's foreign policies are to some extent at the mercy of contingencies: unforeseeable moves or fallings-off, quite apart from secret plans and stratagems, of other powers. But how much more obviously true this is when the different nations are in the process of taking on a new type of political role: are shaping their own new characters by what they learn from, what they make of, and what they succeed in imposing upon their equally active and changing neighbours! This is how

Ranke presents the wars that centred on Italy during the two decades covered by his *Histories*; and he sees clearly that, since the great nations of Western Europe have become what they are largely through what they have done to and suffered from one another, what each nation eventually has become is something that could not possibly have been predicted until it had actually happened.

Ranke's way of expressing this point is all the more persuasive, as evidence of the basically contingent character of history, because of the quaintly providential language that he favours and because he writes, not as a logician or philosopher of history, but simply in defence of his own historical procedure. His intensely religious outlook made him see the hand of God in the main development of European history; and within this development he sees one nation after another taking a dominant role, for a while impressing its force and character upon the others, attracting or dominating them, then lapsing into relative quiescence while another nation occupies the main stage. 'Therefore', he writes, 'instead of starting with a general description of the political institutions of Europe . . . I have preferred to discuss in detail each nation, each power, and each individual only when they assumed a pre-eminently active or dominating role.'[4] In other words, the possibility of deducing what took place from a general background picture is entirely repudiated. Hence, if Ranke's initial presumption could be granted that the interaction of nations is the great theme of modern history, it would follow that the historian's attention must be focused upon what this or that nation proved itself capable of doing and being in this or that particular conflict or alliance or state of subjection: something that could not possibly be imagined until it had actually taken place. We could therefore truly say that in history the characters exist in and for the action: and that until the action is *followed*, the characters cannot be *understood*. In one passage in the *Histories* Ranke actually succeeds, by a curious *tour de force*, in combining this insight with his providential view of history. Thus, after describing the dispute between the Spanish and Portuguese kingdoms as to how the new worlds which their navigators were discovering should be divided, he comments: 'But Providence wanted something quite unexpected to arise from this controversy; and what actually happened went far beyond what anyone could have foreseen.'[5]

So far, then, as the slogan 'the primacy of foreign policy' has any value–and its value certainly varies for different historical periods–it witnesses to the dominant role of contingencies in history.

CONFLICTS AS THE KEY TO HISTORY. This thesis is so familiar, and has been accepted by so many historians in either a more general or a more restricted form, that we can pass at once to the question: Does it serve to confirm or does it weigh against the above view of the role of contingency in history? It will be useful to break this question down and to deal with it under the heads of (i) the origins of conflicts, (ii) their persistences, (iii) their resolutions.

(i) In the main, conflicts occur because they are unforeseen. Men stumble into more quarrels than they pick deliberately; and often, when they appear to pick a quarrel, this means that they have decided upon an open show of hostility as the best means of settling some long-standing and imperfectly understood cause of conflict. Common desire for or interest in certain rare, competitive goods is sometimes cited as the prevailing cause of conflict between men; and certainly such competitive relations are the natural condition of mankind. But equally, once any form of civilised order is established, they do not necessarily result in conflicts, either overt or covert, between either individuals or groups or nations. It would be truer to say that, however great the importance of competitive interests as a permanent background motive for conflict, open conflicts tend to break out because two parties are suddenly brought into close relations for which they have in no way been prepared, or because of the unnoticed break-up of some long-standing condition of mutual adjustment between them. In either case, the factor of contingency is apparent.

But to this answer it may be objected that what we are concerned with in this discussion is 'objective contingencies'–if such things there be–not with subjective or seeming contingencies: not with what some individuals could not possibly have foreseen, given their historic situation, but with what could not (if anything could not) be foreseen given ideal conditions of knowledge–i.e. knowledge of all the relevant universal laws and preceding and surrounding factual conditions. But this objection itself rests on a crucial misapprehension, the correction of which will enable us to see, perhaps more clearly than we could in any other way, the basic mistake of most defenders of historical determinism. They seem to envisage historical understanding as consisting, in any typical case, of knowledge of what actually caused the different thoughts and actions of certain parties, irrespective of the ill-informed or downright erroneous beliefs of other (usually opposed) parties as to what the first parties had done, were doing or were proposing to do. On this view, 'subjective contingencies', due to ignorance and error, would therefore play no indispensable role in any historical narrative: at best they would help us to see why the actually operative causes were as they were and so determined the actions that followed. But, as historical determinists might have learnt long ago by reading Dilthey–or still better by a careful study of a fair sample of historical texts–what we understand in history is seldom a specimen case of a clear causal sequence, that is, a clearly inferrible result of certain already known or established conditions. Historical understanding of the relation between actions A and B is achieved whenever we are in a position to see these actions as contributing, in any of an indefinite number of possible ways, towards a single, followable narrative whole. For example, if we are to understand how X cheated Y of Z, it is much more important for us to have followed Y's misjudging of X's character or his failure to appreciate Z's worth, than to possess the established sufficiently determining conditions–assuming such to exist–of X's actual act of cheating. Indeed, it is quite a common situation in history for a succession of events to be followable only as a succession of misunderstandings or errors–things which we have no difficulty in following since we are all of us only too well acquainted with them. Thus the 'subjective contingencies' which bulk so large in every rapidly changing situation are highly pertinent to an understanding of how the issue is finally decided. History, to be sure, is not confined to telling how ignorant armies clash by night, for it commonly shows us the less ignorant army (or army commander) exploiting the greater ignorance of its opponents. But such exploitation itself is, as military theorists all agree, very much a matter of flair, of seizing the main chance, of picking the moment to risk winning or losing all: certainly it can never be based, in any quickly moving situation, on a rational review and assessment of all relevant factors. Here we have the background of General de Gaulle's dictum: 'C'est sur les contingences qu'il faut construire l'action.'[6]

(ii) What, then, of the situation once conflicts are in existence? We tend to say: either they work themselves out, the participants exhaust themselves; or else, quite as likely, they will continue indefinitely, every latest move from one side stimulating a new counter-move from the other side—subject, of course, in either case, to contingencies, i.e. to the arrival of some new, unpredictable factor which will help to resolve—or explode—the conflict in question. Now admittedly the tragic persistence, the unending grinding-out of a bitter conflict is one of the most typical themes of history: for example, the war that drags on and on by the fatal war-orientated character of all the machinery of the states involved. But such tragic chapters of history are always written, it seems to me, against the chance or hope of some kind of intervention from outside: some contingency that will divert or arrest or in some way alter the insensate struggle. For in the end sheer repetition ceases to be history: other eventual names for it are obsession, madness and death.

(iii) What kinds of contingency, then, do we have chiefly in mind when we think of the cessations or resolutions of conflicts? Of course, a conflict may be crushed out of existence by the superior force of one party; or both parties may be diverted from it because of some far greater threat from a new quarter. But the sort of action that can be said to settle a conflict is usually one of which some degree of initiative, of original thought and of sustained effort is required. A bold political solution shows a certain analogy to an invention; a new way of looking at old quarrels can result in something comparable to a discovery. Thus, when an historian records a constructive settlement of some important conflict, he is pointing, among other things, to a point of transition in men's habits of thought and action. This is the hall-mark of any really original achievement, and it is as a particular point of transition, and not by any parallel which it shows to previous achievements–for there may be no such parallels, there may be no generally accepted function which it can at first be seen to have performed–that men begin to feel its force and that historians must seek to convey its significance. But here we touch on a manifestation of contingency, or at least of unpredictable novelty, which we shall be discussing further in connection with our third historical slogan.

Meanwhile it is only proper to ask: why should some of the deepest and most influential historical thinkers, and in particular Marx, have believed–or perhaps simply have taken it for granted–that the predominance of conflicts in history was evidence of, or at least was clearly compatible with, the doctrine of historical determinism? For Marx I suggest three main reasons. First, his almost exclusive interest in one aspect of recent European history: the ever-accelerating development of the capitalist system of production, and in particular the industrialisation that this involved. This movement, with its relatively clear outlines and unmistakable impetus, suggests, more than any other movement recorded in history, the possibility of explanation in terms at once historical and, as a result of simple extrapolation, prophetic. Second, the extraordinarily simple and strictly determinist pattern of that part of his economic theory which provides the framework of Marxian prophecy. Needless to say, its simplicity and its determinist character are alike the result of enormous oversimplification– neglect of possibilities of economic self-renewal and of political readjustments of the economic system–which Marx shared with almost all his contemporaries. Thirdly, Marx's failure to recognise the utterly contingent fact–designated by Trotsky, with characteristically Marxist pedantry, 'the law of inequality of Capitalist development'–that capitalistic developments are or have been at different stages, and advancing at different speeds, in different countries at one and the same time. In a world partially unified by commercial enterprise, this trite fact has constantly made nonsense of Marxist extrapolations which would have great plausibility if confined to a single economic community or set of (culturally as well as economically) comparable communities. The crude variety of the world is the despair, and in the end the undoing, of all monolithic social theories.

TECHNOLOGICAL PROGRESS AS THE KEY TO HISTORY. This thesis might be summarised as follows. All history seeks to show how important changes in human societies came about; but among such changes advances in technology–in men's knowledge of how to control material objects and forces to serve their purposes–play a crucial role. For it is these that decide which of mankind's other interests and hopes and aspirations are realistic: what kinds of social reform, for instance, are feasible and what kinds of compromise are possible between class and class or nation and nation. Therefore all history should be related to the condition–to the progress or lack of progress or even the regress–of the technology of its period. And the most crucial works of history are those that explain how great technological advances were made possible, or how, despite apparently favourable circumstances, important chances of advance were retarded or even permanently lost.

We need not here attempt any general judgment of this attractive if somewhat brash historical programme. Suffice to say that a good deal of recent economic and social history seems to have been written in conformity to it or to something very like it. All we have to decide is whether it appears to favour the doctrine of historical determinism, or, on the contrary, to confirm the all-important role of contingencies in history.

From the determinist side it could presumably be argued that social needs and opportunities *plus* accumulated practical knowledge together suffice to explain the development or lack of development of technology in any community. As against this, however, it might be argued that all technology is the result of what was originally discovery, and that discovery (as a number of contemporary philosophers have pointed out) is the kind of thing whose occurrence can never be predicted, even on the basis of the most ideally complete relevant knowledge, before the discovery is actually made. For, of course, to predict a discovery would be in effect to make it before it was made, which is self-contradictory and absurd.

To this argument, however, the determinist might retort that two very different claims are here being confused. One is a metaphysical claim: that discoveries have a peculiar status, that every discovery is unique, unexplainable, marking a kind of *saltus* or discontinuity in technological or intellectual history. The second claim is much milder and more acceptable. It is that, before a discovery is made, men, of course, lack the means of describing, and indeed of envisaging, the state of affairs which the discovery would reveal. But this is a fact about men's capacities for description in a particular situation, not a fact about the inherent contingency of the discovery itself. Once the means of describing it are to hand and have been fitted into our general conceptual apparatus, we can perfectly well set about investigating into, and may reasonably hope to establish, the necessary and sufficient conditions of the discovery in question.

But this retort evidently rests on the assumption that we *can*, reasonably, hope to find the explanation of a discovery in the sense of obtaining knowledge of its necessary and sufficient causes. But is this assumption plausible? No doubt we do sometimes read an account of how an invention or discovery was made, and say after reading it: 'Ah, now I see how the idea came to him . . .' But does not this mean simply that we now follow how someone came to do such and such things and think such and such thoughts, in exactly the sense – and no more than the sense – in which we follow the actions and plans of a character in a story? The forward 'qualitative leap' that *was* the discovery or invention seems no longer a mystery or a miracle, a sheer discontinuity in the history of thought. We have realised, perhaps, that it was natural to expect something rather like the discovery – anyhow to expect news of some striking development–in such and such an area of thought or as a result of applying such and such a technique: or we may have come to recognise, for the first time, the relevance of the discoverer's interests in some partially analagous field, or the relevance of some trait in his character which helps to explain his almost 'irrational' persistence, and so on. But understanding in this sense of becoming able to follow is, as we have amply demonstrated, something entirely different from a knowledge of the sufficient and necessary causes of an event or sequence of events. And if to explain a discovery means simply to enable us to understand it in *this* sense, then the above objection loses all its force.

We are left, then, with the seemingly difficult–and as some will think, intellectually defeatist–claim that in every genuine discovery there is some element, some residue of contingency, of what could not conceivably have been deduced, even under ideal conditions of knowledge, from what had gone before. Personally I see no necessary sign of defeatism in this claim: I think, however, that it can usefully be given a form that has a less pretentious metaphysical ring. I suggest that when we call a discovery genuine or fundamental, what we chiefly have in mind is that we intend to use it to mark a transition in the ways we think about the development of knowledge (practical or, as it may be, purely theoretical) before and after its occurrence. On the one side of it we tend, in describing men's achievements and failures, to make use of certain terms and categories; on the other side it is natural to employ other terms and categories. On the one side of it, certain considerations are apposite or apropos, on the other side they are not, and so on. That this is commonly the situation in describing developments in the history of science and of technology is, I think, unquestionable. And it is the clearest possible testimony that, for historical understanding, later developments are not to be conceived as obviously deducible from what went before. This is not a piece of defeatist or soft-minded metaphysics: it is a direct lesson of the practice of history.

Having stressed throughout this chapter the paramount

importance to history of events of peculiar human interest, and more particularly of contingent, essentially unforeseeable events –whether of the sort we commonly attribute to chance or of the sort that displays genuine originality, inventiveness, initiative– I must now enter a *caveat*, in case this emphasis should be misunderstood. I am not claiming that historians either do or should exert themselves particularly to emphasise, in the course of their narratives, the presence of the sorts of features that I have just mentioned. It is no more the job of the historian to underline, or to insert philosophical glosses upon, the contingent character of the crucial events in his narrative than it is the job of the physicist to insert into his proofs logical or methodological notes as to the character of these proofs. Again, as we noticed above with regard to the 'sensation of the past', we should not expect historical writings to be particularly effective in making us realise, or in making real to us, the contingent character of the main events with which they are concerned. The basic and constant aim of the historian is to present an acceptable, because evidenced and unified, narrative: chance developments, creative developments, routine developments, necessary or foreseeable developments must alike be woven into the whole design, and their categorical diversity is indeed liable to be lost under the even texture of a great historical style. Hence the partial justification of those who, like Charles Péguy in his *Clio*, have accused history of an inevitable blindness to life and to living values, and in particular to the mutual impingement and attraction of what is timeless and of what is most obviously temporal, because most particular, most chancy, most growing, in human life. Poetry, in its great classic forms, was evidently far better suited than is history to emphasise these aspects of life: while a certain kind of prophetic writing (such as Péguy's), or for that matter the kind of philosophical discussion in which we are here engaged, is much more suited to advertising them or to suggesting their significance than is any sober down-to-earth work of history. At the same time, even if it is true that historians tend to blanket or to gloss over the categorical variety of the facts with which they are concerned–letting free-will and determinism rub shoulders, as Ranke expressively put it–this in no way invalidates our constant emphasis upon the contingency of crucial historical events, and upon the contrast, within histories, of events whose followability allows and indeed requires contingent elements and those whose followability consists in their strict or approximate deducibility from certain general laws. Our examination of historical understanding has not been based upon, or suggested by, the verbal surface qualities of historical writings: it is neither an essay in literary criticism nor an exercise in linguistics. Its concern is with the character of the facts, the characteristic followability of narrated or narratable facts, which presents itself to, and indeed imposes itself unsurmountably upon, writers of history and readers of history alike.

Chapter 5

EXPLANATIONS IN HISTORY

HISTORICAL understanding is the exercise of the capacity to follow a story, where the story is known to be based on evidence and is put forward as a sincere effort to get at *the* story so far as the evidence and the writer's general knowledge and intelligence allow. But to follow an historical narrative always requires the acceptance, from time to time, of explanations which have the effect of enabling one to follow further when one's vision was becoming blurred or one's credulity taxed beyond patience.

This, I maintain, is the peculiar and all-important role of explanations in history: they are essentially aids to the basic capacity or attitude of following, and only in relation to this capacity can they be correctly assessed and construed. But it is not from this standpoint that problems of historical explanation have usually been approached in the philosophical literature. There has been a persistent tendency, even in the ablest writers, to present historical explanations as so many curiously weakened versions of the kind of explanation that is characteristic of the natural sciences. To speak more exactly, it is claimed or assumed that any adequate explanation must conform to the deductivist model, in which a general law or formula, applied to a particular case, is shown to require, and hence logically to explain, a result of such and such description. Working from this point of view a number of recent writers have carefully exposed the following defects in most historical explanations.[1]

(i) Since we cannot isolate or reproduce experimentally actual historical situations, it is seldom possible to decide whether a given generalisation applies to a particular situation at all exactly. Indeed we find that most so-called 'covering law' explanations in history terminate in a number of alternatives, none of which is definitely ruled out by the evidence, and between which the historian is left to select in the light of what his particular narrative requires. Alternatively, and more optimistically, we may say with Professor Hempel that most historical explanations are really only 'explanation-sketches', pointing to the possibility and the need of further more detailed research which may eventually give us more nearly complete and exact explanations of the facts in question.

(ii) Frequently, in order to get his available generalisations to apply at all, an historian has to suppose the existence of some unobserved or at least unrecorded factor in the situation that he is seeking to explain. In this respect, his position seems at first sight not unlike that which often faces a chemist, for example, when he is trying to apply general physical formulae in some highly complex experimental situation. But there is a crucial difference between the two kinds of case: the unobserved factors, which the chemist supposes, must be of a kind that can be tested, in respect of their observable consequences, both in this and other theoretically comparable instances. But for the historian there can usually be no comparable tests of his particular suppositions, for the simple reason, which we have just noticed, that the situation which he is explaining cannot be experimentally reproduced. The historian's suppositions, therefore, must inevitably seem to any critic trained in the natural sciences to be of a dangerously *ad hoc* character. To give a simple example: the hypothesis that a particular politician's actions over a certain period must be attributed to his temporary insanity is not one that we can imagine historians proceeding to test, systematically for truth or falsity, on other partially similar manifestations of political ineptitude on the part of other politicians.

(iii) A surprisingly large number of historical explanations of the 'covering law' kind turn out, on investigation, to do no more than point to some *necessary* condition of the fact or event to be explained. The condition selected and emphasised will usually have the merit of suggesting a continuity with earlier events. This is no doubt of importance for the construction of an historical narrative, but it does not amount to explaining an event in the sense of enabling us to infer or predict its occurrence.

(iv) Again a great many explanations (or seeming explanations) in history do little more than remind us that a particular action is quite in keeping with what we know of the behaviour and purposes and standards of the agent, and perhaps of his age and circle as well. By this means surprise and incredulity may often be eliminated, and a basic first step taken towards organising the materials of a narrative: but again to take this necessary first step is not, in any usual sense, to explain.

I have deliberately tried to suggest in the above summaries the different ways in which a number of recent analyses all point to the basic need of a discussion of what an historical narrative is, and what following a narrative means. But, to mention some examples, none of the writers who have contributed to Mr Gardiner's *Theory and History* has *in fact* pointed to this need. And this is true even of Professor Dray and of Professor Popper, whose respective accounts of historical explanations seem to me ideally designed to fit into more general accounts of historical thinking, based on the idea of narrative. In other words, we are faced with a persistent neglect of the pragmatic aspect of explanations in history—of the characteristic context within which they occur and the characteristic functions which they are intended to fulfil.

Once we consider their pragmatic aspect, however, we can hardly avoid the conclusion that the characteristic function of explanations in history is an ancillary one. It is, to repeat, to enable us to follow a narrative when we have got stuck, or to follow again more confidently when we had begun to be confused or bewildered. Hence explanations in history, like the explanations we ask for or volunteer to fellow spectators at a game, are in the nature of intrusions: they are not what we primarily came for—the play, that is the basic thing. Or, in old-fashioned logical parlance, explanation is a *proprium* of the basic activity of following an historical narrative: but a *proprium* to whose relative importance or complexity or bulk within any given narrative no *a priori* limits can be set. This view seems to imply that, unless or until it needs to be 'righted'–as well as logically endorsed–by a helpful explanation, every historical narrative is, in an appropriate sense, *self-explanatory*. It is now essential for us to see what this implication amounts to.

Evidently, to follow an historical narrative requires familiarity with, and unquestioning acceptance of, any number of generalisations, of very different kinds, about human behaviour. Some of these generalisations will be simply classificatory, some will be causal, and others may form part of some general theory of human action. The question that we have now to consider is this: does the occurrence of any such generalisation in an historical narrative necessarily provide an explanation of some kind, and does acceptance by writer or reader of any such generalisation mean necessarily that part of a narrative has been explained? It will be useful in answering this question to consider in turn a number of different kinds of generalisation which different authors have taken to be characteristic of historical explanation.

In the first place, then, we do occasionally find in the course of reading histories–although much less frequently than certain philosophers assume–incidents and sequences of incidents which exemplify well-established causal relationships between variable factors, whether economic or sociological or psychological. But in accepting such sequences, and in accepting the way they contribute to the development of the narrative, are we *necessarily* accepting an historical explanation? Surely not, if the sequence in question is of an altogether banal character: or if its components are so familiarly connected in everyday experience that it would be sheer pedantry to remark that one might have predicted the occurrence of its earlier components. This negative answer will hold, I suggest, even in most of those cases in which an historic incident or development provides a model instance of some scientific law, Malthus's for example, or Gresham's, or any well-established principle of, say, the Freudian psychology. In such a case, the historian may, of course, remark that the developments he has described conform exactly to the law in question. But there is no compelling reason why, in his role of historian, he should do so; and if he does, he will mention it as something incidental to his main job, which is to present the development as part of a followable, and on the evidence acceptable narrative. In other words, a causal sequence may perfectly well occur and be recognised within what could be called a self-explanatory narrative. Of course, in saying this I am not denying that a causal sequence within a narrative may not contribute towards an explicit explanation of certain other items in it, given that the right pragmatic conditions are fulfilled. But this brings us back to the fact that the pragmatic aspect of historical explanation has been so strangely neglected, with Professor Dray providing the one outstanding exception to this rule.

Again, in reading a work of history, we quite commonly follow and consider together a sequence of incidents, each of which severally or all of which conjointly amount to an obviously important necessary condition of some further incident or result. Is it not natural to say in this kind of case that the resulting incident has been explained – and explained by the very process or build-up of the narrative itself? We can, of course, speak like this if we like, and in doing so we should be pointing to the kind of fact which more than any other suggests the notion of a self-explanatory narrative and (although here we reach a much more dangerous notion) that of a narrative explanation. The advantage of these ways of speaking is that they remind us of the gradual transition, which exists within all historical thinking, from less to more completely intelligible and followable narrative. Their disadvantage, however, is that they suggest that all explanations or explanatory factors in history are so many threads within, so many component contributions to, a self-explanatory whole. But, in fact, no historical narrative is self-explanatory: every historical narrative stands in need of the kind of explanation which is intruded into it because it has failed to be self-explanatory, because it needs to be righted, needs to be got back on to the rails again, so that we can follow its progress as before. But why, it may be asked, do I regard explanations of this latter sort as all-important in histories, in contrast to those that we find intimately woven into the fabric of a narrative? My answer – which has still to be justified–is this. We are looking for a reasonably clear general rule for deciding when a causal sequence, or a set of necessary conditions of some result, plays an explanatory role in history and when it does not. And a clear and serviceable rule is provided by answering the following question in any perplexing case. Does the causal sequence or set of necessary conditions fall within, or is it mentioned in an explanation which evidently intrudes into, the course of the narrative, with the kind of corrective purpose I have described? If so, I shall argue, it is explanatory; if not, not.

Thirdly, a brief comment on those disclosures of the *rationality* of some action–in particular the considerations and calculations lying behind it–which Professor Dray takes to be the most important and characteristic of all the different kinds of explanation that we find in histories. Admittedly, such disclosures can amount to explanations, for example, when the considerations and calculations in question are obscure, or when the evidence for them is incomplete or when the timing or manner of the action that follows has something incongruous or mysterious about it. But very often they should not be regarded as explanations at all. They simply describe or refer to the fact, which may be perfectly intelligible or self-explanatory in the context, that certain actions are the fulfilments or expressions of already known intentions, plans or policies. Very often we 'see' from the context the evident intentionality of an action, or appreciate the sagacity or firmness of some choice or policy, quite as directly as we 'feel' the fear or anger of a character in fiction in some typically fear-arousing or anger-arousing situation. Or, to use again the analogy of watching the cricket match; we see the bowler consult the captain, we see the field changed, we see the catch taken. Evidently with regard to 'rational explanations' also, we need a clear rule for deciding in what circumstances they really are explanatory.

Our argument to show that the pragmatic aspect of historical explanation calls for much more careful attention than it has hitherto received, admits of a final powerful reinforcement from the linguistic side. As they occur in historical narratives such words as 'hence', 'thus', 'therefore', 'because', etc., evidently lack the clarity and fixity of meaning which they possess in formal logic and in the natural sciences. Very often in an historical narrative a 'therefore' or a 'because' serves simply as an aid to the reader, urging or reminding him to hold together under his attention a succession of incidents which, in fact, need no explanation at all. Consider, for example, the following statements: (*a*) The news had now reached the President, who therefore gave the following orders. (*b*) Because of Grouchy's error the Prussians were again threatening Napoleon. Is it not clear that in (*a*) the 'therefore' means little if anything more than 'thereupon'?—i.e. it points to an intelligible or followable next step, but makes no claim that the main clause is or contains a sufficient condition of the subordinate clause which follows. Nor, I think, is there any presumption that the main clause expresses a necessary condition of what follows. Conceivably the President would have given the same order if slightly different news, or even if no news, had come through. It is even clearer that the 'because' in (*b*) could have been wholly dispensed with had the writer inserted a few lines earlier an evidently narrative sentence to the following effect: 'Meanwhile Grouchy had lost track of the retreating Prussians, who had re-formed and were marching on Napoleon's flank.' The whole hapless tale of Grouchy's mistake is as directly followable, and in an appropriate sense as self-explanatory, as the outcome of a children's game of hide-and-seek to a well-placed observer. In sum, what appear to be explanatory sentences—or what might be taken to be such by overzealous logicians—can often perfectly well be replaced by a number of narrative sentences which no one would dream of regarding as explanations. The need for a rule for deciding what are to count as explanations in history—a rule grounded on pragmatic rather than on purely logical or even linguistic considerations—could scarcely be plainer.

What I have to suggest in this situation may sound absurdly simple. It is that we should look for the required rule in the kind of historical passage in which the writer evidently stops narrating and proceeds to do something else—something that will often contain an element or an embryo of historical explanation. Thus, when an historian begins to speak in the first person, in order to indicate his own standpoint, he is almost certainly moving towards an explanation of why he is going to present certain events in an unexpected or controversial way.[2] The same result is often to be expected when—in what would seem to be the exactly opposite mood—he substitutes for the familiar concrete language of narrative, the abstract and pontifical tones of the sociologist or theologian.[3] A still more obvious sign of the need and imminent approach of an explanation is a direct attack, on the part of the historian, upon the methods, presuppositions or bias, ignorance or bad logic of traditional accounts or of his rivals.[4] Finally, an historian may put all his cards on the table. He may explain to us the whole course of his interest and reading and puzzlement in connection with a particular problem, and lead us, step by step, to that assessment of the evidence, and that interpretation of the events which finally commended themselves to him.[5] Such a subordinate narrative—somewhat in the style of the summing-up by the great detective at the end of a mystery thriller – may, in fact, provide a perfect explanation of the kind of facts that here, in the historical case, need to be explained.

From this point of view there can be no question of confining the idea of explanations in history, as is commonly done, to such actions or circumstances as have not as yet been successfully brought under some generally accepted explanatory law. Any item in an historical narrative may need explanation—to ensure that the progress of the narrative is not blocked or will not escape the normally intelligent reader. The contrast between explanations in history as thus conceived and the kinds of explanation that are characteristic of the sciences is clear and basic. Explanations in the sciences, we may say, play a supreme creative role: they mark the vital growing-points as well as the points of positive achievement. It is they that express the kinds of increase of knowledge that we look for from the sciences, and they do this because they are in essence answers to problems which challenge scientific men to expand and refine and unify the existing corpus of their laws and theories. But, by contrast, no one expects an historian to be an originator or unifier of the laws and theories which are exemplified in his work. What we expect from him is the ability to use other men's laws and theories, as and when they are relevant for his own purpose: which is to help us to see which is the most likely of a number of conceivable or followable developments in the difficult because imperfectly evidenced narrative that he is trying to present. In doing this the historian assumes that the scientific theories he is using are true; and if by some strange chance his use of them should have the effect of confirming them or of throwing doubt on their truth, this is an accidental product, it is no part of the use to which he puts them in the service of history.

Again, from the point of view here advocated, there can be no question of identifying historical explanations, as Professor Dray has done, with those which provide us with or enable us to appreciate the *rationale* of certain actions or policies. Irrationalities, deviations from rational or moral or traditional norms may well provide explanations: explanations in which, however, a reference to relevant norms may admittedly be essential.

But it is now time that we attempted a more positive account of this characteristically historical function of explanations. To this end it will be useful to work with a new model, to replace the deductivist model which has so long dominated discussion in this area. The model I suggest is that of the philologist's gloss, understood in a broad sense, to cover not simply minor detailed elucidations and corrections of a text but large-scale, often quite revolutionary, re-orderings, re-interpretations and hence re-assessments of a text as a whole.

The first thing to be said in favour of this model is that it accords with the facts of the history of historiography. It is commonly asserted that Niebuhr showed how history could be made into a 'scientific discipline'—or, as I should prefer to say, showed how history could be made a discipline with rational standards of its own—by applying to it the techniques of criticism, interpretation and emendation which had been developed by classical and biblical critics since the Renaissance.

The establishment of a correct text, be it of Homer or Tacitus or some book of Scripture or of church history, calls for an exercise of general intellectual and cultural capacity, whose basis no doubt is an exact knowledge of the language of the text, but which can include any relevant piece of historical knowledge relating to the subject of the text and to the conditions under which it was written and copied and re-copied. Clearly there is a considerable, although admittedly an incomplete, analogy between this exercise of scholarly gifts and the exercise of historical understanding. What we have now to show is how this analogy illuminates the question of historical explanation.

It lies in the fact that in work of either kind the need to explain arises most obviously when the textual critic or the historian is compelled to depart in some marked and important way *from the received* text or from the historical interpretation which has been traditionally, or which would be most naturally, placed upon it. When the textual critic proposes a drastic new reading of a key sentence, or a drastic re-ordering of certain lines or scenes or chapters of the text which he is editing, then evidently he must explain what he is doing and why. Similarly with the historian, whenever he departs from the commonly received account of certain famous events, or whenever his interpretation or assessment of events that he is presenting for the first time runs counter to our natural custom-born expectations and habits of judgment. These are the most obvious occasions which call from the historian as from the textual critic a full explanation: of what *he* is saying–contrary to other things that he might have said–and why.

This way of regarding the matter suggests the need of a drastic correction of some of my previous references to historical explanation. In these I have written as though, in introducing explanations into his narrative, the historian is simply supplying us, his readers, with some generalisation whose relevance to the immediate situation in his narrative we could not be expected to notice for ourselves; but that once the appropriate generalisation is supplied, once the situation is recognised as a case of such and such a general kind, we can happily see how it followed or what will follow from it as the narrative proceeds. This was, however, only a provisional account, useful and excusable because of the widespread assumption that to explain always means to bring some fact or event under some general law or formula. But now we can abandon that naïve assumption. Conceivably an historian's explanation could take the form of simply applying a little-known generalisation to elucidate an otherwise obscure or baffling set of facts: and in such a case the historical explanation would show an affinity with the explanations of natural sciences. But in general the historian's task of explanation arises for reasons that differ profoundly from those that apply in scientific work. A sense of implausibility in the received account, a suspicion that many possible motives and opportunities for action have hitherto been neglected because of bias or unimaginativeness or both—such are commonly the beginnings of an historical explanation, which will conclude by endorsing a much more acceptable account of what *must* have happened.

Let us now glance at a number of stock instances which illustrate our general claim regarding historical explanation. Folklore, tradition, personal memories even, commonly present us with an event that seems an enigma, something quite out of the ordinary, almost a miracle. Obvious examples are the great romantic success stories of history. How did the great conquerors, the great national heroes, the great missionaries succeed as they did? How was it that such very different people, from humblest to highest, at once recognised their greatness, their rightness, the truth of what they said, the invincibility of their cause? Such enigmas are the stuff of historical romance, but to the historian they present a challenge—to his standards of what is historically followable and acceptable. And very often such enigmas can be removed, without any irreverence towards the great, by recognising that they are due to the endemic human thought-habit of putting the cart before the horse. The hour, the call, the combined demands of many different types of person together make a chosen individual great. The urgent historical question about a Cromwell or a Washington or a

Napoleon is not concerned with their personal qualities, astonishing though these must have been: it is the question why and how circumstances combined to give them the scope and the motive to do what they did.

It is for this reason that we commonly find historians torn between more dramatic-sounding and more scientific-sounding explanatory terminologies, and tending, often a little brashly, to replace uses of such dramatic concepts as mission, task, and destiny by more prosaic references to the actual possibilities and opportunities inherent in some situation, together with some individual's persistent presumption that he must act and present his actions as conforming to a single role. Yet it is worth noticing in this connection that an individual's capacity to conceive of his life as a fulfilment of a particular destiny (which means, virtually, a role in a particular story) may be a necessary condition of his being able to exploit the opportunities which the situations facing him have to offer.

But it is not only individual achievements that are liable to seem much more inexplicable than they actually are: the same is true of many mass movements, of general trends, of social causes. We are commonly asked to stand in wonder before, for example, the rapid spread of primitive Christianity, the enthusiasm for the crusades, the spread of nationalist ideals in the nineteenth century, or even, in, the contemporary scene, the astonishing momentum gained by the movement for the European Common Market. And in the face of such 'phenomena' as these, historians are easily tempted to fall back on question-begging descriptions and explanations, in terms of the spirit of the age, and the common aspirations and needs of people who to all appearances had very little in common. But, exciting and impressive though the above-mentioned 'phenomena' undoubtedly were, there is nothing to prevent us following and accepting their developments with the aid of a little analysis and explanation. Each of our examples displays, in some degree, the property of the snowball and the attraction of the bandwaggon. More precisely, it is quite commonly the case, in human affairs, that a minor success by a handful of individuals is the necessary condition of the enlistment of greater numbers in their causes, which is in turn the necessary condition of a major success – or at least great notoriety – which is in turn the necessary condition of attracting still greater numbers, and so on almost indefinitely. In this kind of case, therefore, what is required is not simply to get the cart back behind the horse, but to get the bemused reader to recognise that the cart's seemingly miraculous progress has, in fact, been due to the work of a succession of perfectly natural horses.

These examples help us to understand why so much re-writing of history – and especially of national histories – takes the form of de-bunking. But serious re-writing of history is de-bunking aimed largely at making hitherto enigmatic, romantically mysterious events more acceptable, because more intelligible. The result will no doubt be a narrative which, when read in the light of the accompanying discussion and explanation, can be seen to conform to accepted general laws better than – i.e. with fewer strains and clashes than – the original account. But this will be due to the historian's success in getting the cart back behind the horse, it will be a result of a new 're-write' which replaces the old enigma. The motive of the new re-write, and the nerve of its accompanying explanation, is always the desire to see things straight, to get – on the basis of the known facts – a narrative that can be properly followed; its initial spur is always the feeling or hunch that things have hitherto been presented the wrong way on, not that an exception has been found to some hitherto generally accepted generalisation or theorem.

Another cause for the re-writing of histories is our tendency to oversimplify issues, for example, to see important historical conflicts in terms of black and white, as duels rather than three- or four-cornered fights. Although Marxism exalts this tendency into a heuristic principle, there can be no doubt that it is very often misleading. Thus, Marx and his followers, insisting on the primacy of the capitalist-proletarian conflict of interests, have grossly neglected the further complicating conflict between long-term and short-term (annual) productive processes and interests, e.g. between those of engineering and heavy industry on the one hand and agriculture, especially by peasant producers, on the other. It is no doubt true that every genuine fight is, at any particular moment, primarily between two contestants; but the existence of third and fourth parties, especially when their attitudes are in some degree uncertain or ambivalent, may markedly affect the way in which one party actually engaged in fighting another will launch his attacks or pursue his advantages.

Three- or four-sided contests are, however, only special cases of a wider topic which Professor Popper has aptly entitled 'situational logic'.[6] Much history has to be re-written, as against earlier less reflective accounts or against the grain of the presumable prejudice of readers, in order to make clear exactly what possibilities of action a particular situation contained. Failure to see what the objective possibilities were in a given historical situation is probably the commonest cause of miscalculating or for failing entirely to appreciate the intentions and plans of the agents involved. (This, of course, is not to deny that historical misunderstandings do occur from lack of specific –say psychological or military or medical–knowledge about the facts in question, but only to suggest that lack of scientific knowledge is not the usual cause of historical misjudgments and that the provision of it would not by itself provide a cure for every historical error.) As a rule we offend against situational logic by oversimplification, by not recognising the complexity of the factors that must have affected the decisions of any rational agent in a situation of the kind under review.

Two fairly specific applications of situational logic may usefully be mentioned here. First, the classification of conflicts in respect of their possible solutions. A conflict–be it political, military, economic or doctrinal–can from one point of view be regarded as a problem that might possess one solution or no solution or many solutions. There are conflicts to the death, given the mutual relations and the claims of the contestants. There are again conflicts to which the only possible solution must be one imposed by a third, outside party; who will perhaps sufficiently satisfy both contestants because he deliberately overrides the cardinal claim of each. There are, on the other hand, conflicts in which any interference from outside can only serve to exacerbate, conflicts of which the only possible solution must come from the participants' own recognition of the origin and nature and prospective results of their quarrel. But when an historian recognises that some conflict is of one of these patterns, his recognition does not result from trying out a number of well-established generalisations to see which of them applies best to his particular case. It results rather from his examination of the logical possibilities of the particular case, the logically possible outcomes which a particular complex of conflicting claims and aims and interests will allow. All good historians possess a strong native sense of this kind of situational logic; but they have usually lacked the philosophical framework of ideas, as well as the terminology, that would help them to describe what they are doing when they do the kind of thing that results in an historical explanation.

'Situational logic' has also a close connection with what Popper calls the 'method of rational construction, or the zero method . . . I mean the method of constructing a model on the assumption of complete rationality . . . on the part of the individuals concerned, and of estimating the deviation of the actual behaviour of people from the model behaviour, using the latter as a kind of zero co-ordinate".[7] Popper cites certain parts of economics as illustrations of this method: but it seems to me that historians have always employed something like it, although, of course, in a rough and qualitative way. To explain the bizarre action of some potentate, an historian may remind us how any normal judge or administrator or strategist might have chosen to act in similar circumstances. Then, by making clear to us how much the potentate's choice deviated from the normal, he prepares us to accept some–probably rather surprising–hypothesis that will account for this oddity: perhaps chronic jealousy, perhaps a temporary euphoria, perhaps isolation, perhaps hereditary disease. It is in this kind of way that, for the most part, 'covering-law' explanations are inserted into histories. They are not simply laid on to otherwise baffling cases, like a plaster on a boil: they are selected and applied in connection with, or as part of, the historian's insight into possible ways in which the events that he is describing could have gone forward to produce their independently known result.

But probably the most important and interesting cause for the total re-casting of particular narratives, and therefore for propounding ambitious and complicated historical explanations, is the fact that the passage of time forces us to attend closely to certain features of a particular period which had no great significance to those who lived in it. In this kind of case the historian will no doubt bring the feature in question under a number of generalisations which have indeed never been applied to it before. But by attending almost exclusively to this part or aspect of what he is doing, philosophers have missed what is of peculiar interest and importance in the historian's procedure: namely, the way in which he distinguishes his own historical standpoint from that of his predecessors. He explains that—and later why—he cannot see things as they did, cannot find things acceptable or followable in the way that they did. What to them was a matter of course is to him worrying or completely unintelligible: what to him is evidently the key to the whole situation they did not even trouble to investigate or perhaps even to mention. Examples of this sort of contrast will readily occur to students of the English seventeenth and eighteenth centuries. But a most powerful expression of it is that given by Fûstel de Coulanges in his Inaugural Lecture at Strasburg and in his introduction to La Cité Antique.

It does not take much serious thought [he tells us in the lecture] to perceive that this (ancient) history presents us with innumerable problems and difficulties. I do not speak only of the uncertainty of primitive times; that is, as far as I am here concerned, a minor point: I am referring to institutions, and I feel that even the best-documented institutions are no sooner scrutinised closely than they are seen to be obscure and unintelligible. Open any work on Roman, or still more on Greek history, and you will stumble over contradictions and difficulties on every page; and almost inevitably at each of the terms consul, senate, assembly, republic, liberty, democracy—you will find yourself amazed and bewildered, and will ask yourselves, can this really be the truth and do we understand it properly?[8]

Fustel proceeds to illustrate this general claim from his own difficulties, particularly with the concepts of liberty and of property entertained in the ancient world and then goes on to explain his own new standpoint—in that sense of 'explain' which means to justify a reorientation of historical attention, with consequent new groupings of questions and generalisations of the known facts, and with the introduction of new methods of approach and new types of hypothesis. His resulting ambitious explanation of *all* that is baffling in ancient civilisation has, of course, long since proved unacceptable; but the discussion that leads up to it—Fustel's indication of the need for a general re-seeing of a whole historical epoch—provides a perfect example of that function of historical explanation which I have been trying to expound.

Before concluding this chapter I want to consider three criticisms which the above account of historical explanations is likely to evoke from philosophers.

The first is that I have trivialised the issue, or that I have evaded the serious philosophical issue which is raised by the existence of historical explanations. This has nothing to do with the pragmatic aspect of explanation; it is the question whether explanations of the logically complete and therefore incomparably important characters that have been achieved in the sciences are to be looked for or hoped for or approximated to in works of history also. This objection evidently assumes that any intellectual activity in which scientific or logically complete explanations are accorded a secondary or ancillary role cannot be serious. But, the objection continues, history is a serious intellectual activity; therefore it must seek to use scientific explanations—presumably in a manner close to that of the applied sciences, which are, of course, concerned, as history is, with *particular* tasks and problems.

My answer to this objection is that it expresses, on behalf of the sciences, a claim which the scientific spirit must learn to disown. To de-limit the sphere of relevance of any kind or style of explanation is not to belittle it. Certainly, I would say, we do no dishonour to the genius of scientific explanation by withdrawing the very dubious claims that have been made for it in the field of history.

The second objection is that my account of explanations in history rests on an obvious procedural inconsistency. In effect, it will be objected, I have contrasted historical explanations in their pragmatic aspect (by stressing the function that they fulfil in historical thinking) with scientific explanations considered in their logical aspect (by stressing, or presuming, their conformity to the deductivist model). But this contrast is quite inapposite, the objection continues. What should be contrasted are scientific explanation and historical explanation each in its pragmatic aspect or else each in respect of its logical completeness or incompleteness. Thus suppose that, emphasising the pragmatic aspect, we try out the model of the scholar's gloss. Then we should ask: do we ever find in scientific treatises explanations that have the effect of a gloss, viz. that of helping the puzzled reader to apply a scientific theory to seemingly recalcitrant cases, or even in the face of apparent exceptions to its claims? The answer must be that we sometimes do; that scientists do from time to time explain their theories in a sense which, as with historians, comes very close to justifying their continued use after certain adjustments have been made and certain causes of confusion have been cleared away. Hence, from the pragmatic side, there is a parallelism between the two cases. But similarly, from the logical side, there are at least parallel questions in the two cases. We can ask of scientific and of historical explanations alike whether or to what extent they conform to the ideal of a statement of necessary and sufficient conditions of a given result. There is therefore nothing odd, nothing basically 'different' about historical explanations. They only appear different or peculiar when they are contrasted with scientific explanations in a peculiarly misleading way.

But this objection, although it may seem natural and persuasive, is not really to the purpose. For my thesis is not simply that explanations in history have a pragmatic aspect in respect of which they obviously look very different from scientific explanations considered in their logical aspect: it is that, unless their peculiarity from the pragmatic standpoint is recognised, assessments of the strength of historical explanations from the logical standpoint are liable to involve gross misunderstanding. A proper understanding of the function of explanations in history is a necessary pre-condition of a correct assessment of their adequacy. By contrast it would be pointless to call attention to the gloss-like explanations that occur (though very rarely) in scientific treatises with a view to helping their readers to a better appreciation of scientific standards of argument and explanation. Every competent scientist knows well enough what scientific explanations are meant to do; he knows in most cases whether and why one explanation of certain phenomena is superior to another. And a long and distinguished succession of philosophers of science have struggled to give exact and comprehensive accounts of what the standards of explanatory force are in the different sciences. The whole burden of the present chapter, however, has been that since explanations are not the main goal and the main hall-marks of achievement in history, and since the standards of efficacy of historical explanations have certainly not been made clear by philosophers, it is necessary for us to take a step back and to describe clearly the characteristic functions of explanations in history before we can discuss in general terms what makes some historical explanations superior to others.

But it may be urged that my account, placing as it does so much emphasis on the pragmatic aspect of historical explanations, lies open to a still more serious criticism. In any situation where an historical explanation is needed, there could on the face of it be any number of possible explanations which would have the effect of removing the crux (like a plausible scholar's emendation) and getting us back comfortably to the job of following the narrative. But the question would, of course, remain whether any explanation selected to fulfil this purpose was logically acceptable or was the most logically acceptable of all those that might have been considered. More simply, was it justified; was it, in the appropriate sense, true?

The question thus raised is certainly pertinent. But, in fact, it serves to support rather than damage my central thesis. For the fact is that the kind of explanation that I claim to be characteristic of histories cannot be confirmed, or even be preferred against other possible explanations, except *via* the acceptability of the narrative which it enables the historian to reconstruct or resume. If the narrative has now been made consistent, plausible, and in accordance with all the evidence, if it is the best narrative that we can get, then the explanation that helped us to get to it is the best explanation as yet available. Unlike scientific explanations, the kind of explanation that I have been describing can neither be tested nor confirmed by its successes with other parallel cases. To revert yet again to one of our earlier examples, the explanation that will make sense of the enormities—and of the successes—of a Stalin will not necessarily help historians to make sense of the enormities of a Tiberius or an Ivan the Terrible. And again, unlike particular narrative statements, historical explanations cannot be directly supported by 'hard' historical evidence, since the question about any historical explanation is not a question of fact, but of the best way of arranging the facts.

Finally, two considerations which, in my belief, weigh greatly in favour of my account of historical explanations. It helps us to see past a paradox that must figure in some form in any acceptable account of historical thinking. Every genuine historian must write as a representative voice and eye of his own age, inevitably expressing its concerns, conforming to its standards, using its analytical skills and its fund of general information. And yet, at the same time, he must write annoyingly against the pet prejudices and received opinions of his age, showing that they cannot be sustained, that they must be replaced by better, more truly acceptable accounts, and so on. Now in no part of the historian's task can these two apparently conflicting tendencies be shown more clearly to be complementary than in those tasks of explanation which, I have claimed, are at once all-important and peculiar to historical thinking.

Secondly, my account of historical explanation helps us to see why, from the point of view of most practising historians, the issue of historical determinism is a mere red herring. The historian wants explanations, certainly. To this end he makes use of any number of causal generalisations, certainly. But he uses these to help him to produce a convincing narrative, the metaphysical status of whose links, or of whose explanatory endorsements, is in no way his concern. Ranke's dictum that in history free-will and determinism rub shoulders together is no doubt philosophically unpalatable; yet it expresses very well the practising historian's carefree attitude to metaphysical questions.

Chapter 6

THE USES AND ABUSES OF HISTORY

O UR account of explanations in history serves to reinforce the more general and familiar thesis that historical understanding is of a basically different kind from that achieved in the natural sciences by the discovery of new laws or by learning how to apply established laws to what seemed to be exceptional cases. At the same time, our account includes–and indeed stresses the indispensable service–of such general laws in supporting any new interpretation of the logic of some particularly puzzling historical situation. And equally, our account of historical understanding–of what it means to follow an evidenced narrative–certainly permits the use of any such narrative as a source of supply from which particular cases can be abstracted to suggest or to support this or that general law of the social (or in some cases the physical) sciences. In both these ways, therefore, historical understanding has important links with the kind of understanding that is gained in the sciences. But to grant this is in no way to subtract from our basic claim that historical understanding is something *sui generis*, inasmuch as it is the understanding of how some particular outcome came to be.

But if historical understanding is essentially of this kind, are we not forced to confess that the long-cherished idea of history as a guide to the future has been a sheer illusion? Must we not concede that history is, in itself, useless, or that its value is confined entirely within itself–to the intellectual satisfaction and self-discipline of those who study it, steeping themselves in a past whose intelligibility offers us no positive guidance for the ever-emerging future? Certainly, it seems to me, we should have to consent to this conclusion if the only way in which knowledge can be used or can prove itself useful were that exemplified by the application of scientific laws and formulae to help us meet the problems of practical life. Engineering, medicine, and the rapidly developing social sciences are in action every day before our eyes, to remind us of the importance –and indeed of the magnificence and the, humanly speaking, providential character–of this sort of 'useful knowledge'. But perhaps because of the very massiveness, as well as the comparative novelty, of what we owe to and expect from the applied sciences, we are all of us today liable to neglect other forms of useful knowledge: and to neglect them to our peril. Historical understanding, I shall now argue, can be of use to us, and needs must be used by us, in a variety of ways that are of the first importance to any form of civilised life.

In the first place, historical understanding can teach us, especially with regard to the institutional sides of life, what we are or where we stand in the light of where we have come from; more particularly understanding of what we are in the light of whence we have come can explain why there are certain things which we *cannot* do, let the future develop as it may. Secondly, historical understanding can assist us, somewhat in the manner of practice for games of skill, not indeed to foresee and forestall the difficulties that will face us, but to meet and cope with them, whatever forms they may take, with a kind of confidence, a kind of necessary carefreeness, such as no degree of scientific preparation can provide. Thirdly (and this will no doubt cause some eyebrows to rise) historical understanding can help us to see and can give us justifiable assurance regarding, not simply what we can or cannot do, but about what we ought to do or must never do in many important kinds of moral situation.

With regard to the first of these claims, that to understand any institution or practice or doctrine it is necessary to know something of how it came to be, it will be useful to glance for a moment at *its* history, at how it has come to be in the very uncertain, ill-defined and rather neglected condition in which we find it today. There are a few suggestive adumbrations of it in Plato, but it is nowhere seriously developed in the thought either of the ancient world or of the renaissance. But early in the eighteenth century it found in Vico its first and still in many ways its incomparable prophet, and in the 1760s it found in Justus Möser its first fully conscious and disciplined exponent. Thereafter it imposed itself rapidly on almost all forms of social thought–legal, political, economic (at least in Germany) and educational–although, curiously enough, despite the efforts of Hegel, it had very little effect on the practice of philosophy; at the same time, it was responsible for that most unphilosophical and unnatural of intellectual abortions *Naturphilosophie*. By the mid-nineteenth century it had become virtually a canon of intellectual orthodoxy: Renan's *The Future of Science* is a prolonged hymn to the historical method; Comte's *Positivist Philosophy* is almost a paradigm of what is today commonly meant by historicism; while Marx's social thinking is quite as much an historical interpretation of economics as an economic interpretation of history. Perhaps this genetic approach (as it came to be called) to all human institutions and conditions reached its apogee in the teachings of Freud; but thereafter, especially in Anglo-Saxon philosophical circles, a definite reaction against it set in. Here is a good representative statement of the 'anti-genetic' attitude–of the attitude which repudiates the claim that we are discussing–written with Freudian teachings particularly in mind. It comes from the introduction to C. D. Broad's *The Mind and its Place in Nature*.

We are all extremely liable to confuse a history of the becoming of a thing with an analysis of the thing as it has become. Because C *arose out of* B, and B out of A, people are inclined to think that C is *nothing but A in a disguised form*. Thus, suppose we could show that action from a sense of duty developed out of action from fear of public opinion, that this developed out of action from fear of the ghosts of dead ancestors, and that this developed out of action from fear of living chiefs. . . . We should be very liable to think that we had *analysed* the sense of duty as it now exists, and proved that it is just a disguised form of fear of punishment by tribal chiefs. This would be simply a gross mistake. To analyse anything you must examine and reflect upon *it*; and the most elaborate account of what preceded it in the course of history is no substitute for this. At the best a study of the history of a thing may make you look for factors in the thing which you might otherwise have missed. But, on the other hand . . . it is just as likely to make you turn a blind eye to factors in it which were not present in the earlier stages.

At first sight it seems impossible to disagree with anything that Broad says here; and yet, on careful reflection, we can see that his criticism is pertinent only to the most grossly exaggerated examples of the genetic approach. Everyone will agree that to understand a thing you must reflect about *it*: but what is in question is whether such understanding is possible, with regard to any human institution or condition unless some account is taken of how it came to be the way it is – and when and where and how it is. To distinguish 'analysis' from 'history' as Broad does is simply to remind us that we have two words for two kinds of description or understanding, and to suggest – as yet without any show of proof – that these words stand for altogether different operations, the first of which can proceed adequately in all cases without any assistance from the second. But this is exactly what is in question. Do things – in particular do human institutions, practices, beliefs, creeds, etc. – always lie entirely open to our analytic inspection, revealing all that they are in a single instant, provided that our analytic inspection is powerful enough? Are not institutions, for example, constantly being adapted, so that their identity can hardly be of a simple, directly recognisable kind? Quite often considerable historical study, not to mention great intellectual perceptiveness, is called for before we can establish the identity, or the continuity through remarkable developments, of an institution – or a practice, or a belief, or a creed, or even the meaning of a word. And yet once such an identity or continuity of development has been uncovered, we may be absolutely certain about it: what has been disclosed is so unmistakable that it can be accepted as part of the definition or analysis of the institution in question.

A second latent weakness in Broad's argument is this. In his final sentence he seems to be mixing up a question of intellectual principle (which is here our only concern) with one of prudence in intellectual practice. It is true that we sometimes possess some knowledge of an institution's present condition whilst we as yet know almost nothing of how it came to be in that condition. In cases of this kind it would clearly be absurd to attempt to interpret or explain the former knowledge by the latter ignorance. But what should be considered, with regard to the question of principle, is a case in which we have valuable but imperfect knowledge of a thing's present condition and considerable although no doubt still more imperfect knowledge of its recent development into that condition. And the question to be decided is whether in this kind of case the genetic approach has something of quite special value to contribute to our understanding of the thing's present character and behaviour. More particularly we ought to ask: What sorts of insight, what sorts of otherwise neglected truths about human actions and institutions, can an historical or genetic approach, and only such an approach, provide? What are the kinds of factor which, unless picked out and appreciated in their historical development, are liable to be misjudged or ignored in any direct functional analysis of an actually existing situation? These questions are of crucial importance for the critical philosophy of history: but to date they have never received the attention that they deserve, either from the enthusiastic nineteenth-century advocates, or from the somewhat panicky twentieth-century detractors, of the genetic approach to human affairs. In the rest of this chapter I shall try to sketch out the broad lines of an answer to them, chiefly in terms of some familiar although all too easily neglected features and problems of political life.

First, then, the historical approach often helps us to see the importance of features of an institution which at first sight seems unjustifiable or arbitrary, since (apparently) they in no way help to fulfil the institution's most obvious functions or purposes. Nevertheless such factors may be among the necessary conditions of the institution's survival or efficiency. They may even—paradoxical though this at first sounds—express the very quick of its existence; that which not only keeps it in being but contains the seeds of its main future developments; that which will be remembered and cherished long after its currently accepted functions and purposes have become outmoded or forgotten.

Thus, for example, every political movement or party embodies, in addition to its official platform and its plans for legislative reforms, a number of vague, emotionally charged reminders of the past from which it has sprung. These may take the form of styles of address, the repetition of slogans and sacred names, ceremonies of remembrance, badges, banners, marching songs–all of which serve as cues for articulate or silent mass affirmations of loyalty and cohesion. The origin of such emotional cues may be remote or forgotten or fantastically misunderstood; or they may enshrine and echo personalities and incidents whose relevance to the practical issues of the day seems almost nil. Hence to practical forward-looking men the retention of these emotional cues may seem to be not simply useless but positively embarrassing and frustrating–it may seem describable only in pathological terms, as the expression of childishly wishful fantasies, or of unacknowledged aggressive-nesses and phobias, or at best of ossified survivals from a more ignorant age. But the aptness of such descriptions does not mean that the emotional cues so described can be easily dispensed with. They may be essential to the party's continued existence as a reliable, recognisable unity. For, broadly speaking, every human association is formed to meet some particular need or danger or opportunity; and if it is really successful in uniting men for this first purpose, it will tend to be kept in being and made use of for other related purposes. Again, very broadly speaking, the greater the number of different purposes that a particular association can be used to serve the greater its chances of persistence, despite inward strains and anomalies and contradictions. It would therefore be the height of folly to regard all seemingly arbitrary features of a political movement or institution as negligible. They are there: and they cannot be ignored or disowned or flouted or sneered out of existence. Of course, it may always be possible–indeed, it is often a crucial task of statesmanship–to develop them, to canalise or direct them, to utilise them (or their names) for very strange purposes. But before any of these things can be done, such seemingly arbitrary features need to be understood: in particular the ways in which they have become interwoven with other aspects of the movement need to be understood. And it is difficult to see how such understanding is to be had, except by an historical appreciation of how the movement has developed, and by assessing, in the light of that development, the different relations of its many different strands. Such an appreciation will commonly show that the apparently arbitrary survival of some emblem or dogma from long ago in fact points back to some choice or alignment which was quite essential to the accepted orientation of today's rational and practical policies.

A closely similar point can be made from the other side, i.e. in terms not of popular acceptance and support of a particular institution or movement, but of its first, and subsequently, legendary founders or leaders. Admittedly, every political movement starts from some widely recognised danger or opportunity: but precisely which individual, of all the many individuals who might well give the new movement leadership and direction, will in fact be there and available, on the spot and with exactly the right status and record to meet the call of the hour – this is indeed almost entirely a matter of chance. But, on the other hand, once a first leader is recognised: once the movement has begun to develop under his hand and under his name, to be symbolised by his face or voice or known character and way of life, then commonly it will begin to take on features and qualities which had no necessary connection with the danger or opportunity which first brought it into being. Such personally attributable features, it might be thought, must be superficial and quickly lost and forgotten. But to assume this is to give way to a culpably shallow rationalism. The capacity of mankind, in its political actions, to make legends out of its leaders is a factor of immense historic importance. To admit this is not to subscribe to the foolish doctrine that great men make or determine the histories of the movements they initiate or the nations they lead. Every important chapter in human history is, of course, made by successive generations of men in their thousands or millions. But very commonly in making such a chapter together, and in order that they shall succeed in making it together, men must imprint upon it the image, complete with some arbitrary as well as with politically requisite features, of its first spokesman or protagonist or guide.

Besides helping us to see what we can and what we cannot do

with our institutions in view of the ways they have come to be what they are, I believe that a study of their history can assist us in a more direct and positive fashion towards a wise use of them. Not, to be sure, by enabling us to foresee the dangers or difficulties with which our institutions may in future be faced, but rather – paradoxical although this again may sound – by preparing us to maintain and adapt them in the face of changes that are entirely unpredictable. History reveals on its every page the importance of contingencies – accidents, coincidences or other unforeseeable developments – in every human enterprise, relationship and institution: it would therefore be utterly illogical to expect it to aid us in anticipating and forestalling specifically predicted developments. Nevertheless, in spite of the seeming paradox, it can and does assist us to achieve a 'masterful manipulation of the unforeseen'.

As a rough analogy, to indicate how this can be, I would cite the use of practice in games of skill. To some extent, of course, practice is preparation for broadly predictable situations: it includes the building up of habitual moves and responses which are appropriate to recurrent features or moments of the game. But practice is something much more than this, especially for a player of some skill. Its chief purpose is to get the player into a state of general preparedness – of 'form' as we say – which means an all-round readiness, quickness and flexibility of responses which enable him to introduce or combine moves or strokes or feints or what not as occasions demand, and such as he has never tried out before: to prepare him, in a word, so far as this is possible, for *whatever* shall happen. Now the oddness of such practice – and of its effectiveness – deserves far more serious consideration than it has hitherto received from either philosophers or psychologists. Here it will be sufficient to make good its reality by pointing to two of its principles or quasi-principles,[1] which to date have remained nameless, but with which we are all perfectly familiar.

The first of these I shall call the principle of the reserve: the second, which looks, at first glance, the direct opposite of the first, I call the all-or-nothing principle. History affords us innumerable examples of both: indeed, to follow and to appreciate an instance of either principle is to enjoy one of the keenest and most characteristic pleasures that historical study can afford.

First, then, the principle of the reserve. When faced with any task, problem or impasse, we must be prepared for the possibility that the best, the most rationally and scientifically laid plans that we can contrive may go awry. We should therefore, if possible, retain the means and materials—or at the very least keep in mind the possibility—of other methods of pursuing our aim: methods that may be less convenient or less desirable, rougher or costlier, and whose working out we may have only vaguely envisaged. But, whatever their drawbacks, we must have them to hand, to avoid being guilty of that worst of practical shortcomings, being found entirely unequal to the event, being found entirely resourceless before the situation—no matter how freakishly fortuitous—that actually faces us. It is as a safeguard against such a contingency, which always threatens those who put their faith in some theoretically water-tight project, some prediction of how things are bound to turn out, that the principle of reserve is of such great practical value.

It is worth noting that, although this principle is most obviously pertinent to the conduct of public affairs, it has some perfectly good analogues among maxims or considerations which apply to the most personal and private sides of our lives: for example, that we must work, but without allowing ourselves to be entirely used up by our work; that while we should give all that we have to give in many of our personal relationships, we should never, so to speak, identify our lives with a relationship of any one particular kind; and that we should always keep something of our own—despite the principle of frankness and self-giving to others—that we 'scarcely tell to ony'. Quasi-principles of this kind are most easily stated in negative form: they are essentially vague, and it is inconceivable that we should ever be offered statements of the sufficient conditions of their just or appropriate employment. They have to be discerned and recognised through successive examples. Our endeavour to master and apply them is the very antithesis of any habitual or automatic application of a rule. Yet by means of the examples which histories afford, we certainly can create and constantly improve our capacity for dealing with tomorrow's contingencies when they arrive.

The all-or-nothing principle seems, at first, to make altogether contrary demands upon us. It rests upon recognising that, in certain extreme situations, it is necessary to put all one's fortune on a single cast, to dare to put it to the touch to win or lose it all. But how can such heroic recognition be squared with the cautious, the realistically adaptive, the sometimes (inevitably) opportunist spirit of the man who works on the principle of the reserve? This seeming contradiction can be removed, however, if we recall the special character of the two principles – they are expressly intended to deal with the contingent aspect of experience – and if we contrast them, in this respect, with other empirically grounded rules of prudence. The latter, which we find embodied in countless proverbs, maxims, practical tips, etc., are propounded as rules known to be true on the whole, or in the great number of usual or normal or standard cases, if not of this particular case; they are known to be true in the long run even if acceptance of them should prove disappointing in the short run in which we are actually engaged. But practical decision, although it will normally base itself on such generally true maxims, has also its own natural anxiety over the particular case with which it is currently engaged. To the man of action there come moments when the long run and the majority of cases begin to mean nothing, when his whole concern is with this particular case which is proving itself an obvious deviant, a twister, a freak, and upon whose outcome, good or ill, his whole future, his life, the cause he lives for, may depend.

This kind of situation might be illustrated by that of a skilled and usually reliable and indeed conventional card-player who for some personal reason must win a particular game, irrespective of distressing his partner, violating the usual conventions, etc., and equally irrespective of the extent of his loss if he loses. We may assume that he will begin play in quite orthodox fashion, e.g. in conformity with his bids if the game is bridge. But after a very few rounds it may be clear that orthodox play, although it may here as always minimise losses, is not going to guarantee victory. What, then, is to be done? If our player has the lead, we can imagine him proceeding to open up the game in a new and quite surprising way, in view of his earlier leads. And should this tactic disappoint, he may change yet again, despite raised eyebrows from partner or opponents. The unorthodoxy of his procedure, his offence against the conventions, may, however, be entirely justified in view of his own peculiar aim. Alternatively, we might imagine him staking all upon one enormous bluff at the outset; a bluff which might well cost him almost every trick in the game, but from which there is a real chance of attaining the narrow victory that he requires. On the former supposition he exemplifies the principle of the reserve; on the latter he exemplifies the all-or-nothing principle. Use of the former principle depends upon the ability to judge, in terms of one particular situation, the relative values of a number of approaches all of which are no doubt theoretically commendable: the latter depends upon the ability to see where the one small chance lies in a complex situation, and upon the ability, which Cardinal de Retz took to be the hallmark of practical genius, to distinguish the chance that is extraordinary from the chance that is truly impossible.

Now it requires no further arguing, I think, to derive from this description the conclusion which history is continually illustrating, although a too narrow logic may dislike it: namely that every successful man of action brings with him a mastery of both the above principles, and an almost instinctive skill in applying them, to any complex and serious situation.

Finally I want to suggest that historical understanding can often help us to decide which courses of action we are morally obliged to follow and which we are obliged to shun. This assistance is particularly important for those moral choices and resolves that arise because of our involvement in institutions, or our adherence to some important movement or cause: in a word, to the institutional side of morality, which contemporary moralists tend either to neglect or else to treat in the most perfunctory and hackneyed manner.

My claim in this connection can be introduced by recalling that we can hardly hope to man or serve an institution worthily unless we believe in it. Now, what does believing in an institution amount to? Not necessarily to believing that it has a future or that the future is with it; but rather that it deserves to have a future, that it has potential life in it and therefore might well have a great future if only we and others give it the support, and apply to it the energy and the intelligence, that it requires and deserves. But how, it may be asked, can historical understanding contribute to such positive, practical beliefs?

Certainly historical understanding will not suffice to ensure loyal support, intelligent service, faithful defence or careful development of any institution or cause. Nor, perhaps, in strictness, is it a logically necessary condition of such service, which conceivably might be given by some simple soul who had virtually no historical understanding of the institution that he was serving. For ultimately, it might be argued, loyal adherence to any institution or cause must be based upon some intuition or revelation of its worth, some direct and original appeal which it exercises upon the practical and imaginative sides of our natures. I am not myself altogether happy with this view, but for the argument's sake let us accept it. But now it must be admitted that the kinds of intuition or revelation that are here alleged, are notoriously—and indeed sometimes cruelly and even hideously—fallible. How, then, are they to be tested and secured? Not simply by a consideration or calculation of the foreseeable consequences of the actions and attachments which they commend; for some of these consequences will themselves have to be judged by the way they will play back upon and affect the future of the institution or cause whose value—or the rightness of our adherence to which—is the very thing that we are trying to confirm. Moreover, there are notorious practical difficulties in the way of such calculations of foreseeable consequences, unless made on the broadest and crudest scales. But by what other means can our moral intuitions and revelations be tested or confirmed? It is here, I believe, that historical understanding can make its contribution.

This can best be explained by an example. Suppose one had

had the extraordinarily good fortune to be one of the original disciples of Socrates, considered as the first exemplar of the spirit of free criticism deployed to vindicate the autonomy of morals, or of Galileo, conceived as the first clear exemplar of the true method of hypothesis and experiment in physical inquiry. If one had had a modicum of intelligence, one could not but have recognised in either case something of immense importance, something most certainly with life in it and deserving a future. One would certainly have believed *in* what one heard and saw; and one might well have been fired to devote one's life and energies to furthering the aims and methods which either of these intellectual masters had begun, however laboriously and imperfectly, to disclose. Yet, in attempting this task, one would almost inevitably have run into innumerable and enormous difficulties: difficulties of a kind that would not simply have brought progress quickly to a halt, but would have made one feel entirely at a loss, in doubt, and intellectually and morally forlorn. What light, what guidance, one might well then ask, could the first fragmentary findings of either master afford to us when faced with *this* incomparably more complicated problem? How would *he* have envisaged the difficulties of applying here the method which seemed to him so lucidly inevitable in the first chosen simple cases?

But now, contrast this imaginary situation with that which we, in fact, enjoy: we who can look back across centuries of the continuing struggle for freedom of thought, containing so many noble reaffirmations of the autonomy of morals, or at the astonishing developments and successes of the method first descried by the genius of Galileo. Is it not far easier for us to see what Socrates and Galileo were respectively about than it was for the first of their disciples? Looking back along the line of development that stems from either name, surely it is now far easier for us to know what we mean by the spirit of free criticism or by the method of ideal and real experiment. And is it not now, correspondingly, far easier for us to know what it is that we believe *in* when we say that we believe in the spirit of free criticism or in the spirit of experimental inquiry? I do not say that our beliefs in these excellent things are necessarily stronger or more effective in producing appropriate attitudes and actions, or that they are more trustworthy, more deserving of faith and hope, than were the original beliefs first fired by the examples of Socrates and Galileo. What I claim is that any such belief, when it has been to some extent articulated through the history of its vicissitudes and revivals, its unexpected implications, its revolutionary extensions and triumphant re-affirmations, has one immense advantage over any direct, original acceptance of it—no matter how powerful, how pene-trating, how full of prophetic promise the original apprehension and acceptance of that belief may have been. When our beliefs have been to some extent historically articulated we are in a very much better position to *describe* them, to indicate the differences—perhaps the many ranges of differences—that an acceptance of them makes to the rest of our conduct or view of the world. We are thus not only better equipped to defend the institutions and causes we believe in against polemical attacks, we are also in a better position to defend and discuss and reaffirm them *to ourselves*, to our critical perplexed selves, in moments—or decades or centuries—of difficulty, doubt and discouragement. In a word, it is often easier for us to act rightly because we have historical understanding to help us; or, conversely, historically understanding can sometimes help us to decide what we ought to do and to do it.

I do not think it is necessary to pursue this argument beyond the example I have given. Certainly it is a form of argument that might admit of grave abuse, since it presupposes that we can distinguish those traditions which embody and develop an idea of unquestionable value, from those which may simply express some deep-seated and perhaps evil tendency in human nature. But despite this possible danger there can be no question in my mind, of the moral illumination which, conversely, historical understanding can sometimes provide.

Chapter 7

THE HISTORICAL UNDERSTANDING
AND PHILOSOPHY

THAT adequate understanding of any political, legal or social institution calls for some knowledge of its history–some appreciation of the main changes and chances through which it has come to be what is it now–would generally be granted, even if for the wrong reasons. The same holds true, *a fortiori*, of religious creeds and practices, especially those that claim a definite historical origin and depend upon a long tradition of interpretation. Can the same be said of philosophical practice and doctrines? Before attempting to answer this, I want to consider briefly the parallel question with regard to that wide and variegated field of researches which we bracket under the rubric 'natural science'.

Most scientists of the nineteenth, like a good many of the present century, would quite certainly have rejected the suggestion that an understanding of its history was necessary or even useful for an understanding of a particular branch of science. These scientists would have maintained–as some still would maintain–that their work is in no way assisted by a study of its past, since whatever was valid and valuable in earlier scientific investigations is always embodied in currently accepted laws, methods and techniques; whereas, on the other hand, the rejected hypotheses or principles or prejudices of earlier scientific generations are, from the scientific point of view, simply so much lumber and of no scientific significance. 'A science which hesitates to forget its founders is lost'. The whole genius of scientific research lies in its essentially progressive forward-looking character: its confidence that it will continue to bring more and more unexplained phenomena under its general laws, and to unify these laws within more and more logically complete and unified theories; a process in which nothing of value inherited from the past is lost, but in which the value of that inheritance has constantly to be tested by its capacity to meet the problems of the future.

It is not difficult, however, to show the inadequacies of this point of view. Persistent progress in science is certainly not something that can be taken for granted: it is not even something natural or normal like growth in many living creatures from birth to their prime. It is therefore of the first importance to point again and again to the main social, political and economic conditions upon which, during the past three and a half centuries, progress in the sciences has depended, and to insist that if these conditions—e.g. freedom to teach and to publish, the availability of sufficient funds and other material facilities—were to fail, then science of any kind could very quickly come to a standstill: as it virtually did in Italy from the late seventeenth to the late eighteenth century. Detailed study of the history of science is important if only because it re-enforces this lesson, by showing how far from a steady rational unfolding of universally acceptable truths that history has been. Like the history of any other great movement—e.g. movements towards rationalisation in legal or administrative systems—it constantly hinges on contingent factors, lucky coincidences or unlucky failures of communication, the requisite data meeting with the right technique or with the right man of imagination at the right time, and so on. Certainly every great chapter in the history of science points to the chanciness of particular scientific developments, a chanciness which makes the speed and magnitude of those developments all the more breath-taking.

But this is not the only service of the history of science to the actual practice and advancement of the different sciences. Just because of the essentially progressive, forward-looking character of scientific work—or just because science today means research science—it is impossible to provide a finally sufficient or conclusive set of conditions or criteria of what makes a particular study scientific. The differences between the aims, foci of interest, standards of achievement, presuppositions—not to mention techniques, postulates and conventions—of the sciences of today and those of the science of a hundred years hence are entirely unforeseeable. On the other hand, certain necessary conditions of scientific work can, it is generally believed, be asserted with complete confidence: e.g. the requirement that any theory, if it is to rank as scientific, must be in principle falsifiable, or that it is to be tested not by its most hopeful-looking but by its least likely-looking logical consequences. This is indeed a necessary condition of the acceptability of any scientific hypothesis considered as a candidate for a place among properly and rationally, although only provisionally, accepted scientific truths. But in conceding this we must not forget that the question of acceptability is itself dependent upon other phases of scientific work, e.g. the invention of notations, the suggestion of frames of reference and description, the decision to accept certain conventions, aspects of scientific thinking with regard to which it would be entirely improper to ask pre-maturely—where and what are their testable, their conceivably falsifiable consequences? Neglect of this truth is only one form of what has been called the 'theorem and experiment' account of scientific thinking: an account which misses the heart of what it seeks to describe, namely that the life of science exists between the established theorems and experiments of today and the half-formulated hypotheses and thought experiments of tomorrow.

Emphasis on this point does not mean, however, that the future of any particular branch of science is an entirely open one. On the contrary, it is largely determined by a number of aims, standards, presuppositions, etc., which are firmly embedded in this or that particular genre or style of scientific work. A not entirely imaginary example will help to make this clear.

Let us imagine the classical theories of light being presented, with the necessary experiments and calculations, to a student of good general intelligence, who claims at the end of the demonstration to have followed everything all right, but then proceeds to ask: Why did we approach the problems in only this way? Why (perhaps) did we approach them in this way at all? Why shouldn't we have begun in some altogether different way, with altogether different postulates, and favouring altogether different kinds of experiment? (Roughly the questions underlying Goethe's objection to the Newtonian theory of colours.) Well, how *ought* a physics teacher to treat such a student? Harsh though it sounds, I believe that the only possible treatment would be to advise another subject of study: perhaps the psychology or the physiology of colour vision. For, whatever the value of the student's suggestions, it is virtually certain that what he wants to do 'isn't physics'. But now what are the grounds of this judgment? They are that any particular physical experiment or piece of theory is an example of a certain style or *genre* of explanation that has been developed successfully to deal with a wide variety of phenomena – and developed not only in the way of internal unification of its theories, codification of its tests, etc., but in the way of an ever deepening and ever more firmly entrenched sense of its own proper possible aims. More simply, work in physics as in any other science has come to mean work done within a tradition.

For this reason acquaintance with the history of science could also help to prepare scientists for revolutionary changes in their basic aims and standards and presuppositions – as well as in their techniques and postulates – as their own special fields continue to be extended or to be understood at ever deeper levels. Admittedly the history of science can do nothing to help scientists to predict such changes, but it can exemplify them, and can explain their 'naturalness', by many past instances. Consider in this connection the presumption that scientific work is essentially progressive, that science means the continual achievement of new truths. On this issue the crucial historical facts are these. The earliest indisputable scientists we know of, the Greek geometers, seem to have had no idea of science as an essentially progressive intellectual activity. For them to do science meant to produce their demonstrations of the few demonstrable truths they had so far hit upon, and then to search around in the hope that they might hit upon others of the same logical status, belonging to the same (one and only) infallible system. Nor had inherent progressiveness any place in Aristotle's, or for that matter in Bacon's or Descartes', conception of science. On the other hand, since early in the eighteenth century, and more particularly since Kant, acceptance of inherent progressiveness as the hall-mark of scientific work has become steadily more widespread. How did this idea take such firm root in the deepest of eighteenth-century minds?

Part of the answer to this question is suggested by three of the best-known heuristic maxims that had guided the development of early seventeenth-century physics. (i) All recorded or presumed changes were to be expressed in quantitative terms. (ii) No metaphysical divisions were to be admitted within nature, so that conceivably any physical phenomenon might prove itself a 'retainer', in Locke's phrase, to any other. (iii) All classifications were to be made on a nominalistic or provisional basis. Now, for simplicity, let us assume that these principles were accepted by all early seventeenth-century physicists for either Cartesian or Baconian reasons, i.e. on grounds of clarity or with a view to predictive power. (In fact, they were commonly combined with others connected with the revival of corpuscular theories of matter.) The point I wish to make, however, is that the reasons why they were accepted neither included nor were thought to imply the requirement that physical investigation should prove to be inherently progressive. Quite the contrary: the common assumption–traces of which are still evident in Locke–was that physical investigation was, for one reason or another, an essentially limited task, such as might theoretically be completed either by a single man of genius or by a few generations of researchers working under the direction of a master mind. And yet each of these principles naturally–although indeed not necessarily–points the way to the idea of science as an essentially progressive activity. Thus, (i) every method of measurement admits, as a logical possibility, if not in practice (and even if not in connection with currently accepted physical theories) of indefinite refinement. (ii) As scientific theories connect more and more distantly related phenomena, our original descriptions of these phenomena are likely to stand in need or progressive revision. (iii) While a nominalist attitude to classifications will bring to an end all quarrels as to their real or essential basis, it will in no way discourage—quite the reverse—the search for more and more powerful systems of classification and explanation.

Where this highly schematic account falls short is, of course, that it tells us nothing, in positive historical terms, of how and why this all-important change in scientists' attitude to their work came about. And the same complaint would properly be lodged against any chapter of alleged 'history of science' which simply recorded that, in the work of a succession of thinkers, proofs became more rigorous, tests more efficient, notations more general or more intuitively revealing, explanations and theories more comprehensive and unified, and so on. For such an account would express no understanding of how and why these advances took place. Such understanding would begin, however, the moment the historian conceived such advances as so many fuller articulations or deeper recognitions of the reasons that had inspired previous researches or of the criteria by which successes in previous researches had been gauged. And such understanding would advance the more we came to appreciate the particular needs, spurs and challenges—including the recognition of errors, inconsistencies or incompletenesses in previous research—by which the new advance was kept in movement. Thus by coming to appreciate, in the theoretical sense of that word, any important line of growth in any part or aspect of science, we—or the scientist—are *eo ipso* learning to appreciate, in the appraisive sense of the word, the richness and variety of the development and hence the richness and many-sidedness of the achievement of the natural sciences.

If historical appreciation is of such importance in the fields that we have so far discussed, it would be natural to expect it to be of no less importance for philosophy. But here the situation is strangely confused. On the one hand there is the vulgar belief that philosophers are much too historically minded, that they are excessively concerned with the past (generally regarded as the dead and erroneous past) of their own subject. This view might seem to gain support from the fact that most philosophers certainly devote their energies to questions that are very like those that exercised their predecessors of more than two hundred or even more than two thousand years ago. But, as against this, we should notice that a number of recent or contemporary philosophers have maintained, both in precept and practice, that philosophy could and should be taught *de novo*, dealing with problems and employing techniques that belong to the contemporary world, and with as little reference as possible to the cramping influences of its past. Those who have favoured this latter programme have undoubtedly regarded themselves as innovators and have usually believed that they were at last putting philosophy on to the sure path of a science. They have failed to notice, however, that in propounding their radical thesis they have been conforming to the main pattern that philosophy has followed since Descartes: radical innovator following radical innovator, true new method proclaimed hard upon true new method, so that it is small wonder if to the intelligent outsider movements in philosophical thought seem almost as variable as fashions in women's clothes. The truth of the matter is that, with comparatively few exceptions–Aristotle, Leibniz and Peirce being the greatest– philosophers have displayed a fantastic lack of historical- mindedness and an almost total lack of interest in their own historical role within intellectual life. Admittedly most philo- sophers study the arguments of their predecessors, often with the utmost care, but mainly in the spirit in which a prosecuting council attends to the arguments put forward by the defence. Typically, philosophers regard their problems as challenges– challenges to their own intellectual virtuosity–which face them with the same timeless quality, and hence the same immunity from all historical considerations, that mathematical problems appear to possess. And in so far as the great philosophers of the past are important it is–or so we have been taught for some two hundred years–chiefly as the originators of great errors, giving rise to those puzzles which it is the main business of the current philosophy, with its improved methods, to disentangle and dispel.

In the present century the claim to have started philosophy afresh, to have swept the boards clean of old and unnecessary lumber, has taken a variety of forms; but quite the most influential has been that which stems from the claim of Lord Russell (in his pre-1914 period) that logic is the essence of philosophy. This claim, to be sure, has taken on a number of different forms, as the meaning given to the term logic has been progressively widened; but at every stage its propounders, with a very few exceptions, have continued to claim for their current version of it the exclusive prerogative of complete and final philosophical sufficiency. But the very number of claims to this effect that have been made since Descartes's day, and the extraordinary rapidity with which one school or style replaces another during periods of philosophical activity,[1] surely suggests an historical problem. How are we to explain the paradox that the one branch of serious intellectual study in which continual revolution in aims and methods is the rule should also be the one branch in which the central problems show an astonishing similarity, if not a complete identity, from generation to generation? What, let us therefore ask, was the origin, and what has been the growth of the habits of mind and of the institutional frameworks that have been associated with the practice of philosophy?

The suggestion that their problems and functions call for historical examination will no doubt seem to many philosophers a sheer insult. But if so, this only shows their lack of understanding of what historical understanding and explanation are. The main if not the sole point of such understanding would be to help philosophers to see better the kind of thing that they habitually do, and no doubt will continue to do, in the light of the way that job has persisted, with all its peculiarities and all its irreplaceable value, down the centuries. A good example of the way philosophers misunderstand the history of their own subject is provided in the preface to Lord Russell's *The Philosophy of Leibniz*, where he contrasts the understanding (sc. the real philosophical study) of different philosophers and philosophical problems with a study of their 'historical relations' (sc. to other philosophers and their problems), and remarks that the latter study can be made 'with little or no regard to their meaning'. As though any kind of history, political or economic or cultural, could be written without considerable understanding of the meaning of the activities in question! But nowhere is this more obviously necessary than in the case of philosophy. To understand, e.g., why Plato wrote as he did in a particular passage means thinking with him – at the very least trying to see what he was trying to say in the first instance. But it is also quite likely to involve thinking against him: refusing what he proposes on the ground, say, that it is inconsistent with other positions that he maintains. It is usually at this point that the historical question, that the need of historical understanding, will arise. But the question why Plato thought (or mis-thought) as he did in one particular passage is likely to expand into a much larger question as to why his thinking on this kind of topic took the general shape that it did. And this, which is certainly an historical question, involves no denial or disregard of Plato's philosophical genius.

I propose, therefore, in the remainder of this book to consider from an historical point of view first a number of institutional features of philosophy as we know it, and then, also from an historical point of view, a number of key concepts and key problems in philosophy: the aim being, in either case, to explain the most striking paradox of philosophy – continual revolution in its means of settling, or of hoping to settle, perennial problems, combined with the persistent resurgence of these problems, if not in wholly identical, yet always in more than merely nominally identical forms. I undertake this task in no derisory or disrespectful fashion. On the contrary, to those who have the patience to allow me a fair hearing, it will become plain that I am offering a justification of philosophy that is much more confident and I trust much more persuasive than those negative and defensive and often highly eccentric elucidations of it with which an unhappy and unconvinced public has been fobbed off for the past few decades.

We can usefully begin by noticing that, to a much greater degree than either history or the natural sciences, philosophy has throughout its history been an academic subject, pursued for the most part within universities or prototypes of universities, and usually as adjunct or hand-maid to other studies – theology, the law, ancient literature, mathematics and natural science – which evidently possess a more direct and practical importance. Now universities are in many respects highly conservative institutions: an intelligent undergraduate, if transported from thirteenth-century Paris to twentieth-century London or New York, would have had no great difficulty in distinguishing their student populations and recognising the kinship of their studies with his own. This is true despite the drastic and nowadays continual changes in and additions to university curricula, especially in the natural sciences. Yet even here changes are perhaps more superficial than we care to believe. The most difficult and most precious ingredients in scientific research and in education in scientific research remain surprisingly constant: I mean, in particular, clarity of intention in connection with experiments, the virtues of patience and accuracy and utter honesty, and above all the capacity to be infected by, and so to sustain and transmit, the various moral and temperamental as well as intellectual qualities that make a great investigator or a great team or tradition of investigators. And what holds of science in this respect holds even more certainly of the humanist-historical disciplines, and perhaps most obviously of philosophy. For, besides sharing in the generally conservative atmosphere of university teaching, philosophy is, by general agreement, concerned with questions of 'second intention': questions that relate to or arise from some of the key concepts and puzzles and valuations of other disciplines. Today this is perhaps most clearly seen in the tendency for philosophy to proliferate into so many kinds of 'philosophy *of* so-and-so'; be it mathematics, or science, or law, or language or art or history or whatever. But for our present argument it is more important to stress the 'second intention' character of what have been the three central strands of academic philosophy since the Renaissance, viz. logic, epistemology and ethics. That logic should have a central and on the whole constant place in the body of university studies is both natural and desirable, since logic is concerned with the canons of validity of inference in any branch of inquiry. And it is noteworthy that, despite the prodigious developments of formal logic during the past century, it could still be claimed by those who favour well-established terminology and have not been entirely carried off their feet by the modish 'logicising' bandwaggon, that the demarcation problems connected with formal logic remain today very similar to what they were for Aristotle: they are the question of its relation, on the one hand, to mathematical and on the other hand to plausible or practical reasoning. At the very least we need not be surprised that the question of the place and scope of formal logic has greatly exercised philosophers in almost every great creative period of philosophy from the twelfth to the early twentieth century.

Very similar considerations apply to both epistemology and ethics. The former is concerned with the relation between those of our thoughts (judgments) which are in some degree subject to logical self-criticism and control, and their basis in perception and sensation (or perhaps in reactions below the level of self-consciousness altogether). Wherever authority is being questioned, wherever credentials are being demanded–be it in physics or history or penology–epistemological questions are being raised and principles invoked. The subject-matter of ethics has traditionally been conceived as those very special rules or norms of conduct which are presented as if they possessed, of logical necessity or right, universal application. Possibly the discussion of moral principles and their presuppositions may not seem so essential to the general advancement of academic studies as the discussion of logical and epistemological issues. And in one great period of philosophy, the mediaeval, there was very little direct discussion of what we should call ethical terms, problems and principles.[2] On the other hand, from the sixteenth century onwards there has been, I think, not a single philosophical school or movement of any significance in which the discussion of ethical problems has not played a central role.

It is not, then, difficult to see why these central philosophical studies should persist–and should be raised in suitably refashioned form in every generation–in any institution or community devoted to the transmission and advancement of learning, and to the maintenance of standards, including standards of intellectual integrity. Indeed, from this point of view the constant and seemingly unprogressive concern of philosophy with certain basic problems is almost as natural as the constant—and largely unprogressive—care of intelligent and devoted parents and teachers in every generation to their children and their charges.

So much then by way of explanation of the constant or unprogressive character of the most central subjects of philosophy. But so far we have done nothing to explain why such constancy should be accompanied by seemingly never-ending conflicts between different philosophical schools as to how these central issues should be settled. Only too often these conflicts have a rigid and sterile quality. But then occasionally there is a phase of great new hope, of revolutionary hope, that seems to be consolidating itself as a new orthodoxy. Not for long, however; seldom, in fact, for more than two decades (the average span of a great teacher's effectiveness), whereupon it begins to crumble before some new assault, the force of some new voice or the lure of some promised vision. How is this second and equally characteristic aspect of philosophical endeavour to be explained?

We may begin by recalling that philosophy seems to have contained an 'agonistic' or competitive element from a very early stage in its history. The great fifth-century sophists were quite as much competitive performers as rival pedagogues. Indeed, their paradoxes and riddles, and the peculiar style and methods of discourse affected by a Gorgias or a Protagoras, suggest the virtuoso much more than the teacher or investigator. In this respect the sophists were certainly drawing on their philosophical predecessors, Xenophanes and Heracleitos in particular; and anthropologists could no doubt suggest analogies between this aspect of early Greek philosophy and the parades and competitions of verbal and mental gymnastics that are common to many primitive peoples. But secondly, we should notice that this agonistic element seems to have persisted, in different forms but with undiminished intensity, in every great subsequent period of philosophy. Wherever philosophy has made itself felt as an intellectual force–and this has often happened *sub rosa*, contrary to the general purposes of the academies within which it has flourished–it has been characterised by an anarchic insistence upon argument on all topics, by its passion for examining the most hallowed credentials and for unearthing seemingly unquestionable presuppositions. In view of its history, the suggestion that philosophy might–or should–some day settle down to a quiet orthodoxy is quite as unrealistic as the hope that it may some day proceed to progress along 'the assured path of a science'.

Considered in itself, this agonistic element might seem a mere peculiarity–sometimes amiable, sometimes otherwise–of the practice of philosophy. Its importance, however, lies in the way in which it was grafted, first in the person of Socrates then in the writings of Plato, on to other intellectual tendencies of a much more positive kind. The effect, as we see progressively revealed in Plato's writings, was to turn the agonistic spirit in upon itself: the endless and aggressive questioning of Socrates is gradually turned into an instrument of continual self-criticism in the service of a number of positive intellectual goals. To speak more technically, philosophy took on the shape and the spirit which it has retained ever since when it came to be articulated as, primarily, logic, epistemology and ethics: i.e. as the study of the canons of valid inference, as the search for the objective criteria of different types of knowledge, and as the examination of the individual's duties to society. That these are essentially continuing tasks, which need to be renewed–rephrased, rediscussed, reslanted–in every academic generation, can hardly be disputed; and it is plausible to suggest that unless they were conducted in an agonistic spirit, they could hardly be discharged at all. A study of basic intellectual standards can scarcely be alive unless it is also kicking: otherwise it would quickly degenerate into the repetition of stale truisms and obedience to methodological dogmas.

In its subsequent history the agonistic element in philosophy has undergone two major, two opposite yet complementary, developments. First, it has spilled over from philosophy to fertilise, and indeed to make possible, rational inquiry in many other fields – the legal, the economic, the aesthetic, and above all in the field of natural science. So powerful indeed has its influence been in this latter field that a good many scientists would probably claim that the ideals of unimpeded questioning on all topics, and of competition between possible explanations and theories, were not simply characteristic of scientific work but unique to it. It is not only in the interest of historical truth that this error should be corrected: it is no less important that scientists should realise that quite a number of the rational-making factors in their methods were originally derived from, and are still shared with, other intellectual disciplines. Moreover, it is a complete mistake to think that there is any clear-cut division between conflicts of opinion among, e.g., physicists over physical theories and interpretations and their differences over philosophical issues. Even in technical publications by leading physicists we find the two kinds of conflict interwoven in the most intimate – although, from an historical point of view, in entirely natural – ways.[3] On the other hand, it must be conceded that, as developed within the natural sciences, the agonistic spirit has been combined with a number of restraints which have moderated its naturally anarchic character. As a rule experimental tests – especially when applied to what seem to be the least probable necessary consequences of the hypothesis under review – serve to decide between rival scientific opinions; and even where decisions cannot be reached by experiment, preferences as between hypotheses can be defended on generally accepted grounds, e.g. manageability, analogy or coherence with other accepted theories, and so on.

These considerations bring us to the second development. Notoriously a number of important theories of knowledge, from that of Descartes onwards, not only show the marked influence of scientific methods and standards but are based on some particular interpretation or explanation of the astonishing achievements of the mathematical and experimental sciences. Descartes and Leibniz, Locke and Kant, Mill and Peirce, Poincaré and Russell, all are impressed by different real and important features of scientific discourse and scientific proof. This tendency has added fresh fuel to the endemic agonistic spark of philosophical debate. On the one hand, scientifically well-equipped philosophers have given us surprisingly different accounts of the essence of scientific method, and indeed of the aims and standards of the most developed sciences. Hence the conflicts between rationalist and empiricist, of quasi-aesthetic and quasi-instrumentalist accounts, first of scientific procedures, and thereafter of human knowledge in general. On the other hand, the facile assumption that scientific methods of proof and rules of discourse provide criteria for the whole range of human knowledge has inevitably, if unfortunately, called out a succession of conservative reactions: namely, refusals to regard scientific innovations or discoveries as having any special relevance to the discussion and criticism of other branches of knowledge.

Finally, we must say something of a form, or an expression, of the agonistic spirit in philosophy, which, when carried to excess, is liable to make a laughing-stock of philosophy, but which nevertheless admits of some measure of explanation and defence. This is the immense influence exercised in the history of philosophy by powerful individual personalities. It is fairly easy to see why this is so. Important philosophical theses rarely admit of logical demonstration and never admit of experimental tests. (Roughly we can say: this is because they are largely concerned with the framework within which, and the criteria on the strength of which, experimental tests are made in the different sciences.) Further, even when important philosophical theses can be shown to be logical blunders or sophisms, this does not necessarily mean that their influence is at an end. For example, Kant's discussions of space and time contain what have seemed to many critics to be almost unbelievable logical lapses: yet this hardly affects their broad philosophical significance, or their crucial role within an important theory of knowledge. In general, philosophers are judged—or, better, are felt to deserve further thought and study and intellectual support—not on the basis of what they prove or even of what they explicitly assert, but rather of what their assertions and attempted proofs seem to *promise* in the way of new illumination of persistent philosophical problems. Now such promises, and the intellectual hopes and enthusiasms which they properly arouse, cannot be graded or measured on any objective scale. It is therefore only natural that they should be recognised in, and even (within sane limits) identified with, the techniques and standards, and even the intellectual style and character of this or that particular teacher. Every serious student of philosophy can recall what might be described as his moment of philosophical initiation: when he was convinced that *this* particular teacher–whose book he is reading or whose lecture or class he is attending–is going to feel out a new path through the jungle or crack open an age-old puzzle because he has the right technique or combination of techniques, and because he has the imagination and the singleness and strength of character to do it. We begin to be philosophers by recognising our masters: too often we are confirmed as philosophers by quarrelling with them.

So far in this chapter I have urged that, in point of historical fact, philosophy has always combined continuing struggles between different schools of opinion on certain central issues with a sense of obligation–be it fatality or vocation–to pursue these struggles despite apparent lack of progress and indeed with no prospect of reaching any ultimately acceptable solutions. But is this combination of characteristics also in some sense necessary? Is philosophical discussion something that, in the nature of the case, must be resumed again and again despite the impossibility of ever reaching final satisfactory conclusions? And if this is true, then why is it true–how can the relevant kind of necessity be displayed and admitted?

I want to show, in the remaining chapters of this book, that in the case of a number of important philosophical problems the combination of characters just discussed can be shown to be necessary because of the history of their terms, or, to speak more exactly, because of the place which their key terms hold in our general conceptual schemes as a result of certain historical developments. In claiming this, I am not claiming, to be sure, to be offering a new brand of solution to these problems. My arguments are aimed simply at showing that, even if these problems turn out to be insoluble, this in no way detracts from their importance, and indeed their indispensability, to the whole of intellectual life.

The problems with which I shall deal fall into three groups. First I consider a number of seemingly inconclusible disputes over the proper definition of certain concepts, including those of science, art (in the sense of the 'fine arts'), religion, justice and democracy. These I call essentially contested concepts; and I shall try to show that their essential contestibility, far from being a cause of philosophical scandal, is rather a proof of the continuing need of philosophy and of vital, agonistic philosophy. Secondly, I consider a field of philosophy (I choose ethics although epistimology would serve equally well) in which philosophers dispute not so much the proper connotation of the key terms involved as the proper method of approach to the whole field. Here, whilst fully assenting to the value of continuing basic ethical controversy, I hope to show that such controversy could be made at once more realistic and vastly more interesting if philosophers would recognise the close affinity between moral and historical judgments; and I shall suggest that the best way of proving that morality is an essential and autonomous feature of 'that historical being, man' is by first showing that some exercise of historical understanding is a necessary prerequisite of every moral judgment and decision. Lastly, and more briefly, I consider Collingwood's astonishing claim that metaphysics is an historical science, one whose work can never be completed, and whose problems, even when they seem to be settled, are bound to reappear phoenix-like from the ashes of some new great conflict so long as the natural and social sciences themselves continue to advance.

Chapter 8

ESSENTIALLY CONTESTED CONCEPTS

THE concepts to be discussed in this chapter relate to a number of organised or semi-organised human activities: in academic terms they belong to aesthetics, to political and social philosophy and the philosophy of religion. The basic fact about them is this. We find groups of people disagreeing about the proper use of the concepts, e.g. of art, of democracy, of the Christian tradition. When we examine the different uses of these terms and the characteristic arguments in which they figure we soon see that there is no one use of any of them which can be set up as its generally accepted and therefore correct or standard use. Different uses of the term 'work of art' or 'democracy' or 'Christian doctrine' subserve different though of course not altogether unrelated functions for different schools or movements of artists and critics, for different political groups and parties, for different religious communities and sects. Now once this *variety* of functions is disclosed we might expect that the disputes in which the above-mentioned concepts figure would at once come to an end. But in fact this does not happen. Each party continues to maintain that the special functions which the term 'work of art' or 'democracy' or 'Christian doctrine' fulfils on *its* behalf or on *its* interpretation, is the correct or proper or primary, or the only important, function which the term in question can be said to fulfil. Moreover, each party continues to defend its case with what it claims to be convincing arguments, evidence and other forms of justification.

When this kind of situation persists in practical life we are no doubt often justified in regarding it as a head-on conflict of interests or tastes or attitudes, which no amount of discussion can possibly dispel; and we therefore feel justified in dismissing the arguments of the contesting parties as at best unconscious rationalisations and at worst sophistical special pleadings. On the other hand, when this kind of situation persists in philosophy (where some disputant continues to maintain against all comers that there is one and only one proper sense of the term 'substance' or 'self' or 'idea') we have recently been encouraged to attribute it to some deep-seated and profoundly interesting intellectual tendency, whose presence is 'metaphysical'—something to be exorcised with skill or observed with fascination according to our philosophical temperament. Now I have no wish to deny that endless disputes may be due to psychological causes on the one hand or to metaphysical afflictions on the other; but I want to show that there are apparently endless disputes for which neither of these explanations *need* be the correct one. Further, I shall try to show that there are disputes, centred on the concepts which I have just mentioned, which are perfectly genuine: which, although not resolvable by argument of any kind, are nevertheless sustained by perfectly respectable arguments and evidence. This is what I mean by saying that there are concepts which are essentially contested, concepts the proper use of which inevitably involves endless disputes about their proper uses on the part of their users.

In order to bring out the importance and peculiarity of concepts of this kind and in particular to show why an adequate understanding of them requires some appreciation of their history—of how they have come to be used in the ways they are, I am going to expound in some detail an artificial example to whose structure and manner of functioning other live and important essentially contested concepts conform more or less closely. The model may well seem trivial, since it is taken from the field of sport—and of imaginary sport at that. But its seeming triviality is in fact an asset; it enables us to appreciate, in a case where bias and passion are unlikely to afflict us, a certain way of meaning, of influencing, of persuading, which has hitherto been either ignored or grossly underestimated.

We are all familiar with the concept of 'championship' or of 'the champions' in various games and sports. Commonly a team is judged or agreed to be 'the champions' at regular intervals, say, annually, in virtue of certain features of its performance against other contesting teams. Then for a certain period, e.g. a year, this team is by definition 'the champions' even though, as months go by, it becomes probable or certain that they will not repeat their success. But now let us imagine a championship of the following quite unusual kind. (*a*) In this championship each team specialises in a distinctive method, strategy and style of play of its own, to which all its members subscribe to the best of their ability. (*b*) 'Championship' is not adjudged and awarded in terms of the highest number of markable successes, or 'scores', but in virtue of level of style or calibre. (No doubt for this to be manifested a certain minimum number of successes is necessary.) More simply, to be adjudged 'the champions' means to be judged 'to have played the game best'. (*c*) 'Championship' is not a distinction gained and acknowledged at a fixed time and for a fixed period. Games proceed continuously, and whatever side is acknowledged champion today knows it may perfectly well be caught up or surpassed tomorrow. (*d*) Just as there is no 'marking' or 'points' system to decide who are the champions, so there are no official judges or strict rules of adjudication. Instead what happens is this. Each side has its own loyal kernel group of supporters, and in addition, at any given time, a number of 'floating' supporters who are won over to support it because of the quality of its play –and, we might add, the loudness of its kernel supporters' applause and the persuasiveness of their comments. Moreover, at any given time, *one* side will have the largest (and loudest) group of supporters who, we may say, will *effectively* hail it as 'the champions'. But (*e*) the supporters of *every* contesting team regard and refer to their favoured team as 'the champions' (perhaps allowing such qualifications as 'the *true* champions', 'the *destined* champions', '*morally* the champions' . . . and so on). To bring out the importance of this point, we may suppose that all groups of supporters would acknowledge that at a given moment one team T_1 are 'the effective champions'. Yet the property of being acknowledged effective champions carries with it no universal recognition of outstanding excellence in T_1's style and calibre of play. On the contrary, the supporters of T_2, T_3, etc., continue to regard and to acclaim their favoured teams as 'the champions' and continue with their efforts to convert others to their view, not through any vulgar wish to be the majority party, but because they believe their favoured team is *playing the game best*. There is, therefore, continuous competition between the contestant teams, not only for acknowledgment as champions, but for acceptance of (what each side and its supporters take to be) the proper criteria of championship.

It is easy to think of a number of sports which, with a little doctoring, could be made to conform fairly closely to the conditions sketched out above. For example, in show-jumping a particular horse is judged to be the champion in virtue of a number of relatively independent criteria: not knocking down any bars, not refusing any jumps, 'dressage', conformity to certain prescribed time intervals between jumps or for different parts of the course, ease of movement and apparent 'comfort', endurance, and so on. We can quite easily imagine a jumping contest in which championship is accorded and acclaimed in the way just described to different horses and their riders by their different groups of spectators, each of which is always winning a few or losing a few 'floating' supporters according to the ostensible performance and 'effective' recognition of their favourite. But for the sake of clarity I prefer to invent or postulate a game of unusual simplicity. The game is a variant of skittles. The only action it demands from all members of any contesting side is a kind of bowling at certain objects. But such bowling can be judged, from the point of view of method, strategy and style, in a number of different ways: particular importance may be attached to speed or to direction or to height or to the use of bounce or to swerve or spin, and we can imagine separate groups of supporters for each team that specialises in one of these main styles. Of course, no one can bowl *simply* with speed, or simply with good direction or simply with height or swerve or spin: *some* importance, however slight, must, in practice, be attached to each of these factors, for all that the supporters of one team will speak of its 'sheer-speed attack' (apparently neglecting other factors), while supporters of other teams coin phrases to emphasise other factors in bowling upon which their favoured team concentrates its efforts.

Let us now try to state, in the light of this imaginary model, the formal—or in a loose sense the logical—conditions to which apparently the use of any essentially contested concept must conform. There would appear to be at least the five following necessary conditions. (I) The concept in question must be *appraisive* in the sense that it signifies or accredits some kind of valued achievement. (II) This achievement must be of an internally complex character, for all that its worth is attributed to it as a whole. (III) Any explanation of its worth must therefore include reference to the respective contributions of its various parts or features; yet prior to experimentation there is nothing absurd or contradictory in any of a number of possible rival descriptions of its total worth, one such description setting its component parts or features in one order of importance, a second setting them in a second order, and so on. In fine, the accredited achievement is *initially* variously describable. (IV) The accredited achievement must be of a kind that admits of considerable modification in the light of changing circumstances; and such modification cannot be prescribed or predicted in advance. For convenience I shall call the concept of any such achievement 'open' in character.

These four conditions suffice to explain how and why the kind of situation might arise in which different groups of spectators would cheer on and comment on their favourite teams for their respective styles of play. But they do not suffice to define what it is to be an essentially contested concept. For this purpose we must add that not only do different persons or parties adhere to different views of the correct use of some concept, but (V) that each party recognises the fact that its own use of it is contested by those of other parties, and that each party must have at least some appreciation of the different criteria in the light of which the other parties claim to be applying the concept in question. More simply, to use an essentially contested concept means to use it against other uses and to recognise that one's own use of it has to be maintained against these other uses. Still more simply, to use an essentially contested concept means to use it both aggressively and defensively.

It is easy to show the necessity of each of these conditions in terms of our artificial example. There can be no question but that my concept of 'the champions' is appraisive; nor, I think, that it is used both aggressively and defensively. This disposes of conditions (I) and (V). What of condition (II) that the achievement of championship (by playing the game best) must be of an internally complex character? Are all worth-while achievements essentially internally complex? That they are seems to me as certain as any statement about values and valuation can be: although why this should be so—whether it is a necessary truth and if so of what kind—is a question of the greatest difficulty. Its truth has been recognised, or at least emphasised, in the history of thought more by aestheticians than by moralists. Few people, I think, would deny that aesthetic value of any kind presupposes some sort of organisation of parts or elements in a whole; but it seems to me equally clear that any valuable forms of action or thought or feeling are internally complex—besides requiring a highly complicated social context. In the case of our imaginary model, think of the complexity involved in the very ideas of playing a game, of playing against different opponents, and of playing in accordance with—or to exemplify—one particular style! And our model really is a simplified model, achieving or expressing a value of a very simple kind.

To see the necessity of condition (III)—the initially (or essentially) variously describable character of the achievement which the term 'champions' accredits—we need only recall that each group of spectators must take some cognisance, however slight, of the factors other than the one (e.g. 'sheer-speed attack') for which they cheer on and commend their own favourite team. Moreover these other factors might well be graded in slightly different orders by different members of a particular support-group—and *a fortiori* by different floating backers: facts which suggest that at the outset—when play began on the first morning of the first day—how supporters would group themselves around different factors would have been anyone's guess.

Finally, to explain the necessity of condition (IV)—that the achievement our concept accredits is persistently open or vague

–let us consider the particular case of the team which concentrates its efforts, and reposes its hopes for the championship, on a 'sheer-speed attack'. The task facing them is: can they put up an outstanding performance in this method and style of bowling, a performance which will make all other methods and styles look 'not really bowling at all'? To succeed in this the bowlers in our team must evidently pay attention to circumstances, and modify their method of play as circumstances suggest or dictate. (We may imagine that certain grounds–or alleys–and certain lights are much more obviously favourable to 'sheer-speed attack' than others.) But whatever the circumstances, our team strives to be acclaimed as 'the champions' in virtue of its characteristic ('sheer-speed') method and style of bowling. In ostensibly favourable circumstances such acclamation could be backed by the judgment: 'They are the champions –they have shown us what speed bowling *really* is.' In ostensibly unfavourable circumstances it could be backed by: 'They are the champions–they have shown us what speed can do when everything seems against it.' In general no one can predict, at any given time, what level or what special adaptation of its own particular style–what bold raising or sagacious lowering of its achievement targets–may strengthen any particular team's claim to be the champions.

So much for the five conditions by reference to which we can, I think, see quite clearly what it means for a concept to be essentially contested. But now the following objection may be raised. 'All that your statement of these formal conditions does is to suggest the kind of situation in which people might imagine that they were using a concept of a peculiar kind, which you call "essentially contested". But the kind of situation suggested is simply a particular variant of those in which people engage in endless contests as to the right application of some epithet or slogan, when the truth is that they are confusing two *different* concepts about which there need never have been any dispute or contest at all. To all appearances your concept of "the champions" not only denotes consistently different sets of individuals (teams) according as it is used by different parties (supporters); it also connotes different achievements (in the way of different methods, strategies and styles favoured by the different teams) according as it is used by different groups of supporters. Is there, then, any real ground for maintaining that it has a *single* meaning, that *could* be contested?'

The easy answer to this objection is that no one would conceivably refer to one team among others as 'the champions' unless he believed his team to be playing better than all the others *at the same game*. The context of any typical use of 'the champions' shows that it has thus far a single meaning as between its different (contestant) users. But to this answer the critic may retort: 'But exactly the same situation *appears to obtain* wherever men dispute over the right use of what proves to be a thoroughly confused concept—or better a thoroughly confusing term which cloaked the possibly quite consistent uses of two or more concepts, which only needed to be discriminated. Your definition of what it is to be an essentially contested concept no doubt covers many facts which your artificial example is meant to illustrate, but it neglects the possibility that among them may well be the fact of a persistent delusion, viz., the deluded belief that the different teams *are* all playing the same game.'

It turns out, then, that this objection is not a request for further refinement of our definition of an essentially contested concept, but for an indication of the conditions in which the continued use of any such concept, as above defined, can be defended. And this is a perfectly fair request, since it is certainly reasonable to urge the parties contesting the rightful use of such a concept to bethink themselves with all seriousness, whether they are really referring to one and the same achievement. For instance, in our artificial example, might it not simply be said that T_1 is trying to put on a first-class performance of (primarily) fast bowling; T_2 of (primarily) straight bowling, and so on, and that these quite proper but quite different aims of our different teams are not essentially, but only accidentally and as a result of persistent confusion, mutually contesting and contested?

I shall at once show in outline how I think this objection should be countered, still using my artificial example; but I must add that until my answer is interpreted in the live examples which follow it may well seem somewhat specious. In defence, then, of the continued use of the concepts 'championship' and 'the champions' in my example I urge: each of my teams could properly be said to be contesting for the *same* championship if, in every case, its peculiar method and style of playing had been derived by a process of imitation and adaptation from an *exemplar*, which might have the form either of one prototype team of players, or of a succession or tradition of teams. This exemplar's way of playing must be recognised by all the contesting teams and their supporters to be 'the way the game is to be played'; yet, because of the internally complex and variously describable character of the exemplar's play, it is natural that different features in it should be differently weighted by different appraisers, and hence that our different teams should have come to hold their very different conceptions of how the game should be played. To this we should add that recognition or acceptance of the exemplar's achievement must have that 'open' character which we have ascribed to every essentially contested concept. A certain kind of worthwhile achievement was presented, and our teams have all been seeking to revive or reproduce it in their play. But there can be no question of any purely mechanical repetition or reproduction of it. To follow an exemplar is to exert oneself to revive its (or his) way of doing things, not only to the utmost of one's ability, but to the utmost that circumstances, favourable or unfavourable, will allow.

We may illustrate this situation in terms of Team T_1 (with its 'sheer-speed attack') and its supporters. All members and supporters of this team are at one with all members and supporters of all other teams in acknowledging the authority of the exemplar; but in appraising the exemplar's achievement members and supporters of T_1 have concentrated their attention, primarily and predominantly, on the one factor of speed. They have conscientiously sustained and perhaps even advanced the exemplar's way of playing as circumstances permitted in terms of their own appraisal of it. Members and supporters of T_1 are therefore assured that T_1 has played the game as it should be played. But just the same holds true, of course, of all the other contestant teams, together with their supporters.

At this point it is worth recalling that in our artificial example championship is not awarded on any quantitative system; we can now see how difficult, if not impossible, such a system would be to work, given the other conditions which we have laid down. For who is to say whether T_1's sustaining and advancing of the exemplar's way of playing is a better ('truer' or 'more orthodox') achievement than that of, say, T_2, whose members have no doubt contended with quite different difficulties and exploited quite different advantages in their concentration upon the different factor of direction? In sum it would seem to be quite impossible to fix a *general principle* for deciding which of two such teams has really 'done best'—done best in its own peculiar way to advance or sustain the characteristic excellence revealed in the exemplar's play.

We have thus taken two steps in defence of the continued use of our essentially contested concept 'the champions': (I) We have seen that each of our teams claims—and can point to facts which appear to support its claim—that its style of play embodies 'the true line of descent' or 'the right method of development' of the exemplar's play. (II) We have seen that there can be no general method or principle for deciding between the claims made by the different teams. To be sure, these steps do not amount to a justification of the claim of any particular team, viz. that *its* way of playing is the best. Indeed, if they did so the concept of 'the champions' would cease to be an essentially contested one. Nevertheless, recalling the internally complex, and variously describable, and peculiarly 'open' character of the exemplar's achievement, we must admit the following possibility: that this achievement could not have been revived and sustained or developed to the *optimum* which actual circumstances have allowed, except by the kind of continuous competition for acknowledged championship (and for acceptance of one particular criterion of 'championship') which my artificial example was designed to illustrate. Thus Team T_1 could hardly have developed its sheer-speed attack to its present excellence had it not been aspiring to convert supporters from Team T_2, which in its turn could hardly have developed its skill in respect of direction had it not been aspiring to convert supporters . . . and so on for all the contestant teams. This result of continuous competition does not justify the claims of any one of our teams; but it might be said to justify, other things being equal, the combined employment of the essentially contested concept 'the champions' by *all* the contesting teams.

It is in this conception of a possible optimum (never finally achieved and approachable by a variety of routes and through a variety of results as between different competing claims) that the unity of an essentially contested concept may be said to reside (or at least to be made manifest) and that, consequently, its continued use can be justified. But this defence of the continued use of an essentially contested concept is conditional in the extreme. It is introduced as a possibility, which the facts in certain cases may at once preclude. For example, it might turn out that continued use of two or more rival versions of an essentially contested concept would have the effect of utterly frustrating the kind of activity and achievement which it was the job of this concept (in and through all the rival contestant versions) to appraise—and through positive appraisal to help to sustain. Even in more favourable cases, the question whether in fact competition between rival claimants has thus far sustained or developed the original exemplar's achievement to the optimum, will usually be a very difficult one to decide. Again, even where the question could be answered affirmatively with regard to a particular kind of achievement, the cost of sustaining and developing it competitively may well be judged too high in the light of its more general effects. In this connection, our artificial example from the field of sport was an unusually favourable one. It suggested one main and at least harmless result—the sustaining and developing of a number of competitively connected athletic skills. Suppose, however, that the pursuit of championship in our example were to result in the impoverishment of all the players and supporters (through neglect of their proper business), or in the formation of savage political cleavages between different teams and their supporters —then our reaction to it would be very different.

To sum up our discussion so far. Conditions I–V as stated on page 161 explain sufficiently what it means for a concept to count as essentially contested. But they do not include any clear suggestion, still less any rule, for distinguishing an essentially contested concept from a concept which can be shown, by a careful inspection of its different uses, to be radically confused. In order to be able to make this distinction, which is in effect to justify the continued use of any essentially contested concept, it is necessary to add two further conditions. These are (VI) the derivation of any such concept from an original exemplar whose authority is acknowledged by all the contestant users of the concept, and (VII) the probability or plausibility, in appropriate senses of these terms, of the claim that the continuous competition for acknowledgment as between the contestant users of the concept enables the original exemplar's achievement to be sustained or developed in optimum fashion. But these conditions evidently embody an historical approach to, and appreciation of, the special character of essentially contested concepts. As we saw in the case of certain institutions, so here again, understanding of how concepts of this kind function or can be used requires some appreciation of how they *came to be* usable in a rather unusual way. The importance of this historical approach and appreciation will at once become plain when we turn to our live examples.

The examples I choose are the concepts of a religion, of art, of science, of democracy and of social justice.

That Religion, when used as an entirely general term, expresses what may come to be – or may progressively be more and more recognised as – an essentially contested concept, seems to me highly likely. Witness the different emphases placed upon elements of cult and of doctrine, of personal salvation and of social cohesion, of moral comfort and metaphysical illumination, in the different world religions and indeed in some cases in one and the same religion at different stages of its growth. But for my present illustrative purposes it is best to concentrate on one particular religion, neglecting its relation to others. For this purpose I choose Christianity. And I want to consider the concept of Christianity in its practical, not its purely doctrinal, manifestations, e.g. as exemplified by what would generally be meant by such a phrase as 'a Christian life'. Let us see how far this concept can be fitted under my five formal and the two broad historical conditions of essential contestedness.

Clearly our uses of such a phrase are appraisive: they accredit a certain kind of spiritual achievement. Equally clearly this achievement is of an internally complex and variously describable kind. Witness the continuing debate as to which element or aspect of Christian doctrine and inspiration is most unique to it—incarnation, redemption, atonement, grace, fellowship, denial of the world or its salvation? That Christianity is also an 'open' concept, in the sense that I have given to that term, seems clear from its history. Thus, e.g., it would have been unthinkable for Christianity in its beginnings to have set out to abolish the institution of slavery; but equally it would have been unthinkable if, at a later stage, Christianity had condoned it. Again, only too often if not always, Christianity has been practised (and conceived by its different adherents) both 'aggressively' and 'defensively' (condition V). And that any proper use of the term must conform to my condition (VI)—derivation from a commonly acknowledged source—is obvious; whilst that it conforms to my condition VII—approach towards an optimum realisation through different competing inter-pretations—might be agreed (although no doubt with many qualifications) not only by liberal Christians but by other liberal spirits of other (or of no) religious persuasions.

The most questionable case, undoubtedly, is that of condition V. Is the concept of Christianity, and its derivatives such as 'a Christian life', *necessarily* used both aggressively and defensively? The familiar pattern of the history of Christianity is certainly that of one dominant church, in any area or in any epoch, *and* usually a number of dissenting or protesting sects. But is there anything inherently necessary in this pattern? Is the Christian kingdom, here below also, essentially one of many mansions? Conformity to my conditions (I) to (IV) and to my condition

(VI) cannot be said, in this or in any instance, to *entail* such a conclusion. But it makes it extremely *likely* that such a conclusion will be found to hold; and given its historical development to date–which is something that Christianity (in this like any other religion) can never possibly shed–its contested character, or the aggressive and defensive use of many of its key doctrines, would appear to belong inherently to it *now*.

Having said this I do not propose to press this example any further, partly because of my ignorance of the relevant apologetic literature, but chiefly because the most important question it raises is one which I shall try to deal with later in a more general form. This is the question, which would be raised by any positivistically minded critic of any religion, whether the so-called arguments by which adherents of one creed seek to convert adherents of other creeds are in any proper sense arguments at all.

When used to stand for a supreme genus or category of human activity, the word Art, and its near homonyms in European languages, has had a surprisingly short history, of at most some three hundred years. The Greek *mimesis* and the Roman and mediaeval and renaissance uses of *artes* had much wider and more practical connotations: the idea of Art in the sense of 'the fine arts' and as the central idea in an autonomous branch of philosophy, 'aesthetics', is a product of the late seventeenth and early eighteenth centuries. Art, as a categorial term –and as an ingredient in the titles of many different institutions –grew up as an answer to Science: just as the idea of 'the fine arts' was an answer to the challenge of 'useful knowledge'.

Serious if philosophically naïve discussion of the canons of excellence in the different arts–plastic, literary, musical, for example–has, of course, had a much longer history; and it might reasonably be maintained that such discussion has to date been of far greater intellectual worth, and has excited greater educational influence, than any philosophical discussion of Art as such. Yet the general philosophical concept of Art, or rather successive philosophical answers to the question 'What is Art?' have had considerable effects not only upon criticism of the arts but upon popular attitudes to the arts and the artistic process. From this point of view successive philosophical definitions of Art (as such) have, I would say, proved a good deal more influential than, to date, have philosophical definitions of Religion or, for that matter, of Science. I shall therefore consider the conflicts between different definitions of Art, taken as an entirely general term, in some detail. But I shall also try to show how these conflicts have affected some of the particular arts (e.g. painting) and certain concepts that belong to the particular arts (e.g. colouration). And it is with these that I shall begin.

Let us imagine, then, an amateur of the arts, with a genuine if puzzled admiration for many recent and contemporary paintings, who seeks guidance in the formation of his taste from the reasoned judgments of professional art critics. And let us suppose that he is rather unlucky in his initial inquiries, and that he hits upon, not the kind of critics who emphasise the one-sidedness of their own sympathies and their own characteristic appreciations of painting, but upon a number of those critics—and there are many such—who either openly or deviously give the innocent reader to understand that there is *one* style or method of painting (the one which the critic in question happens to prefer) which *alone* gives us real paintings— paintings which sustain and advance the great traditions of the past and herald the unborn masterpieces of tomorrow. And, of course, the trouble is that a number of critics or groups or schools of criticism will be saying this about a number of different styles or movements in recent and contemporary painting. In this situation, deafened and confused by the confident voices and commanding jargons of some half-dozen different camps, our simple art-lover will be utterly at a loss. Whom can he trust? Had he not better rely on his own untutored taste, uncertain and diffident though it may be? But suppose that at this point a friendly and modest voice speaks in his ear: 'Heaven knows which, if any, of these conflicting voices is right, or how, if at all, their different points of view could be reconciled. But I think I can tell you how this separation of points of view came to be. I cannot solve your problem, but I can tell you more or less how it arose.' If he is wise, our simple art-lover will grasp at this offer of aid.

We need not go into any of the details of the story which the art-historian would unfold. Perhaps it would take as its base-line that deep division in artistic aims and standards that was effected by the Romantic movement. The reasons for further splinterings within, in particular, the art of painting as practised in particular in France, will then be (as far as possible sympathetically) disclosed. Some of these reasons will be of a kind that would arise naturally from the experience of artists working in a society in which there is no longer a single main type of patronage; others would arise from the increasing availability of specimens of art of the most diverse ages and cultures; others from the teachings of popularized science—as with the first Impressionists; yet others from political and social pressures—as with the Social Realists. But throughout the explanation one point of the first importance would continually be stressed: the spokesman of *most* of the rebel movements or schools would claim, with some show of justice, that the style of painting which they defended was the true inheritor and advancer of the great tradition of painting which had preceded them.

But how, our amateur may ask, could this claim have been made with any show of plausibility from so many different, and often radically conflicting quarters? Chiefly, the answer must be, because painting is essentially a complex activity, which has at different periods admitted of a number of very different but no doubt equally illuminating descriptions. Painting *is* the placing of colour on wood or canvas; it *is* the expression or result of how a given artist sees things—whether in his imagination or in our common world. Moreover, simply because of the character of the medium of expression—the transformation by pigments of the surface of some physical object—this expression of what the artist sees is always potentially a communication. And finally any successful painting is, by definition, a source of aesthetic enjoyment. It is natural and useful to describe paintings—and to encourage or applaud or criticise painters— sometimes in terms of one of the above descriptions, sometimes in terms of another. One of the above styles of description will be best suited to the discussion and interpretation of one school or movement in painting, while a second style of description will be suited to other schools or movements. More generally, painting has a number of aspects; and the relative importance of any of these aspects will be differently assessed according to the beliefs of any painter or critic as to the best way in which the traditional values of painting can be developed or sustained. But there is no certain way in which the correctness or incorrectness of any such belief can be established in advance or on principle. The result is that, so long as there is painting as we know it, there will always be a number of ways (or at least of alleged ways) in which the traditional values of paintings can best be kept alive. The lion and the unicorn—classicists and romanticists, impressionists and post-impressionists, abstractionists and expressionists—will always be fighting for the crown. 'Painting', when used as it commonly is today as an appraisive term, meaning 'real painting', 'genuine painting', 'painting which reminds us of what painting can do', etc., is the expression of an essentially contested concept.

Now, what is true of the general term 'painting' will be matched—in respect of conflicting critical usage and of the way in which these conflicts can be understood—by the case of more specific terms such as, e.g., colouration, depth, composition, etc. Thus from different artistic viewpoints, colouration, when considered as an appraisive term, may be used to refer predominantly either to the arrangement of pigments on a surface, or to the use of pigments to convey certain *other* special effects, e.g. massiveness, distance, etc., or to their use to represent or suggest certain forms found in nature, or to express something peculiar (individual, novel, important) in the artist's general way of seeing things. This being so, it is not difficult to see that the notion of colouration is, in fact, used in an essentially contested manner, even if this fact is not admitted by the majority of critics and aestheticians.

Now, I want to suggest that we should regard the four or five most important classic theories or definitions of Art in a somewhat similar way: i.e. that we should regard them as highly abstract—and often quite unplausibly overgeneralised—attempts to make certain successive preferences in aesthetic appreciation and art criticism conform to the framework of particular philosophical systems. In support of this suggestion, we may recall that the most interesting developments in aesthetics have usually been due to writers who were not primarily philosophers at all, but were men of great insight into some two or more of the arts and very forceful exponents of some new movement of feeling and aspiration in the critical appreciation of these arts. Examples would be Vico, Addison, Burke, Coleridge, Baudelaire, Ruskin, Nietzsche, Péguy, and in our day Mr Eliot and M. André Malraux. Such men as these voice new standards and aims in some group of the arts so powerfully that they exert a considerable influence upon critics of yet *other* arts, so that their teachings and preachings are eventually stretched to apply –often with much decreased plausibility–to the arts in general. At this point, I want to suggest, the philosophic aesthetician commonly picks them up, and proceeds to pack a dehydrated version of some great critic's message into the framework of his system of philosophy.

Let us try, then, in accordance with this hypothesis, to learn through the history of the concept of Art how it came to be the essentially contested concept that it undoubtedly is today. What main advances, since the eighteenth century, has philosophical aesthetics to show? One thing would no doubt generally be claimed for it: its vindication of the autonomy or uniqueness of artistic values. Yet this claim is liable to be very misleading: for it suggests that either artistic excellence consists in one single unique thing or property (intuition-expression *or* communication *or* configurational unity or whatever you please) or else, if it is complex, that its ingredients are one and all confined to the sphere of art: and both these contentions are, I think, certainly false. What is valid in this claim could be better expressed by saying: the history of philosophical aesthetics discloses a growing recognition of the fact that the word 'art' is most usefully employed, not as a descriptive term standing for certain indicatable properties, but as an appraisive term accrediting a certain kind of achievement. This truth (though, of course, differently phrased) seems to me to be made progressively clearer in the writings of idealist aestheticians, from Kant through Hegel to Croce and Collingwood. At the same time none of the idealists, with the exception of Kant, showed any appreciation of the essential complexity of every artistic achievement; and we have still to see how the history of the concept of art forces recognition of this complexity upon us.

Eighteenth-century aesthetics inherited a traditional naïve aesthetic which was already of at least twofold character. It combined an element of representationism (illusionism, imitation of nature) with an element of idealisation (sometimes conceived in terms of 'correct' formal relationships). The first of these elements did not survive long in the history of general or philosophical aesthetics: there are some arts which are manifestly *not* representational. But the second may be regarded as the prototype of later 'configurationist' theories. Now, according to almost all 'configurationist' theories artistic excellence is an inherent or resident property in the work of art itself. The artist must work to get it there; the spectator finds it there; but there it emphatically is – and not in anybody's imaginings or perceivings or judgings. Evidently, on this view, to say of any (presumed) 'good' work of art, that it will therefore be admired by competent judges, is to make a *synthetic* statement. Eighteenth-century subjectivist aesthetic theories denied this, urging very persuasively that any excellence we attribute to a work of art can be more properly described and valued in terms of the states of mind, e.g. certain pleasurable responses, of the suitably situated and educated spectator. Thus the first important step in the history of aesthetics was to shift attention from the thing, the work of art, to the spectator who enjoys it. The second step is the work of the Romantic movement: attention is shifted from the cultivated spectator to the creative artist. Absurdly excessive, useless for all critical purposes though the Romantic cult of individual genius may have been, it nevertheless served to enforce an all-important lesson. Eighteenth-century esthetics had set up the spectator-critic as the proper locus of aesthetic value. But the critics' taste, as such, is for the already achieved, for the *déjà fait*. Hence the justification of Wordsworth's 'Every great and original writer . . . must *create* the taste by which he is relished'. Freshness, originality, spontaneity–creation itself–were admitted to be artistic excellences before the Romantics sang and spluttered: but the Romantics gave to these values an emphasis which they had never before enjoyed and are never likely now to lose. The third important step to be noticed may also be traced to the Romantic movement–to its recognition of the validity of many *different* traditions–for all that the full development of this insight had to wait until the present century. The inadequacy of the individual artist as locus or source of artistic value is to be made good by reference to the traditionally accepted values, in any one style or *genre* of art, with and from which–to sustain or develop or reform or revolutionise which–every genuine artist, every genuine work of art, begins. Only by reference to such values can the original (or the conservative) value of any work of art be appraised. Meanwhile the fourth step had already been taken by the one truly titanic figure in this history. With Tolstoy, attention is shifted–from the object, from the spectator-critic, from the individual artist, and the tradition within which he works–to the proper relationship between artist and public. Art is an achieved communication; and its peculiar value is simply that a certain elementary kind of communication takes place. Art is no longer to be valued as a commodity, as an object of cupboard love, as a display of original virtuosity or traditional discipline. It is proclaimed as an essential bond of union between man and man, as a necessity of human life.

In this abstract of aesthetic history we see the main grounds–and the very real justification–of some five of the main types of theory or definition of Art: configurationist theories, theories of aesthetic contemplation and response (usually couched in psychological terms, usually–though not necessarily–hedonistic), theories of art as expression, theories emphasising traditional artistic aims and standards, and communication theories. Each in its own highly abstract way gave expression to powerful and justifiable movements in the preceding history of the arts and of art-criticism. Each, since it was first propounded, has been a contestant for the title of the true, the only satisfying, the only plausible theory of art. Each is still capable of exercising a certain pull on our sympathies. But each, in respect of its exclusive claims to define the concept of Art, is utterly unacceptable. Its history makes clear what a thorough functional analysis of its uses might have suggested, that the philosophical concept of Art is an essentially contested one, and that so-called 'theories of Art' are intelligible only as contributions to a seemingly endless, although at its best a creative, conflict.

We can usefully conclude this part of the discussion by a summary statement of how our five defining conditions, and our two historically justifying conditions, apply to the general concept of Art. (I) Art, as we commonly use the term today, is mainly, if not exclusively, an appraisive term. (II) The kind of achievement it accredits is always internally complex. (III) This kind of achievement has proved to be variously describable – largely, if not solely, because at different times and in different circles it has seemed both natural and justifiable to describe the phenomena of Art with a dominant emphasis now on the work of art (art-product) itself, now on the response of the audience or spectator, now on the aim and inspiration of the artist, now on the tradition within which the artist works, now on the general fact of communication between the artist, *via* art-product, and audience. (IV) Artistic achievement, or the persistence of artistic activity is always 'open' in character in the sense that, at any one stage in its history, no one can predict or prescribe what new development of current art-forms may come to be regarded as of properly artistic worth. (V) Intelligent artists and critics will readily agree that the term Art and its derivatives are used, for the most part, both aggressively and defensively.

I must admit that my first justifying condition – derivation from a single generally acknowledged exemplar (in this case a single tradition of art) cannot be simply or directly applied. Clearly there have been different, and very often quite independent, artistic traditions. Nevertheless, I think that in any intelligent discussion of works of art or of artistic valuation, it is fairly easy to see what particular artistic tradition or set of traditions is being regarded as the 'exemplar term'. Finally it could at least be argued that the stimulating effects of competition between different artistic standpoints, or different ways of describing artistic values, have done something to justify the continued use of Art as a supremely general or categorial term.

In discussing the complicated, highly emotionally charged, and in practice constantly abused and confusing term Democracy, let me disown at the outset any attempt to 'clear up' its confusions by suggesting or proving its essential contestedness. There are innumerable grounds for confusion, and for the prolongation of confused argument, over the term Democracy, both at the level of global or parochial propaganda and at the level of either philosophical or would-be-scientific political theory. My initial contention, however, is this. If challenged, all those who make different uses of the term Democracy, must be willing to relate their favoured use – or at least make a pretence, no matter how feeble, to relate it – to an unmistakable succession of political endeavours and aspirations which have been embodied in countless slave, peasant, national and middle-class revolts and revolutions, as well as in scores of national constitutions and party records and programmes. These aspirations are centred in a demand for *increased* equality: or at least they are almost always advanced against governments and social orders whose aim is to prolong gross forms of *in*equality. To be sure, when thus conceived, the concept of democracy is extremely vague, but not, I think, hopelessly so, as is, for instance, the term of the 'cause of right'. Its vagueness reflects its actual inchoate condition of growth; and if we want to understand its condition, and control its practical and logical vagaries, the first step, I believe, is to recognise that in this, its basic and most popular use, the term Democracy stands for an essentially contested concept. Continual competition between radically opposed democratic parties in most western countries, as well as the rapidly intensifying competition between different forms of democracy, or of democratising movements, the world over, give this contention an immediate plausibility. Let us therefore proceed at once to see whether our seven conditions of essential contestedness apply in this case also.

(I) The concept of democracy, in the sense in which we are discussing it, is appraisive; indeed, many would urge that during the last one hundred and fifty years it has steadily established itself as *the* appraisive political concept *par excellence*. Questions of efficiency and security apart, the primary question on any major policy-decision has come to be: Is it democratic? By contrast, the concept of liberty, or more accurately, of particular liberties deserving protection irrespective of their democratic spread or appeal, appears steadily to have lost ground.

(II) and (III) The concept of democracy which we are discussing is internally complex in such a way that any democratic achievement (or programme) admits of a variety of descriptions in which its different aspects are graded in different orders of importance. I list as examples of different aspects: (*a*) Democracy means primarily the power of the majority of citizens to choose (and remove) governments – a power which would seem to involve, anyhow in larger communities, something like the institution of parties competing for political leadership; (*b*) Democracy means primarily equality of all citizens, irrespective of race, creed, sex, etc., to attain to positions of political leadership and responsibility in any democratic state; (*c*) Democracy means primarily the continuous active participation of citizens in political life at all levels, i.e. it is real when, and in so far as, there is real *self-government*.

Of these descriptions (*b*) and (*c*) emphasise features of democracy which clearly can exist in greater or less degree and are therefore liable to be differently placed for relative importance. But does not description (*a*) state an absolute requirement and therefore a necessary condition of paramount importance – perhaps even a sufficient condition – of a democratic society? We of the western tradition commonly claim this; but I believe our claim to be confused, for all that our democratic practice may have been, to date, none the worse for that.[1]

Suppose a society which answers in high degree to the conditions required by descriptions (*b*) and (*c*). In such a society government might reasonably be expected to show itself responsive, in considerable degree, to movements of popular opinion. Yet this result does not necessarily require constitutionally recognised means (e.g. universal and secret ballot and the existence of competitive parties) for the wholesale removal of governments. The practice of certain churches which claim to satisfy proper democratic demands, here shows a curious analogy to those governments which insist on their democratic character while denying their citizens the right of 'free election' on the Western pattern. For this reason, as well as for others which space forbids me to elaborate here, I conclude that the popular conception of democracy conforms to my conditions (II) and (III) for essential contestedness.

(IV) The concept of democracy which we are discussing is 'open' in character. Politics being the art of the possible, democratic targets will be raised or lowered as circumstances alter, and democratic achievements are always judged in the light of such alterations. (V) The concept of democracy which we are discussing is used both aggressively and defensively. This hardly requires discussion – except by those who repudiate the suggestion that there is any single general use of the term 'democracy'. My reply here is that such people neglect the possibility of a single general use made up, essentially, of a number of mutually contesting and contested uses of it. (VI) These uses claim the authority of an exemplar, i.e. of a long tradition (perhaps a number of historically independent but sufficiently similar traditions) of demands, aspirations, revolts and reforms of a common *anti-in*egalitarian character; and to see that the vagueness of this tradition in no way affects its influence as an exemplar, we need only recall how many and various political movements claim to have drawn their inspiration from either the French or the American Revolutions. (VII) Can we add, finally, that continuous competition for acknowledgment between rival uses of the popular concept of democracy seems likely to lead to an *optimum* development of the vague aims and confused achievements of the democratic tradition? Is it not, rather, more likely to help fan the flames of conflict, already sufficiently fed by other causes, between those groups of men and nations that contest its proper use? It is not the job of the present analysis, or of political philosophy in general, to offer particular predictions or advice on this kind of issue. But our present analysis does prompt the question, for which parallels could be taken from our other live examples, and which I shall try to answer in generalised form below: viz. in what way should we expect continuing conflicts and arguments over the proper use of a particular concept to be affected if its essentially contested character were recognised by all concerned?

My last live example can be discussed more briefly. It is the concept of social justice, or of the general principles that should govern the distribution of goods and services in any civilised and humane society. This concept shows the following formal difference from those already discussed. Whereas the concepts of Religion, of Art and of Democracy all admit, under my condition (III), of a considerable number of rival descriptions, the concept of social justice seems to admit of only two. Of these the first might be labelled its Liberal or Individualist, the second its Socialist or Collectivist use.

The first of these is the claim that social justice is essentially *commutative*, or that it rests on the fact that rewards should be proportional to merits. This claim, its adherents tell us, is recognised by men wherever they co-operate, whatever the motives for their co-operation may be: indeed recognition of it is involved in any *rational* egoism. The idea of *distributive* justice presupposes the key notion of commutation; for instance, in the economic field the idea of fair shares or fair recompense presupposes the idea of a fair or open market in which the relative merits of different individuals' products and services can be assessed. In fine, from the liberal or individualist standpoint, social justice consists of those arrangements whereby the meritorious individual shall receive back, for his products or services, his commutative due.

From the Socialist or Collectivist standpoint, on the other hand, social justice is essentially a *distributive* concept. It is centured on the question: To what share of the goods and services is any human being entitled simply in respect of his being a member of a human society? Social justice, from this standpoint, does not rest on any of the claims that individuals or groups of individuals have ever made on one another in respect of fair rewards and returns for work done: rather it is an ideal – one aspect of an ideal picture of human living – conceived as a possibility for the future, although already in some measure influencing some men's endeavours and aspirations. Thus, where the Liberal-Individualist looks to *actual* works of merit, the Socialist-Collectivist looks to potentialities of work or service which require just distribution of goods if they are to be effectively realised. This attitude to social justice may seem starry-eyed – until we remember that different socialist régimes have been able to apply different kinds of social pressure to ensure the genuine and effective co-operation of their citizens.

But our two conflicting conceptions of social justice need not be, and should not be, identified with or confined to particular historic forms or ideals of society. They would seem, in fact, to be conflicting facets of any advanced social morality. Witness, for instance, the opposed lessons of the parable of the talents and the parable of the vineyard, or, on a more mundane plane, contrast the ways in which we try to educe the idea of social justice (although not under that name) in young children: now by encouraging them to do something that will prove their worth (by obtaining its due reward), now by encouraging them to pitch in for the sake of the family or the group or the side.

These two contestant versions of the idea of social justice have certainly jostled against each other throughout a long history; and with that their conflict can usefully be compared between the Liberal-Individualist and the Socialist-Collectivist concepts of liberty and of government. These are examples of concepts to which, in my belief, our account of essentially contested concepts can be applied usefully, illuminatingly, but not with entire success. There are good reasons for regarding conflicts over the scope and roles of liberty and government as due in part to sheer ambiguities; and it is very doubtful whether arguments over the proper use of these terms can ever appeal confidently to a single commonly acknowledged source or example. But I shall leave what I have to say about borderline or difficult cases of this kind to the end of this chapter. For I want now to turn to the two outstanding general questions raised by our discussion of the live examples considered to date. Namely, first: Are the endless disputes to which the use of any essentially contested concept gives rise, *genuine* disputes, i.e. such that the notions of evidence, cogency and rational persuasion can properly be applied to them? And second: In what ways should we expect recognition of the essentially contestedness of a given concept by all its users to affect the character or level of the conflicts and arguments to which it gives rise?

The first of these questions amounts in effect to asking whether there is such a thing as the logic of *conversion* either in the religious or aesthetic or in the political and moral fields. Are *some* conversions in any of these fields of such a kind that they can be described as logically justified or defensible? Or on the contrary, are conversions in these fields always changes of viewpoint which can indeed be engineered by appropriate methods, and can be causally explained by adducing relevant data and generalisations, but only in such ways that the idea of logical 'justification' is inappropriate to them? Our previous discussion has certainly established one point: viz. that if the notion of logical justification can be applied only to such theses and arguments as can be presumed capable of gaining universal agreement in the long run, the disputes to which the uses of any essentially contested concept give rise are not genuine or rational disputes at all. Our first task, then, is to decide whether conformity to this condition – the possibility of obtaining universal agreement – provides a necessary criterion of the genuineness of arguments or disputes of all kinds. Now, an affirmative answer to this question certainly requires special defence; for the notion of possible ultimate universal agreement is a highly sophisticated one and does not figure among the familiarly recognized criteria of rational justification. Moreover, I would claim that those, e.g. Peirce, who have urged us to accept an affirmative answer on this issue have entirely neglected the existence of essentially contested concepts, and have failed to examine in any detail the peculiar structures of the arguments to which our use of essentially contested concepts give rise. Pending such examination, therefore, I conclude that this first possible form of the objection need not cause us any great worry.

But now the objection can be put on more commonly recognised grounds, viz. that, as we have explicitly confessed, it is quite impossible to find a *general principle* for deciding which of two contestant uses of an essentially contested concept really 'uses it best'. If no such principle can be found or devised, then how can the arguments of the contestants in such a dispute be subject to logical appraisal? My answer is that even where a general principle may be unobtainable for deciding which of a number of contestant uses of a given concept is its 'best use', it may yet be possible to explain or show the rationality of a *given individual's* continued use, or in the more dramatic case of conversion his *change of use*, of the concept in question. Rational explanation is possible in such cases in much the same way that (to recall our discussion in Chapter 4) an individual's change of social role or of allegiance to a social norm is often something that is entirely intelligible or followable, for all that it cannot be brought under any general principle or law.

For clarity's sake let us revert, yet once again, to my artificial example and consider the supporters of three contestant teams T_1, T_2 and T_3. And for simplicity let us assume that the style of play of T_2 can be said to stand mid-way between the styles of T_1 and T_3. And let us add that in each of these groups of supporters there will always be wavering or marginal individuals, who are more than usually aware of the appeals – the characteristic excellences – of teams other than that which at the moment they favour and support. Let us concentrate on an individual I_2, at present a marginal supporter of T_2. A particular performance of Team T_1, or some shrewd appraisive comment from one of T_1's supporters suddenly makes him realise much more completely than heretofore the justice of T_1's claim to be sustaining and advancing the original exemplar team's style of play in 'the best possible way'. This tips the scale for him and he is converted to being a supporter of T_1. But now we may assume that the same particular performance (or shrewd appraisive comment) has had a comparable, although not so dramatically effective, influence upon other staunch supporters of T_2. It has slightly shaken them, we might say. At least it has made them aware that, in comparable circumstances, T_2 must make a comparably effective adaptation of *its* style of play if it is to keep their unwavering support. Further, we may assume that although supporters of T_3 are less shaken by the particular performance, they have at least been made to 'sit up and take notice'; and similarly, with decreasing degrees of force for supporters of other teams whose styles of play are still remoter from that of T_1.

Put less artificially, what I am claiming is that a certain piece of evidence or argument, put forward by one side in an apparently endless dispute, can be recognised to have a definite logical force, even by those whom it fails to win over or convert to the side in question; and that when this is the case, the conversion of a hitherto wavering opponent of the side in question can be seen to be *justifiable*—not simply expectable in the light of known relevant psychological or sociological laws—given the waverer's previous state of information and given the grounds on which he previously supported one side and opposed the other. It is for this reason that we can distinguish more or less intellectually respectable conversions from those of a more purely emotional, or yet those of a wholly sinister kind. To be sure, our previous wavering opponent of one use of an essentially contested concept would not be justified in transferring his allegiance in the circumstances outlined if he were able, for an indefinite length of time, to withhold his support *from any of its possible uses*, i.e. to take up an entirely uncommitted attitude. But as in our artificial example, so in life, this possibility is often precluded. The exigencies of living commonly demand that 'he who is not for us is against us', or that he who hesitates to throw in his support or make his contribution on one side or the other is lost, not just to one of the sides that might have claimed his support, but to the game and to the day. From this point of view 'the logic of conversion' from one contested use of an essentially contested concept to another is on all-fours with the logic of every unique decision: and as in the latter more general case, so in that which concerns us here, there can be little question but that greater or lesser degrees of rationality can be properly and naturally attributed to one continued use, or one change of use, than to others.

Two points may be added to reinforce this account. It has usually been asserted by 'attitude-moralists' that the sole significant content of any moral dispute must concern the facts, the empirically testable facts, of the matter in question. It is important to contrast this assertion with our account of the conversion of the individual I_2. What I_2 recognises in my account is a fact if you like, but not a mere empirical observandum. It is, rather, the fact that a particular achievement (of T_1) revives and realises, as it were in fuller relief, some already recognised feature of an already valued style of performance, i.e. that of the original exemplar. Because of this particular performance, I_2 sees, or claims to see, more clearly and fully *why* he has acknowledged and followed the exemplar's style of performance all along. The scales are tipped for him not, or at least not only, by some psychologically explainable kink of his temperament, not by some observandum whose sheer occurrence all observers must acknowledge, but by his recognition of a value which, given his particular marginal appraisive situation, is conclusive for him, although it is merely impressive or surprising or worth noticing for others.

While insisting that there may be this much objectivity in the grounds of any particular conversion, we may nevertheless agree with 'attitude-moralists' that fundamental differences of attitude, of a kind for which no logical justification can be given, must also lie back of the kind of situation which we have just discussed. Why should one style of play (as in our artificial example) appeal to one group of supporters and another style to a second group? Why should one facet of Democracy or of the Christian Message appeal so strongly to one type or group or communion, another to a second? At any given stage in the history of the continued uses of any essentially contested concept, it will no doubt be necessary to call upon psychological or sociological theories or – much more likely – the known historical facts of a person's or group's background, to explain their present preferences and adherences. But to admit this is not to deny the existence, or at least the possibility, of logically appraisable factors in an individual's use, or change of use, of a particular contested concept.

Turning now to our second outstanding question, as to the results to be expected from general recognition of the essential contestedness of a given concept, we must first of all distinguish such recognition – a somewhat sophisticated 'higher-order' intellectual feat – from the everyday 'lower-order' recognition that one is using a given concept both aggressively and defensively. The difference is between recognising that one has, and presumably will continue to have, opponents, and recognising that this is an essential feature of the activity one is pursuing. The obvious advantage of the 'higher-order' recognition is (assuming my present analysis to be acceptable) that it makes the parties concerned aware of an important truth. But this will be a truth of higher order, whose significance can best be understood in terms of its important everyday applications. The answer we are seeking must enable us to meet such questions as: How will a Christian of denomination X be likely to be affected in respect of his intellectual allegiance to X (and consequently repudiation of Y and Z) by the recognition which we are here discussing? Similarly, how will the student of the arts be affected by recognising that different groups of critics not only disagree, but in the nature of the case must be expected to disagree in their fundamental viewpoints? And so on for the other cases. It is also important to stress that the results with which we are here concerned are not to be of a predictable or causally explainable character. The practical and theoretical operations which recognition of a concept as essentially contested makes possible are logically appraisable and justifiable operations, such as we would expect from a reasonable being, for all that, for special psychological or social causes, a given individual may fail to entertain them. Examination of these results is therefore an important part of our analysis.

Part of the answer to our question seems to be this. Recognition of a given concept as essentially contested implies recognition of rival uses of it (such as oneself repudiates) as not only logically possible and humanly 'likely', but as of permanent potential critical value to one's own use or interpretation of the concept in question; whereas to regard any rival use as anathema, perverse, bestial or lunatic means, in many cases, to submit oneself to the chronic human peril of underestimating, or of completely ignoring, the value of one's opponents' positions. One desirable consequence of the required recognition in any proper instance of essential contestedness might therefore be a marked raising of the level of quality of arguments in the disputes of the contestant parties. And this would mean *prima facie*, a justification of the continued competition for support and acknowledgment between the various contesting parties.

One important specific form of this result would be the following. Every movement or group or party has its own more or less lunatic fringe–fanatics of their own self-righteousness or dyed in the wool gloaters in their own exclusive orthodoxy. Now, such people do not make good arguers, either against their opponents (whose stronger points they are incapable of distinguishing from their weaker points) or for their own case, at any rate on issues where a certain amount of suppleness is required to maintain some underlying principle. The more therefore the case for a particular use or interpretation of a given concept is regarded as advanceable by argument–even if by argument that can lead to no final knock-down conclusion–the more will its future be in the hands of its moderate and perceptive protagonists. Indeed, one can well imagine cases in which moderate and sane representatives of two or more contestant parties could express agreement as to where the *real* issue between them lies, and agreeing that this issue is simply obscured or debased by the intrusions of lunatic voices, from whichever side. Here we have the best result that, very often in this life, can reasonably be looked for: namely that a given contest can at least be identified with the best elements that take part in it.

But as against this relatively optimistic view the following darker consideration might be urged. So long as contestant users of any essentially contested concept believe, however deludedly, that their own use of it is the only one that can command honest and informed approval, they are likely to persist with argument and discussion in the hope that they will ultimately persuade and convert all their opponents by logical means. But once let the truth–i.e. the essential contestedness of the concept in question–out of the bag, then this harmless if deluded hope may well be replaced by a ruthless decision to cut the cackle, to damn the heretics and to exterminate the unwanted.

This consideration might give us pause until we recall that the demands of Reason have always brought peril as well as light to their hearers. What is being brought to our notice by the present objection is indeed a possible causal consequence or result of widespread recognition of the essentially contested character of a given concept. But it is not therefore a justifiable consequence of it. Those who love the truth in any field will be happy to advance towards it–or in some cases simply succeed in not retreating from it–no matter how long and wearing the effort involved must be. The true religious devotee, like the true democrat or man of genuine goodwill, can never be a believer in 'quick results'. Each, on the contrary, is willing to wait and work till the last day to effect a genuine conversion to his point of view. Each knows that there is no error so fatal as that which insinuates that the only good opponent is a liquidated one.

These are some of the more obvious practical reasons for a careful study of essentially contested concepts. But for our present purpose what has to be emphasised chiefly is that the adequate understanding of such concepts involves some appreciation of their history. At the very least we must accept that every proper contestant use of such a concept can be traced back to a commonly acknowledged exemplar, and can be justified on the ground that, and to the extent that, people can be found who regard it and can rationally defend it as the best possible development of the original exemplar's aims. Evidently among those who subscribe to any particular inter-pretation of an essentially contested concept the amount of such historical appreciation–as well as its depth and scholarly quality–will vary enormously. There can be no upper limit to such appreciation, but in practice we would all recognise the need of a lower limit beneath which the supporters of some exotic interpretation must be assigned to the lunatic fringe. By contrast, one hall-mark of a civilised man is that he possesses at least some sense of the different historic inheritances of the causes to which he adheres.

How wide, it is natural to ask, is the class of essentially contested concepts? Any number of subordinate or more specific concepts falling under the concepts of art, religion, democracy, etc., can be shown to be themselves essentially contested: for example, colouration, dogma, parliamentary immunity. But are there any other essentially contested concepts of the same level of generality, or with the same wide bearings upon human life, as those which we have considered in the course of the present chapter? Possible candidates are the concepts of science and of law, on the one hand, and of liberty and of government on the other. I am doubtful whether any one of these concepts can be brought satisfactorily under the framework of ideas by means of which I have defined essentially contested concepts; but I am quite certain that an adequate understanding of each of these concepts calls for some appreciation of their growth, of their past proliferations and the unifications to which they have been subjected, both by social pressure and by logically tidy and dominating minds. The concepts of law, science, freedom and authority all seem to me to be tied to more specific aims and claims, as well as admitting of more easily agreed tests, than the concepts with which we have hitherto been concerned. In general, I would say, it is in those fields of human endeavour in which achievements are prized chiefly as renewals or advances of commonly accepted traditions of thought and work that our concepts are likely to prove essentially contested.

Of perhaps greater interest is the relevance of historical understanding, as well as the idea of the essential contestedness, to our basic moral notions and principles. What I have in mind is perhaps most easily illustrated by the following dilemma. Most philosophers would agree that to do one's duty in a particular situation necessarily involves some reference to what any other rational being would do in a similar situation. But a great many of our duties arise because of our adherence to one particular interpretation of an essentially contested concept, e.g. social justice or democracy. Thereupon the question arises: Shall such adherence be counted as a necessary part of what is meant by 'in a similar situation'? If so, then the so-called universalisability criterion of duty is rendered logically trivial and practically futile, since the importance of men's differences over the meanings of democracy and social justice cannot be waived aside by a stroke of the 'meta-ethicist's' pen. If, on the other hand, adherence to a particular version of such an essentially contested concept is not regarded as part of the meaning of 'in a similar situation', it becomes very difficult to see how the universalisability criterion can be applied at all in a great many issues of the first moral importance. In order to deal with this dilemma we must, I believe, rid ourselves of one of the commonest and most deeply entrenched prejudices to be found in the history of ethics. To this task I shall devote my next chapter.

Chapter 9

WHERE MORAL PHILOSOPHY RESTS ON A MISTAKE

MORAL philosophers are commonly grouped in two opposed camps. There are the autonomists–those who maintain that morality is something altogether *sui generis*, something that cannot conceivably be described or explained in terms of anything other than itself; and there are the derivationists, who maintain that morality can be described and explained only by showing its connection with–and usually its dependence upon– other parts or aspects of the whole economy of human life. As thus phrased, the familiar division relates primarily to the description or demarcation of the field of morality; and it is from this point of view that I shall first consider it. But the division between autonomists and derivationists is of even greater importance to the central problem of ethics: that of the kind or kinds of justification which our moral judgments and decisions require.

Despite the fundamental character of this division there is, however, one important issue in moral philosophy upon which autonomists and derivationists have, with very few exceptions, been in complete agreement. Most of them (who here are simply following an ingrained habit of philosophical reflection) take it for granted that, whether morality be something entirely *sui generis* or something entirely dependent on other human interests, its *differentia* or explanation–the key notion that gives such theoretical understanding of it as is possible–is something simple and single. Whether this key notion be the goodwill or the recognition of *prima facie* obligations or the idea of intrinsic goodness, or whether (on the other side) it be the maximisation of pleasures over pains or the achievement of personal security or inward serenity, it is usually conceived as something simple and single, and indeed something so obvious that once it is pointed out, no reasonable person can fail to see that here we have the key notion by reference to which all other moral ideas are to be understood. The persistence of this assumption, despite the clear repudiation of it by Butler, and the evident unhappiness about it displayed by Aristotle, is truly astonishing. Yet there it is, one ghostly manifestation of the long-dead Aristotelian doctrine of real essences in minds otherwise thoroughly imbued with the pluralist spirit of scientific inquiry: in Kant, in Moore, in Bentham, in Mill, and indeed in C. L. Stevenson and A. J. Ayer.

The view which I here impute to the great majority of moral philosophers is, of course, compatible with recognising–what is unmistakably obvious–that there may be any number of different material or natural signs (and in some cases useful working criteria) of what is morally obligatory or morally defensible in different kinds of situation. The almost universal view, however, is to the effect that, irrespective of this variety of natural signs or criteria of moral rightness, what *constitutes* the rightness of a choice is its conformity to some single ultimate principle. As we have seen, there is no cause, either historically or logically, for restricting this view to either the autonomists or the derivationists. Nevertheless there is a non-formal possibility of connection and mutual influence between it and the autonomist thesis which particularly calls for attention. Thus, if one is a serious and well-informed autonomist, as Kant was, one is liable to move along the following insidious line of thought. (*a*) Of course there are a great many features of moral situations–of moral judgments, choices, efforts,–which may at first sight seem essential to morality. For instance, the claims of tradition, and many workaday social teleological claims may at first sight seem of considerable, indeed perhaps of paramount, moral importance. But (*b*) if one is as intelligent and well informed as Kant was, one will quickly notice that factors of the kinds just mentioned evidently vary with and appear to depend upon other non-moral interests and values–security, happiness, culture and so on. Hence (*c*) one will be led to presume that the autonomy of morals can best be defended by grounding it upon some one principle, or upon one sort of object of knowledge, which is essentially *sui generis*, evidently independent of all non-moral interests, and allegedly capable of explaining and justifying the multifarious claims and commands of morality.

But however plausible the presumption may sound, it is surely rendered suspect by the results of accepting it. For it has led autonomist moralists to propound a succession of descriptions of the moral field which have patently different denotations, which are logically incompatible with each other, none of which is obviously preferable to its rivals, and each of which is patently incomplete and so unrealistic that it is hard to imagine anyone but a dedicated philosopher trying to embrace it. Think, for example of the kinds of choice or disposition to make certain kinds of rational choice which are basic to Kant's ethics: then of those intrinsically good, intuitively knowable states of affairs which are the basis of Moore's: then of those direct apprehensions of *prima facie* duties which so preoccupied Prichard. Each of these writers has one undeniable merit: his claims, however ill defined, have the effect of revealing the inadequacies of the other two. As to the unrealistic character of their claims, it is enough to recall Kant's blindness to socio-teleological factors in morality, exemplified most powerfully in the value we attach to self-sacrifice; Moore's blindness to traditional and social factors of all kinds; and Prichard's more than normal academic parochialism, exemplified in his remark that the Sermon on the Mount has evidently nothing to do with morality.

Here, then, in the intelligible but logically unwarranted assumption that all morality must have a single, simple basis if it is to be autonomous, we have, I believe, one mistake upon which moral philosophies tend to rest. It is a characteristically philosophical mistake: an expression of that passion for intellectual unity and simplicity which is a familiar, and when properly checked a wholly legitimate, feature of scientific minds. But in philosophy, where there are no experimental checks, it commonly passes through the most careful arguments quite unquestioned, and the only defence against it is philosophical imagination. In the present instance we are being asked to recognise morality as an aspect or dimension of conduct that is autonomous, *sui generis*, irreducible to anything else. But that does not exclude the possibility that morality is an organic whole within which a number of facets may be distinguished and towards which a number of originally independent tendencies may have contributed. An immense array of parallels from the historic and human sciences, headed by the concept of the human individual or person himself, suggests that this may well be so. To my mind the main importance of the mistake we are discussing is that it encourages us to neglect this possibility. I am therefore going to sketch out at this point, very briefly, one possible version of the view that morality, although unique and irreducible to other dimensions of conduct, nevertheless contains a number of distinguishable essential facets; and I shall argue that we can admit this without denying or even doubting the fundamental autonomy of morals.

On the view now to be sketched any moral term, statement or argument possesses its peculiar moral force only so long as it falls within a complex framework of conditions which together define the field of morality. Satisfaction of these conditions does not, of course, ensure the truth of this or that moral judgment or the rightness of any action or the goodness of any character or situation. It merely ensures that what is assessed or described is a fit object for assessment or description in some moral terms or other. Whether the conditions which I propose are the best or logically neatest possible I shall not here try to maintain. Conceivably (although I trust not) they may neglect some important aspect of morality. What I do feel sure. about, however, is that there is a plurality of facets which must obtain, or which are always presupposed, whenever we employ specifically moral expressions, and which must be articulated if moral discourse is to be distinguished from discourse of other kinds. Here are my suggestions:

(1) Moral awareness, effort, discussion and disagreement always presuppose that within a given society certain social arrangements–functional groupings, division of labour, taboos –are currently generally accepted and in some degree approved.

This is an essential presuppositon of all ideas of the general good, the public weal, or what have you, as well as of most moral rules. In saying this I am not claiming that the arrangements in question must have been explicitly accepted by a majority of the society, but only that they have been backed by those who have possessed social influence and power. Nor am I claiming that moral awareness, effort, etc., are necessarily tied up with the *preservation* of traditional agreement and arrangements: on the contrary, they may well be directed towards adjusting or improving these in any number of ways. My point is that, however complicated and qualified the connection may become, every morality, every properly moral judgment or assertion or endeavour must somehow be pegged to a certain on-going pattern of life, because that pattern is regarded either as worth preserving, or as worth changing and adapting in certain specific ways. To emphasise this first facet of morality amounts to affirming that any morality is not only 'pro-life' but is always 'pro' a fairly specific established form of life – maintaining it, adjusting it, often gradually and unintentionally altering its over-all character, but always on the understanding that morality means a concern with what is possible and feasible here and now. Of course, this claim could be substantiated only by conning over a wide sample or moral rules, precepts, proverbs, and establishing (what I think is beyond all doubt) their mainly socio-teleological character. Not that this is the *whole* of their moral character: we have still three other essential facets of morality to consider. And it is largely in terms of these that we can distinguish those socio-teleological rules which have specifically moral force from others whose force is wholly or almost entirely legal or economic or prudential.

(2) Part of what distinguishes moral rules and morally commendable arrangements in any society in their relation to what the social historian Huizinga has aptly called 'ideal pictures of life'. These, Huizinga has shown, have varied enormously, in power, in seriousness, in effectiveness, in different historic periods. But presumably the most important are those that have been provided by either religious or political visionaries – pictures of golden ages, of primitive com-

munisms, of the apocalypse and all things made new, of Utopia within our grasp or the beginnings of truly human history just round the corner. Here we have had and still have ideal pictures of life, serving either as defences or criticisms of currently accepted social arrangements, as well as the moral efforts and standards of individual agents.

This second facet of morality could be regarded as the complement of its first facet. Morality is, to be sure, always concerned with maintaining and adjusting efforts towards what is feasible here and now; but it succeeds in this task only in so far as it hitches the here and now to a star which no one ever expects or hopes to see fully realised in the world of everyday effort. To speak more precisely; our first facet expresses the *conformist* element in morality, our second facet expresses the *melioristic* element of morality. The ideas of obedience, conformity, contribution to the maintenance of an established order, and the idea of a wholesale betterment of society – under the inspiration of an altogether superior vision of life, past, promised or laid upon in heaven – are independent but equally necessary elements in every morality.

(3) No Benthamite, no Marxist, no Christian or Rationalist reformer could conceivably be such a prig as to base the whole of his moral life on socio-teleological or utopian-idealist considerations alone. Besides accepting certain moral targets and horizons and calculating moral means and methods, he has also inevitably learnt, if only by involuntary and perhaps unconscious immitation, to appreciate some of the virtues: those usually visible, but sometimes only inwardly enjoyed qualities and patterns of conduct about which we feel, not simply that certain situations require them, but that they, so to speak, do honour to our humanity in certain situations. Courage is not simply apposite to danger-situations; it is a moving and inspiring response to danger. And the same is true, *mutatis mutandis*, of justice, compassion, loyalty and forbearance. The virtues – and their opposites the vices – would indeed be inconceivable without the two other facets of morality which we have already considered; but their retroactive influence upon these facets is no less obvious and important. For instance, it is

largely thanks to our spontaneous imitation of some of the virtues that we succeed in what would otherwise be the soul-killing task of obeying necessarily stringent moral rules. Or again, it is often through recognising the virtues of others, e.g. the forbearance of parents, that we come to appreciate the contribution to general welfare of certain seemingly jejune social arragements.

(4) Considerations of the kinds just discussed do not suffice to demarcate the field of morality. There remains the will to find the right action for given circumstances, where 'find' connotes some rational method of search, assessment and final decision. Theoretically a number of different factors could be extracted from this 'rational will', but they are always so fused together that I prefer to count rational will as a single facet of morality which becomes prominent whenever we are faced by a novel or complex or otherwise baffling situation. To the question 'How should I act now?' an essential, and peculiarly rational or experimental, part of a proper answer is to put such further questions as: 'How would I regard someone else who in this kind of situation did such and such?' and 'What would anyone else make of my action if in this situation he saw me do such and such?' From such vague and barely moral references to 'someone else' there is a gradation of more and more morally articulated notions–someone whose judgment I trust, someone who is commonly accepted as a good man, a disinterested spectator, a rational being. The facet of rational will begins with fumbling searches for advice and culminates in something like Kant's universalisability criterion of right action.

Here, then, are four facets of the moral framework which, I suggest, we all have at the back of our minds whenever we use an expression that has a distinctively moral force. Each no doubt includes the proper objective of certain 'moral emotions', although none of them provides by itself the proper target of moral endeavour. Each in its own way contributes to that importance which it is only a pleonasm to attribute to moral as against purely prudential considerations. Each is a necessary condition of the moral function of the others, but none of them singly or in any combination is sufficient to define the moral functioning of any of the others. Anyone using the words 'good' (in contrast to 'evil'), 'right' (in contrast to 'wrong'), 'commendable', 'blameworthy', etc., without tacit reference to this fourfold framework, would be using them in a manner that no normal person could understand. Yet it appears to be a kind of professional affliction of moral philosophers to be highly sensitive to one of our four facets of morality, but never to all four together. No doubt, when considered in isolation, some of our moral expressions may seem to belong to one and only one of the facets of morality that I have described. But because a particular kind of moral command or requirement is commonly expressed in terms belonging to *one* of our four facets of morality, it does follow that the other facets have no relevance to the moral case in point. Moral philosophers almost invariably neglect the possibility that in every moral situation there are tacit as well as explicit components, and the reasons for this neglect can easily be supplied. We must not do *this*, we feel, because it would mean sabotaging some essential part of our inherited and shared way of life. We cannot do *that*, we feel, because it would mean violating some of our most cherished visions or ideals. We could not do yet another thing–it would mean being patently vicious. We cannot act in some further way, since we could not rationally expect or demand any other person to do so. Each of these ways of expressing moral judgments is correct and apposite in certain well-known kinds of situation. But none of them should be taken to be or to approximate to being an expression or description of *all* the morally relevant features or facets of the kind of case that it describes. In general, our moral judgments commonly allude to certain selected reasons which support them, and which in suitable contexts may well offer completely adequate support for them; but this is not to say that such reasons are equivalent to the total moral import of the judgment in question. Not only our moral expressions but all our moral thinking tends to be highly elliptical. It is the job of moral philosophy to overcome, or to elucidate and interpret, what our everyday speech here disguises.

What is basically the same point can be made in terms, not of the reasons that support certain lines of action, but of regret or remorse for wrong or inadequate action. Most of us are, by temperament or training, liable to be more responsive to considerations that fall under one or two of our four facets rather than the others. We are, say, predominantly socio-teleological activists, or we are endowed with a Kantian will to find the morally unimpugnable act to match the occasion, or have an unusual sensitivity to ideal values. And for this reason how often, after we have acted for the best–as we see it–and wholly in character, are we not forced to recognise our appalling defectiveness in respect of one or more of the four facets of morality. How graceless or how careless, how small-minded or how damned useless we see ourselves to have been, as we come belatedly to a more complete recognition of the moral situation that faced us and the inadequacy of our response to it.

But why, if all this is true, have moral philosophers, with so few exceptions, fought shy of a plurally based description of the moral field? Chiefly because of the suspicion that a plurally based ethics must mean the abandonment of the autonomy of morals. We must now examine this suspicion more closely; and in doing so we shall pass from a description or demarcation of morality to the question of the ultimate justification of our moral judgments and decisions.

At least three of our four facets embrace considerations, influences, valuations, commands and appeals which, it must be agreed, are very far from being universally accepted in different human societies, and which appear to vary with and depend upon non-moral social interests, aims and rules. There is no need to insist that very different notions of general welfare have cemented different societies and provided part of the reference of their moral codes. What social arrangements and rules are found acceptable or are considered capable of improvement will depend upon a society's attitude towards war, upon its trade with other societies and its methods of production, as well as upon its basic religious ideas and internal class structure. Nor is it necessary to elaborate on the extraordinary varieties of ideal pictures of life which have served as solaces or as spurs to moral initiative and effort in different communities. We need think only of how the ideal pictures of life provided by the Christian religion have at different times supported or elevated, and on occasion debased, the moral codes of its successive flocks. Again, there is little difficulty in recognising what basically different gradings of the virtues have been accepted within different moral traditions. Even between those traditions which have proved themselves capable of fruitful union what astonishing differences there are! What place, for instance, is there in the Christian hierarchy of virtues for the combination of qualities that make up Aristotle's 'magnanimous man'? How differently has the idea of the good citizen been understood in the moral thinking of the Greek democracies, of the Middle Ages, of the Enlightenment, and of the ever-accelerating political vertigo which we must learn to live with today?

It is, no doubt, because of the variability and seeming relativity of each of these three facets of morality, that so many moral philosophers since Kant have stressed the facet of rational will, and have argued that we have here–in choices made in conformity with the principle of universalisability–the one essential distinguishing feature of moral rules as well as the only ground on which moral judgments and decisions can ultimately be justified. But, taken at its face value, could any claim be less plausible than this? Could the inheritance of traditionally approved institutions and arrangements, could the existence of different ideal pictures of life or the infective quality of the virtues conceivably be derived from or be justified by a single highly abstract formula for testing the rightness of our choices and decisions? Besides, most of those who have stressed the facet of rational will have been curiously naïve in presuming that individuals and communities show no variability in the meanings that they put on the idea of rationality, especially as applied to conduct. For, granted that in any serious moral quandary or predicament we would all ask ourselves what we would expect another rational being to do in similar circumstances, yet the usefulness of this principle is easily put in question on the following ground. Many of our most difficult choices arise from our adherence to one particular interpretation of some concept, e.g. that of democracy or Christianity or the scientific tradition, within which the idea of rationality itself figures prominently but within which it is liable to take on perceptibly different shapes. Thus, let us imagine a situation in which three intelligent and sincere men, one an empirically-minded agnostic, one Roman Catholic and one an orthodox communist are faced by a common choice having important social consequences. No doubt, each will apply–whether in anything like Kantian terminology is immaterial–some form of the universalisability criterion of right action; but is it not obvious that, in doing so, each of our three individuals will give to the idea of another *rational* being a considerably different interpretation from those favoured by the other two?

We thus seem to be landed back in the position which the most serious and impressive moral philosophers have been so anxious to avoid. There would appear to be no way of justifying, or of rationally preferring any one moral code to any other. But is this conclusion really necessary?

It rests on the assumption that to justify a particular action means to subsume it under some code of rules which is itself justified by conforming to some over-all defining principle of morals. As against this unimaginative assumption I have every sympathy with those who insist that moral judgments and decisions–and hence the notions of moral goodness, rightness, justification etc.–relate primarily to particular situations, to the demands of the here and now, to what may have to be faced once and not again. Certainly this claim expresses a proper objection to the rationalistic view of moral choices as so many specimen cases for the application of general rules of conduct. But it is also a dangerous claim, since it is liable to lead to sheer irrationalism by neglecting the part played by general rules and considerations in the reaching of any moral decision. But need the rejection of a misplaced rationalism lead us into the opposite error? I do not think so.

In so far as moral judgments and decisions relate primarily to particular situations they can usefully be assimilated to our historical judgments. Now do historians ever succeed in making valid moral judgments about actions that took place in epochs or civilisations that had moral frameworks very different from their own? The answer to this question seems to me perfectly clear: they certainly sometimes do. But this evident truth has often been made to seem questionable because of a variety of confusing factors. First, we may agree that moralising is not the historian's main job. But, second, his moral judgments are often most effective when he lets the facts speak for themselves. And thirdly, a great many basic forms or habits of moral judgment are presupposed in the seemingly value-free terminologies in which the historian describes the actions that concern him. But, putting aside these complications, would anyone deny that historians often succeed in giving us an understanding of the reasonableness or unreasonableness, the prudence or folly, the efficacy or inefficacy of human thoughts and actions occurring in very different social contexts, and at very different levels of general knowledge from our own? And how do historians achieve such understanding? Well, roughly speaking, by digging their way into the situations that they are describing, by trying to live within them, so that they can construct for us a plausible account of the, to us, very odd ways in which things must have appeared and been judged and been done in those strangely different times and places. In doing all this historians make sense, as we say, of the situations and actions in question. Now I ask: if it is possible for historians to establish the rationality, prudence, efficacy, etc., of actions performed against the most varied social and intellectual backgrounds, why should it not be possible to establish the rightness or goodness of human actions performed against backgrounds that vary in respect of inherited moral preferences, articulation of moral aims and development of methods of moral instruction? Why, to particularise, should a true moral assessment of a Themistocles or a Tiberius, a Cromwell or a Richelieu be more difficult for an historian writing today than an assessment of the prudence or imprudence of the policies that they pursued? To make a moral assessment of a character of an action certainly means to assess it in its own moral context, in relation to the moral inspiration, support, education and possibilities of action actually available to the agent. And the historian, no matter how great his gift for getting inside the minds of his subjects, may here be guilty of grave misjudgment. The thoughts of men, and the possibilities of co-operation and of conflict between men, vary immensely from age to age: but not only, and not even especially, in respect of their moral backgrounds and inheritances. The position is not, therefore, that true historical judgments, whether on moral or on other practical issues, are impossible. It is first, that like all human judgments they are fallible; and secondly, that they can be obtained only by discovering the actual possibilities inherent in particular situations, never by the mere application of general rules of conduct to a specimen case.

If this argument is valid for the historian's moral judgments, can it not be generalised to hold for all moral judgments? Do they not require us to take into account the particular moral, as well as intellectual and social, inheritances and possibilities of the individuals upon whom they are directed? More simply, do we not expect—and indeed demand—that all moral judgments shall rest on moral understanding? To be sure, consideration of background differences may often be urged in inappropriate—in morally as well as intellectually sloppy—ways. Again there are cases, particularly those that relate to our own actions, where careful assessment of background niceties would be absurd. Nevertheless, since moral judgment is primarily directed on to individuals and their actions in particular situations, it always presupposes the kind of understanding that is appropriate to individuals, that is, in a broad sense, historical understanding.

The importance of these considerations is clearest in the kind of case in which two individuals reach full moral agreement whilst appearing simply to have agreed to disagree. Imagine, for example, two administrators who are faced in their different fields with what appear to be two very similar problems, yet after consultation, each may wholly endorse the other's decision to pursue, in view of background circumstances, a line of action that is markedly different from the one that he himself has chosen to meet his own case. Or think of two friends belonging to very different religious or political communities. Each may morally endorse the action that the other decides upon in some domestic or educational problem, whilst knowing that for himself, living in a very different type of community, such action would be inappropriate or perhaps impossible.

Again, if we did not take into account differences in moral background and opportunity, how could we commend, or even recognise, what may well have been among the most significant moral advances ever made by men—for instance, the crucial first steps towards the elimination of cannibalism or the enforcement of the incest taboos. These steps must have been taken against a background of moral presumptions which we should today find unimaginably repellent. For example, the demand that cannibalism should be limited to certain special cases has implications too loathsome to imagine. Yet who knows but that in its day this moral demand required as much courage and insight as we would attribute, say, to the prophet Amos or the tragedian Euripides.

A last argument to the same effect is as follows. If moral judgments amounted in all cases to the mere application of universal moral rules, taking into special account only the peculiar *non-moral* features of each individual case, it would follow that all moral questions either are or might well be wholly decided already. In this case, of course, a large part of moral endeavour—that which seeks for new moral insights to match new moral problems—would be at best an exercise in misplaced energy. An ideally wise moralist, like an all-knowing morality-ordaining God, would already know what ought to be done in every situation whose non-moral features were fully described to him. Now this suggestion is certainly morally repugnant; and it is worth asking why. The answer is that morality is a matter of particular issues, meaning by this not simply particular problems and predicaments but also particular efforts—including efforts to judge rightly—in the life of every human being.

The above arguments seem to me to be satisfactory when applied to our first three facets of morality. Differences in social arrangements, in ideal pictures of life, and in the grading of the virtues, do not necessarily mean–and in fact have not always meant–that agreement in moral judgments is impossible, even when these judgments are made across the widest and deepest cultural divides. But when we turn to the facet of rational will, I must confess that we are faced with peculiar difficulties. When two or more individuals differ in their working criteria of what a rational being is, can it plausibly be suggested that each should try to understand–and no doubt make allowances for–the other's imperfectly developed rational norms in the hope that they may come to agree on some long-disputed moral issue? Does not this suggest the kind of stretching of liberal attitudes that comes close to both a moral and an intellectual sell-out?

Admittedly we are always well advised to be on guard against this danger. But the risk of it is considerably lessened if we get clear just what is required in the way of a concept of rationality if one is to make use of any form of universalisability criterion of right action. First of all, we can cut ourselves free from some unnecessarily restricting Kantian equipment. Any man asking himself, with regard to a proposed action, how he would regard it if performed by another is thus far showing himself rational, and *a fortiori* he is rational if he asks how an ideally impartial spectator would regard it. But this does not imply that what he comes to see to be right by these means is demonstrated or seen of rational necessity to be so. Moral judgments, as we have seen, are to be assimilated to historical judgments rather than to *a priori* intuitions or necessary deductions.

The basic question regarding rational will, therefore, comes to this: how can we tell whether a given moral judgment or decision is rational in the way that the actual existing moral situation demands or will allow? Or, alternatively, since in moral issues demonstrative proof of the rightness of any proposed action is not to be looked for, we must ask what are the essential marks of a rationally made choice or decision. But this way of putting the question has a somewhat unnatural ring to it. For it is not particular acts and choices, but rather general policies and principles and above all *persons* that we think of primarily as rational. Let us therefore concentrate on the crucial case of the person. I suggest that we regard a person as rational in respect of moral issues when he is prepared to discuss, or has the habit and equipment for discussing, the morally relevant *pros and cons* of any proposed line of action. In morals, as much as in religion and politics, the notion of discussion is of far greater importance for the definition of rationality and rational will, than is the notion of demonstrative proof. For in each of these three spheres changes of judgement or decision come about, admittedly as a result of and in an atmosphere of discussion, but sometimes with the force and immediacy of conversion, at other times by an almost unconscious evolution, but seldom or never as a result of actual demonstration. We are brought to see the point or the possibility of a certain way of acting in a situation which, as a result of discussion, has been revealed to us in a somewhat new way.

Let us now consider the special features of rationality as thus conceived. Some of them will be as universal, and therefore as formalisable, as traditional rules of inference; and we may leave it to logicians to list and systematise them in the most convenient way. Clearly they will include principles for ensuring identities of meaning as well as consistency and unity of aim in argument.

But in addition to formal principles, necessary to discussion of any kind, there are special principles—or special features of rationality—required for the discussion of specifically moral issues. First, for example, a properly moral concern about the consequences of any line of action which one has advocated or endorsed. This principle cannot be identified with or brought under that general concern for social welfare which is expressed in our first facet of morality. Its peculiarity—the peculiar habit of rationality which it requires—is best brought out by an example. We all know the kind of 'scientifically minded' pundit who will blandly admit his past mistakes or miscalculations, reminding us that science cannot be advanced without mistakes and indeed all but maintaining that mistakes are fine so long as they are eventually recognised. This kind of pundit performs at least one kind of useful function. He reminds us that there are forms of rationality, closely connected with the notion of responsibility, which are not included in the scientist's conception of reason. Or again, what would we think of a moral or political commentator who, while eager to press his views about what should be done in some situation, is nevertheless unwilling to *bet* on the outcome that he envisages? We might call such a man insincere; but he need not necessarily be so. The point about him is that his rational faculty is defective in a way that matters profoundly in all moral issues. He does not recognise that one can rationally recommend a certain line of action only if one is willing to commit oneself in some way with regard to it.

Secondly, there is what I will call the will-to-agreement between the disputing parties over any moral issues. At its best this manifests itself in an unusual degree of intellectual sympathy and co-operativeness between the disputants; at its worst in the persistence of the insensitive proselytiser. But the essential point about it is this. If we cannot persuade an opponent in an aesthetic or a scientific dispute, we may feel vexed and frustrated; but we will hardly have that sense of utter dismay that comes upon us when we fail completely to reach through to our adversary's position on some moral issue. We here see that the will to understand a morally alien point of view–if only in order to refute it–can be itself an all-important part of morality.

What specific forms can the will-to-agreement most usefully take? I will mention two, one readily admissible, the other perhaps more questionable. First, the willingness of a disputant to consider, where the situation allows, any number of partially parallel cases showing a progressively lessening analogy to the case under discussion, with a view to eliciting the logically initial point of cleavage between the conflicting points of view. This is, of course, simply an abstract formulation of something that all courteous and intelligent people would be willing to do in their moral disagreements and disputes. But I doubt if it is covered by any known philosophical definition of rationality.

A second example. Very commonly moral disputes are waged over some traditionally accepted practice or belief whose *rationale*, if it has any, its defenders are no more able to articulate satisfactorily than its assailants. There is thus no possibility of rational discussion: the belief or practice has to be accepted blindly, so it seems, or not at all. In such a situation traditional conceptions of rationality will assign victory to the assailant and defeat – along with a very black mark – to the seemingly irrational defender. But once we have replaced the idea of rational proof or justification by the idea of the habit of rational discussion as the hall-mark of rational will, any such talk of victories and defeats seems almost irrelevant. From our point of view something like the following procedure would be more appropriate. The rationally undefended 'moral' practice or belief should first be considered under our first three facets of morality. If, when it is judged or tested in this way, it appears to be beneficent it surely becomes incumbent on both parties in the dispute *equally* to look for and propose possible rationalisations of it, so that fruitful discussion of its grounds and implications can begin. Meanwhile, pending the required discovery or proposal, the assailant party, while, of course, entitled to reject the belief in question, will also be wise to acknowledge that his rejection of it is provisional and to express this rejection with a decent respect.

We have now discussed three classic mistakes of moral philosophy: (*a*) the assumption that moral autonomy requires a singly based system of morals or that the moral field can be demarcated by a single sufficient principle; (*b*) neglect of the affinity between moral and historical judgments, with the consequent persistent use of the wrong model for moral certainty (*c*) the identification of rationality in moral matters with demonstrative insight rather than with the habit of discussion. And in the light of our corrections of these mistakes, we can now turn back to the question which we left outstanding at the end of the previous chapter. This arose from the fact that many moral conflicts appear to be due to our adherences to different particular uses of some essentially contested concept e.g. that of democracy or of social justice. And the question was whether, if we tried to apply some form of universalisability criterion in cases of this kind, we must include adherence to our particular interpretation of e.g. democracy in our idea of that 'similar situation' in which we would expect other rational people to act or choose as we do. This question seems an embarrassing one, since at first sight an affirmative answer will render the universalisability criterion trivial, while a negative answer will render it inapplicable to what may seem to be among the most important moral choices we are ever called upon to make.

Let us begin by transposing the problem and ask how adherence to a particular use of some essentially contested concept should be regarded in the discussion of moral problems. From this point of view what is most striking is the recognition, which such a use implies, that there are other historically and logically permissible uses of it which work in opposition to our own. We want to see democracy advanced in a certain form and in certain directions; but we recognise that others have very different ideas about it—ideas which they are, logically and historically, entitled and indeed committed to defend. No matter, therefore, how feeble we find their defences to be, we cannot baldly assert that others ought, morally, to regard and to practice democracy as we do; for here also, although in a somewhat unusual sense, 'ought implies can'. Or alternatively we could say: the use of characteristically moral terms presupposes not only the possibility, but the actual hope and will for moral agreement even in situations where this seems improbable or in which it can only take curiously self-disguising forms. (As in our examples of the two administrators or of the two friends belonging to widely differing cultures.) By contrast, anyone who recognises that his own use of, say, the concept of democracy is essentially contestable, will, of course, believe that his own use of it is the right, in the sense of the orthodox one, but he will not be in a position to arraign other contestant uses and users of it as morally wrong and therefore to be won over simply by moral argument to his way of thinking. His attitude can only be that, while logically and historically permissible, these other uses of the concept are mistaken and their users unfortunate.

This does not mean, however, that recognition of the essentially contested character of the concept of democracy is something entirely negative or irrelevant from the moral point of view. Such recognition is of great moral importance, since it points to an area which calls for moral tolerance and, more specifically, for the abatement of the normal exercise of the will-to-agreement. Thus it would almost certainly be useless for a Western democrat to urge or implore a convinced communist by moral arguments to abandon his particular way of regarding democracy. But it could be most useful to get the communist to admit that there are historically and logically permissible uses of the term democracy over and above the one which he himself favours. To admit this would not be, of course, to take any positive step towards moral agreement; but it could mean the removal of one important barrier to the possibility of such steps being envisaged or attempted.

Thus to return the question whether in applying the universalisability criterion we must in some cases consider an individual's adherence to one particular use of an essentially contested concept, we can now answer: the question, although apparently so crucial, and in truth so morally suggestive, is nevertheless inapposite and confused. The peculiar complex of loyalties, oppositions and recognitions of permissibility, which make up the use of any essentially contested concept, represent a stage in the moral dialectic at which direct yes-or-no moral questions cannot be significantly put. Does this mean, then, that the moral demand for agreement or hope of ultimate agreement must here be abandoned? The answer is: yes, so long as the terms of the dispute remain fixed—as in most cases they are likely to do for the foreseeable future. Theoretically, of course, it is always possible that the contesting parties will, whether in the interests of moral unification or for other reasons, agree to a moratorium on competition between their respective uses of the concept in question; and they might thus attain by degrees to the kind of position indicated by our examples on page 204. And something like this position, in fact, exists, rarely and morally precariously no doubt, but more often and morally much more vitally than the language of our main intellectual conflicts would lead us to believe.

Chapter 10

METAPHYSICS AS HISTORY

MORAL judgments, I have argued, can usefully be assimilated to historical judgments inasmuch as their ultimate concern is with individual choices and actions, taking place here and now or there and then. To be sure, the historian's interest in a particular action is directed on to much besides its moral worth or appropriateness – always supposing that this interests him at all. But let his interest be solely in an action's political or economic motives, its dramatic appeal or its technical competence or tactical efficacy, that interest will develop towards final judgment and appreciation by a process of following, understanding and assessing – always in the light of a complex framework of criteria – such as we have seen to be necessary to moral judgment. In both cases we achieve a kind of understanding which cannot be reduced to the application (or applicability) of a set of general rules to certain 'cases' or 'case histories'. Yet it is one of the curiosities of the critical philosophy of history, and equally of moral philosophy, that this important point of resemblance should generally have passed unnoticed; and that the claims of the historical approach, in connection with philosophy, should have been pushed most vigorously in an area from which the notion of individual choice and action seems particularly remote, viz. in metaphysics; the study of those strangely insubstantial yet all-pervasive beliefs which are so much part of the intellectual air we breathe that some philosophers have tried to deny their existence, while many have dismissed their practical import as nugatory. The verbal forms and associated imagery in which metaphysical beliefs can be expressed vary greatly from age to age and from civilisation to civilisation. But what seems common to all metaphysical statements is their concern with the kind or degree of intelligibility which we can hope to find within given areas, and also between different areas, of our experience. And it is characteristic of metaphysical statements that they claim to show us why there can be just such and such a kind or degree of intelligibility, within or between different areas, and no other. They claim to tell us what in these very general respects must be so, if we are to understand adequately anything that actually is. Unfortunately, as our understanding of what exists in any given field increases, our respect for its formally accepted metaphysical conditions is likely to dwindle.

A bold and suggestive case for the historical character of metaphysics was put forward by Collingwood in his *Essay on Metaphysics*. His thesis can be summarised as follows. Every statement of science or history or common sense arises in answer to a question, or presupposes a question which may or may not be actually articulated. Similarly that question rests on the real or assumed acceptance of certain facts or truths, each of which in its turn can be shown to be an answer to, and hence to presuppose, some prior question. Hence acceptance of any statement as true can be shown to rest upon a train of questions and suppositions which we must recognise and organise if our thinking is to be logically controlled. But this train of questions and suppositions cannot go back for ever. Ultimately we find ourselves accepting, or find that people in other ages or civilisations have accepted, certain absolute presuppositions, i.e. suppositions with regard to which it is impossible, in contrast to everyday 'relative' presuppositions, to ask what prior question or assumption they presuppose; for absolute presuppositions provide the basic framework within which, and only within which, all the questions of a particular period or civilisation can be significantly put.

Metaphysics, according to Collingwood, is the study of absolute presuppositions. And in so far as it is a valid form of study, metaphysics is an historical study. When properly conceived and conducted, its job is, first, to establish what absolute presuppositions were made or accepted by men who thought in such and such fashions at such and such a time, and, arising out of this, to show how men's absolute presuppositions change in relation to other changes in civilised life and thought. Collingwood has surprisingly little to say about the historical character of the first of these tasks, and what he says suggests the methods of a Socratic philosopher rather than of a thought-historian. His account of the second task, although more adequate, is also curiously telescoped. I shall therefore set out in my own words the kind of explanation and defence which his position on both these scores seems to require.

Collingwood asks us to imagine a metaphysician pressing an experimental scientist back step by step by a succession of demands of the form 'And what prior belief or supposition enabled you to ask that question?' Collingwood assumes that the successive answers from the scientist will become progressively more and more abstract in character until at a crucial point, say when he answers, 'Because, of course, I believe there are universal laws of nature', the scientist will not consent to be questioned further, and will in effect confess that this all-important statement is *not* the answer to any prior question itself resting on some further supposition. Therefore, apparently, the metaphysician has performed his first task and may, so to speak, chalk up one clearly established absolute presupposition. But there is nothing suggestive of historical inquiry in the procedure described so far. Evidently Collingwood had something else in mind, viz. that once the *absolute* character of a particular presupposition P appears to have been established by the scientist's inability to cite a question which evokes it, this presupposition must thereupon be considered and appreciated from an historical point of view. But what exactly would this mean? Presumably that the metaphysician-historian will now be in a position to characterise *historically* the whole body of knowledge which presupposes P, i.e. to appreciate its inherent limitations, and to ask and to discover why these limitations were acceptable to thinkers of a certain period, and so on. The general character of Aristotelian science, for example, will best be disclosed by an understanding not simply of the existence, but also of the acceptability of its absolute presuppositions. And similarly, *mutatis mutandis* with Newtonian science.

But why, to turn now to the second part of Collingwood's historical claim about the nature of metaphysics, why do scientists in every age accept certain presuppositions as absolute, i.e. as without the possibility of further question and still prior presuppositions? Collingwood's answer is that the absolute presuppositions of a given stage in science serve to express the condition within which its questions and hypotheses can be significantly put forward and its tests significantly applied. Collingwood goes on to point out that leading scientists today, while accepting certain absolute presuppositions, are aware of the fact that they or their predecessors have dropped or adjusted certain others. Now metaphysics has sometimes been conceived, e.g., by Kant in some of his writings, as the study of the absolute presuppositions of science, but always with the presumption or hope that the absolute presuppositions to be disclosed are the right ones, the final ones, the only necessary and sufficient ones. What is original in Collingwood is his total rejection of this hope, and his bold assertion that metaphysics must be an historical study, i.e. must be content simply to explain how and why successive sets of absolute presuppositions came to be believed, or to be rejected and replaced by others. Finally, Collingwood argues that any absolute presupposition, e.g. the statement that every physical event must be explicable by some set of universal laws, is always found as a member or element in a loosely organised whole which he calls a 'metaphysical constellation'. The absolute presuppositions which make up such a whole must evidently be – or at least must appear to be – mutually compatible. But, he insists, none must strictly or logically require or be required by another. Otherwise the constellation could be reduced to a small number of 'primitive' absolute presuppositions. In rejecting this possibility Collingwood rejects the common metaphysical practice of seeking to assimilate metaphysics to a deductive system. Quite the contrary, in his view, since history is essentially open-ended, the essentially historical function of metaphysics is one that can never be completed.

Collingwood's defence of this thesis was, as he himself would have admitted, brief and programmatic. And the examples by which he tries to clarify it are by no means equally happily chosen. (Despite the astonishing width of his culture and of his intellectually creative powers, Collingwood shows little detailed knowledge of the history of science, and little perceptiveness where scientific aims and methods are concerned.) But the criticisms now to be made against his thesis are not intended in any way to belittle its value. On the contrary, their purpose is to indicate the kind of work that will have to be done if Collingwood's insights, suitably modified and extended, are to win the recognition and continuing support that they deserve.

(a) What exactly is the force of the adjective 'absolute' in Collingwood's key notion of absolute presuppositions? He tells us that he is referring to the kind of presupposition that is not and cannot be questioned at a given stage of scientific thinking. Now, the term 'absolute' usually means 'subject to no conditions'. But in order to propound his theory of metaphysics as history, Collingwood has to admit that all the suppositions which he calls absolute are, in fact, absolute only under very special conditions of general information and of analytical skill. They are, in brief, absolute relatively to a given stage of science. But in the history of science stages are not so clearly marked off from each other as Collingwood's account suggests. Queer people in all ages succeed in asking queer questions, and are not always successfully 'shut up' by the orthodox. But, to press the point more specifically, how (in defence of Collingwood's account) would one set about trying to demonstrate that a particular presupposition really was absolute at and for a particular stage of scientific thought? Presumably by attempting an imaginary logical experiment, by trying to see what would happen if we tried to explain, say, the movement of bodies without presupposing a certain geometry or to discuss changes in living forms without presupposing that larger-scale forms can always be explained in terms of smaller, and not *vice versa*. No doubt in the course of trying to effect the proposed logical experiment, we should in most cases find our capacity to speak and think about the field in question quite quickly crumbling into a senseless chaos. But, apart from the possibility of cases where the experiment might at once yield fruitful results, there would also certainly be borderline cases: presuppositions which everyone took to be absolute a decade or so ago, but which sensitive intellects are beginning to find irksomely restrictive and whose possible abandonment revolutionary spirits are beginning to prepare for and perhaps even to work for. In fine, the notion of absolute presuppositions is not as clear as Collingwood believed; and what is more important, there is something arbitrary about the place where the line between absolute and relative presupposition is to be drawn. But this very arbitrariness adds to the persuasiveness of Collingwood's general thesis, that the existence and acceptance of a given metaphysical thesis in a particular age or circle is something to be described and explained historically rather than justified by some kind of deductive or quasi-deductive proof.

(b) Being himself an historian of distinction, Collingwood was well aware of the fact that historical stages or epochs are not the neat tidy things that writers of historical textbooks may lead non-historians to imagine. 'One phase changes into another,' he tells us, 'because the first phase was in unstable equilibrium and had in itself the seeds of change, and indeed of that change. Its fabric was not at rest: it was always under strain.' And again, 'When there is no strain there is no history.' And again, 'A reformed metaphysics will conceive any constellation of absolute propositions as having in its structure not the simplicity and calm that characterise the subject-matter of mathematics but the intricacy and restlessness that characterise the subject-matter, say, of legal or constitutional history.'[1] All this is well said, despite its Hegelian ring, against those metaphysicians, Hegel included, who have presented their metaphysics as a complete quasi-deductive system. Nevertheless Collingwood retains more than a trace of the Hegelian tendency to see the strains and conflicts in the history-that-is-to-be-metaphysics as so many necessary hurdles or turn-styles along the one main line of intellectual advance. And if the history of philosophy teaches us anything, it is that we cannot truly describe metaphysics in this crudely progressivist way. The characteristic metaphysical situation is not that of one dominant constellation of absolute presuppositions, in temporary if uneasy equipoise, giving some kind of unity and direction to particular scientific theories and experiments. It is rather that of one absolute presupposition ranged against its contrary, or of some well-marked 'constellation' ranged against its rival. Moreover, these conflicts between absolute presuppositions, far from being invariably absorbed or 'uplifted' in some more developed and reconciling unity, seem rather to be repeated again and again in the history of philosophy, perhaps most obviously in periods of greatest intellectual vigour. Collingwood's presumption that metaphysical 'constellations' show a process of change that keeps step with every major scientific advance here does a disservice to the history of ideas by prolonging the myth of a single European tradition, or of a single rationalist movement or perennial philosophy. His conception of metaphysics as an historical study is a heroic attempt to break away from the kind of intellectual overlordship which metaphysicians have traditionally claimed and tried to exercise over other intellectual disciplines; but the task of breaking clean away from tradition is, here as elsewhere, more difficult than at first appears.

(c) Lastly, how exactly did Collingwood see the kind of relationship which holds between an absolute presupposition (or constellation of absolute presuppositions) on the one hand and a scientific theory or style or group of theories on the other? On this issue what he says is so crudely oversimplified as to endanger the value of his whole thesis. He talks of the 'logical efficacy' of suppositions, absolute or relative, meaning by this their power of 'causing questions'.[2] But this is a hopelessly vague as well as unnatural way of talking. A presupposition can properly be said to be necessary to, or to permit, the putting of some question; but no sense can be given to the idea of a presupposition as a sufficient condition or cause of the putting of a question, or alternatively of the putting of a question as being a necessary consequence of some particular presupposition. The fact is, of course, that every question has an enormous number of presuppositions, most of them far too trivial or obvious to be worth stating. But one simply cannot conceive of a situation in which acceptance of no matter how many presuppositions could be said to cause or necessitate the putting of a question. The most that could ever be expected – and this is something which Collingwood ignores – is that certain presuppositions not only permit but have the effect of encouraging questions of a certain kind. Such presuppositions (which are for the most part if not entirely absolute ones) operate, therefore, as regulative principles or maxims. They guide us along certain lines of thought, they prompt us perhaps to put certain questions, but they cannot cause us to think or to ask anything. Or, to speak more exactly, metaphysical propositions, or statements of absolute presuppositions, do not entail any specific scientific consequences. Nor is it at all obvious that any particular absolute presupposition (or constellation of absolute presuppositions) is ever uniquely required by any specific scientific results. On the contrary, at various times in the history of science two or more incompatible sets of absolute presuppositions have been held by scientists who were virtually at one as to the acceptability of the scientific discoveries whose metaphysical presuppositions were in question. This situation is perhaps most likely to arise in the early phases of any science, e.g. in Greek astronomy; but it is hardly less marked in the case of eighteenth-century dynamics which seemed to different minds of outstanding clarity and candour to presuppose positions as radically different as theistic panpsychism, common sense (including deistic) dualism, and an aggressively atheistic materialism. But further, we should recall that scientists, when they turn for support to metaphysics, tend to do so in a most *ad hoc* and opportunist fashion, more in the manner of a man who is rummaging in the rag-bag of currently acceptable proverbs to find one that will suit his cause than of one who is convinced that there must exist, ready to hand, some constellation of absolute presuppositions which will match his own preferred scientific methods and conclusions. Quite commonly indeed a scientific revolution has had to wait many generations before the true shape of its metaphysical presuppositions could be described. This was certainly true of the idea of the electric field; and who will claim that the metaphysical presuppositions of contemporary physics and biology have been effectively canvassed, still less generally agreed?[3]

What do these criticisms add up to? And how much of Collingwood's thesis do they leave intact? I would say that, whilst showing that it requires drastic revision and modification, they do not detract greatly from its importance. Most of them could, I believe, be woven into a strengthened version of the Collingwood thesis, which might run somewhat as follows: Metaphysical statements make up an important, indeed an essential, although all too easily misinterpreted, strand in the general history of ideas. This strand consists of those presuppositions of science or of any disciplined thinking which are generally accepted in a given period and which cannot be effectively questioned (and *a fortiori* cannot be effectively tested) in that period. The historical study of metaphysical statements is naturally and normally carried right up into the contemporary scene; and doing metaphysics means trying to appreciate, trying to see the general influence of certain temporarily absolute presuppositions, whether of contemporary physics or of eighteenth-century psychology or of the classificatory sciences of earlier epochs. The relations between temporarily absolute presuppositions and the inquiries and theses and theories which find support in them are, indeed, far more complicated and erratic than Collingwood recognised. Not only may radically opposed metaphysical constellations claim to give needed guidance and support to one and the same set of scientific procedures and conclusions, it may well be that such conflicts, the claims and counterclaims of different metaphysical voices, have a stimulating effect upon the science in question. Metaphysics, although it has its effective existence in relation to science and other intellectual disciplines, is certainly not itself a science; nor has it ever been, in fact, of great or sustained interest to practising scientists. It has been advanced by philosophers, not least those who have maintained an almost continuous barrage against its pretensions, but only to give it new life—like that of a mildly chastened phoenix. But neither, on the other hand, is metaphysics logic, in the sense that the relations of its statements to the statements of the sciences are ever those of logical entailment. Nor is it a primarily linguistic study, since its main job is to pick out and in a proper sense explain the characteristic function of those verbal expressions that we call metaphysical. That function is, broadly speaking, of the kind that Kant and others have described as *regulative*. Metaphysical statements commend certain lines or styles of research and discourage others. This function cannot be expressed in a single supremely general formula, applicable to all specific cases. On the contrary a metaphysical statement can be understood only (*a*) in contrast to other opposed metaphysical statements, including in particular those which it has itself replaced or drastically revised, (*b*) in the light of the reasons which led to that replacement or revision, and (*c*) in the light of its actual *modus operandi*, i.e. the ways in which scientists use it to justify their preference for a particular way of formulating or a particular method of interpreting, some outstanding problem. In fine, the temporarily unquestioned and indeed unquestionable character of metaphysical statements, which suggest dogmatism or intellectual defeatism when these statements are considered simply in relation to the sciences which presuppose them, can be rendered perfectly intelligible, followable, acceptable – in the only sense of these words that is here appropriate – when they are considered from the historical point of view.

But this account provokes an obvious objection. This cannot be the *whole* truth about metaphysics. When philosophers are 'doing' metaphysics they are not simply trying to understand their predecessors' or their contemporaries' or even their own metaphysical theories. The metaphysical activity must *be* something, must be intelligible in terms of what it actually is, before it can be appreciated historically. Or, to urge the point in more colourful language, before it can be appreciated and assessed historically, metaphysics must be *created*. Strange that Collingwood should here have neglected creation – as completely as any nineteenth-century positivist could ever have done! But, of course, to forget the reality of intellectual creation, to confine one's description of intellectual achievement to already created doctrines is absurd: as absurd in its way as the behaviourist error of equating the living thoughts and deeds of men with certain of their audible and visible bodily manifestations. This objection seems at first blush as forceful as it is natural. But as applied specifically to metaphysics it can, I think, be countered as follows.

As we saw in Chapter 6, it is a mistake to imagine that any human activity can be understood in a functional yet entirely non-historical manner, i.e. in terms of the specific way in which it fulfils its allotted task, without any reference to how and why *that particular* way came to be preferred or accepted. If, on the other hand, by 'doing metaphysics' is meant 'creating metaphysics', i.e. doing what Aristotle, Spinoza and others did in their inspired moments, then possibly a purely descriptive account of what then 'went on in their heads' would not include any specific reference to the historic doctrines which they were replacing and revising (those of Plato and the Eleatics in the case of Aristotle, those of Aristotle himself, of the Stoics, of Maimonides and of Descartes in the case of Spinoza). But if asked, after their creative visionary moments had passed, what they had seen in the course of them, their only possible answers would have been–and were–that *in contrast to what their great and revered predecessors had taught,* the absolute presuppositions of all then existing science (and in Spinoza's thought of all rational conduct) were of the kind that we now know as Aristotelian or Spinozist. What matters in philosophy is not what is seen but what can be said–what is sayable and therefore intelligible–after the seeing.

One further consideration predisposes me strongly towards Collingwood's account of metaphysics, for all that he himself might well have rejected it. Readers of his *Essay on Metaphysics* will recall that, although in its brilliant opening section the main target of Collingwood's criticism is traditional quasi-deductive metaphysical systems, yet he devotes much of the second part of his book to an angry attack on the Positivists' rejection or refutation of metaphysics. It seems to me, however, that Collingwood's conception of metaphysics as a uniquely important strand in intellectual history is one which the Positivists could perfectly well have accepted with gratitude, or might well have propounded for themselves had they been inventive or learned enough to think of it. There is, of course, a sense in which all human activities and institutions, including all the systematic sciences, can be brought under the purview of history.[4] In the case of the systematic sciences, however, there are agreed criteria of their proper achievements, irrespective of their origins in and influences upon the history – the progress or the mêlée – of intellectual endeavour. But the only way, on Collingwood's account, of seeing the sense, the force, the significance of metaphysical statements is by following their track here below, by seeing how they came to be, what they did, how they guided one piece of scientific theorising or frustrated another, how and why they came to be modified or discarded. In this way Collingwood has succeeded in putting salt on the tail of Kant's soaring dove and has found her a niche which, if narrow, is nevertheless respectable and indeed indispensable in the general structure of knowledge.

Alternatively we can say: Collingwood and the Positivists are at one in rejecting any *metaphysical account* or *justification* of metaphysical statements, whether of the straightforward would-be-deductive kind offered by Spinoza or of the 'transcendental' kind offered by Kant and his followers. That there should exist metaphysical moods, longings, speculations; that these curious interpersonal drives should have existed and should have found such expression as has enabled them to serve as regulative principles and so play an important part in the development of scientific theories – these are things for which it is idle to look for a demonstrative explanation or justification. (All Spinoza-type metaphysical deductive systems are fallacious, resting as they do on innumerable suppressed premisses: all Kant-type transcendental proofs are circular, for all that they may contain important insights into the conditions of acquiring different types of knowledge.) The simple truth is that we were not in at the emergence of mind or the creation of the cosmos and we only became aware of metaphysical issues – and became aware of them through developments of language primarily serving very different practical interests—at a very late stage in the process. By that time all our basic metaphysical tendencies, pulling us now this way, now that, were already in place, and all that we can hope to do with them is to distinguish the different uses— some fruitful, some barren, some absurd—to which they have been and are currently being put. Hence, on the view here defended, the task of metaphysics is simply to give us a follow-able and acceptable account of how certain regulative principles (often unhappily articulated and therefore capable of gross misuse) arose, came to dominance and perhaps declined during a certain period of intellectual history. I can see no reason why such straightforward contributions to intellectual history should be unacceptable to Positivists. If, on the other hand, Positivism be taken to involve a denial of the existence of regulative principles in the sciences, then this affinity between Collingwood and the Positivists ceases to hold. But so, in that case, does the claim of Positivism to be a serious philosophy of science.

This account of metaphysical statements and systems is bound to seem disappointing to some readers, since it amounts to a promise or a project, viz. that intellectual history could be developed in such a fashion that it could take the place of, and (among other things) fulfil the only valid functions of traditional metaphysical statements and systems. On this issue, I am sure that Collingwood's guess was right, but until the task is actually done there is no possible way of proving this. Again, it may be felt that in reducing metaphysics to one strand in the general fabric of intellectual and cultural history, we are ignoring what is most peculiar to them: the grotesque, pedantic, violent, pretentious, paradoxical yet unquestionably heroic intellectual achievements which they express. At the very least (it may rightly be felt) metaphysical statements stand up like monu-ments, marking certain extreme positions, the attainment of which can never be repeated or equalled. No one will ever again step out in the same untried direction as Parmenides did, and no one will ever go farther in that direction than he did. And what is true of Parmenides is true, *mutatis mutandis*, of Democritus, of Aristotle, of Aquinas, of Spinoza and even of

Hume. Metaphysical statements may be construed by historians of thought and culture as regulative principles: but taken literally or at their face value, they express total intellectual outlooks, which, however logically defective, have a sublimity of their own. We can certainly admit the propriety of such feelings: indeed they are to be expected in any intellectually sensitive reader of the great metaphysical systems of the past. And we may hope the special quality or pathos of great metaphysical systems will long continue to 'come over' in historical accounts of how they arose and what they did within intellectual history. But if we want a *salutation* of their greatness, rather than a description of what they said and why, we had better turn to poetry–to Lucretius or Dante or Yeats–than to intellectual history.

A similar point arises over the educative value of metaphysics. Besides understanding them–understanding what they said and why, and what influence they exercised and why–we may also, if our temperaments are so inclined, gain a great stimulus from the very arrogance of the intellectual aspirations which metaphysical systems express. (Kant felt this to the full, if any man did.) And similarly we may gain something of immense value from living within some of the endless conflicts to which metaphysical theses and systems almost invariably give rise. To have succeeded, no matter how precariously and briefly, in seeing the point of Scholastic Realism although we are born within a Nominalist tradition, or to have felt the spell of Monism whilst we remain fettered to the pluralist spirit of the empirical sciences, is to have experienced, in a particularly telling form, the kind of self-transcendence which is the supreme reward of historical study. That human thought and aspiration should have been pulled now this way and now that, and should have been whipped forward by so many conflicting intellectual demands and tendencies, is not only a truth worth knowing; it is a matter for wonder and for a proper humility. Thus metaphysics also, despite its seeming aridity, can reflect the tragic conflicts and divisions that are inherent in all re-inspiration of civilised life. And metaphysics also can encourage us to strive for that ideal of generous-mindedness which Hegel glimpsed, only to distort so monstrously to meet the needs of his system, but which his friend and fellow student Hölderlin had already expressed with incomparable power in the lines quoted at the beginning of this book.

> Therefore, since round us are heaped
> The summits of time,
> And those that are dearest are near yet languishing on
> Most separate mountains,
> So give us innocent water,
> O give us wings of the mind most faithfully
> To cross over and to return.

NOTES

Chapter 1

1. Antoine Augustin Cournot, French mathematician and economist (1801–1877). Cournot's most important treatments of our topic are to be found in Chapter XX of *Essai sur les fondements de nos connaissances*, 1851 (English translation *An Essay on the Foundations of our Knowledge* by Merritt H. Moore, Liberal Arts Press, New York, 1956, see pp. 435–89), and in Chapter I of *Traité de l'enchainement des idées fondamentales dans les sciences et dans l'histoire* 1861. The latter treatment has been historically the more important and is referred to by, e.g., Collingwood and J. B. Bury; but the suggestive image of the chess game comes from Chapter XX of the earlier work.

2. See p. 452 of Moore's translation of the *Essai*.

3. See *Gesammelte Schriften VII Band*, especially pp. 191 ff. For an excellent exposition of Dilthey's mature views on our topic, see *The Philosophy of Wilhelm Dilthey* by H. A. Hodges, 1952, especially Chapter IX.

4. For a short and readable account of Rickert's views, see *Kulturwissenschaft und Naturwissenschaft*, 1894. For a fuller treatment, embodying Rickert's general theory of knowledge, see his major work *Grenzen der Naturwissenschaftlichen Begriffsbildung*, especially pp. 294–430.

5. See especially Part V, Sections 1–2, but Collingwood's best ideas are scattered right through the body of his book.

6. See, e.g., the essays collected in Part II of the composite volume *Theory and History*, edited by Patrick Gardiner, The Free.Press, Glencoe, Illinois, 1959.

7. See *The Poverty of Historicism*, especially pp. 140–1.

Chapter 2

1. This conclusion can usefully be applied to the classic philosophical problem of our knowledge of other minds. Three theories are today commonly canvassed on this issue. First the traditional theory that, whilst we all learn to read the thoughts and purposes of others with a seeming directness, anyhow in familiar circums-

tances, yet this capacity is based upon and can only be justified by its analogy with our knowledge, which *is* direct, of our own thoughts and purposes. Second, that our knowledge of the thoughts and purposes—if not of the private feelings—of other people *is* as direct as our knowledge of our own: since what we call the thoughts and purposes of others (or of ourselves) are simply certain selected parts of their conduct considered and gauged in respect of certain 'mental marking schedules', in particular intelligence and retentiveness. Now this kind of considering and gauging, it is urged, is done quite as directly, and often much more easily, in the case of other people's conduct than of our own. And thirdly, that since the language by which we describe our own minds and conduct is, disregarding a few minor adjustments, identical with that which we use to describe the minds and conduct of others, we inevitably think of our own mind and that of the next man in the same general way. Despite differences in the cues for our ascription of mental qualities in the two cases, the kind of judgment that results is of the same general kind because it must be expressed in the same general terms: hence the other man's thoughts and purposes (assuming that I can learn how to describe them) are as directly *intelligible* to me, and therefore as directly knowable by me, as are my own.

Recent philosophical discussion shows that there is something to be said for each of these theories; but it should be equally clear, if only from our recent discussion, that none of them comes near to being the whole truth. This is, rather, that the capacity to read other people's intentions 'directly', and to construe their intentions in the light of our own, and to know truly what we ourselves are about, and to apply 'mental' words correctly and perceptively whether to ourselves or others, are all parts of facets of a single process that is never complete. There is always room for improvement in our appreciation of the thoughts of others and indeed in our awareness of the reality of others: always room for improvement in our most 'humanistic' use of language; and always room for improvement in our self-knowledge. My suggestion is that the experience of following stories provides, in peculiarly concentrated form, all the ingredients of this process, which is the process of growing up—or, more literally, of at once growing *out* and growing *in*.

Chapter 3

1. See *The Idea of History*, pp. 246 ff.
2. See Ibid., pp. 257 ff and index.

NOTES

Chapter 4

1. Quoted from *The Task of Cultural History*, translated from the Dutch text to form the first essay of *Men and Ideas* (see p. 54), London, 1960.
2. From a fragment written in the 1830s and published in translation as part of Section 3 of Part I of *The Varieties of History*, edited by Fritz Stern, see p. 59.
3. Quoted from Section 5 of Part II of *The Varieties of History*, edited by Fritz Stern, see p. 291.
4. See Preface as translated to form part of Section 3 of Fritz Stern's *The Varieties of History*, quoted at page 88.
5. G. R. Dennis's translation, London, 1909, p. 68.
6. See *Le fil de l'épée* (1959 edition), p. 98. Compare some of the opening sentences of this extraordinarily penetrating work. 'L'action de guerre revêt essentiellement le caractère de la contingence. . . . A la guerre comme à la vie, on pourrait appliquer le: "πάντα ρεῖ" du philosophe grec; ce qui eut lieu n'aura plus lieu, jamais, et l'action, quelle qu'elle soit, aurait fort bien pu ne pas être ou être autrement. . . . Ce caractère de contingence, propre à l'action de guerre, fait la difficulté et la grandeur de la conception.'

Chapter 5

1. See the essays contributed to *Theory and History* (ref. footnote 6 on page 14) by Hempel, Nagel, Gallie Frankel, Donagan and Scriven.
2. See, e.g., Fustel de Coulanges' Inaugural Lecture at Strasburg, reprinted as part of Section XI of *The Varieties of History*, edited by Fritz Stern, pp. 179 ff.
3. See, e.g., Ranke's preamble to Book V of *The Papacy*: pp. 394–5 in E. Foster's translation.
4. See, e.g., Peter Geyl, *Debates with Historians*, esp. pp. 156–72.
5. See, e.g., Sir Winston Churchill's treatment of the Camaret Bay letter episode in *Marlborough, His Life and Times*, Vol. I, chapters 21–25.
6. See *The Poverty of Historicism*, pp. 149 ff.
7. Ibid., p. 141.
8. See Inaugural Lecture referred to in footnote 2 above.

NOTES

Chapter 6

1. I say principles *or quasi-principles* because, of course, there is something strange about an alleged principle which is concerned, not with such and such a kind of case or situation, but expressly with those particular situations which escape the net of our usual classificatory and predictive systems.

Chapter 7

1. Lord Acton calculated that the average period of dominance of a philosophical school or movement was about twenty years: presumably made up of ten years of dominant teaching by a master and ten years of still fertile practice of his methods by his disciples.
2. Abelard is an exception to this rule. And, of course, it might be held that many of the great mediaeval thinkers embodied their ethical views in their contributions to political and social philosophy.
3. See Professor S. Körner's 'On philosophical arguments in physics', pp. 97–101 of *Observation and Interpretation*, A Symposium of Philosophers and Physicists, Butterworth Scientific Publications, 1957.

Chapter 8

1. I call this claim confused for the following reason. The claim that description (*a*) is of absolute, paramount (and perhaps also of logically sufficient) character is commonly grounded upon two *liberal* principles or beliefs, viz. (1) that those political liberties that are enjoyed by all (or almost all) our citizens deserve protection primarily because *all* traditionally accepted liberties (no matter how restricted the enjoyment of them) are things that *prima facie* deserve protection, and (2) that the existence of a wide variety of liberties (enjoyed by different ranges of our citizens) has been historically and remains today a *necessary* condition of our specifically *democratic* values and achievements. Both these claims, I would say, reflect our grasp of a particular historical truth of immense importance, viz. as to how democracy has taken root and flourished in the west. But if they are put forward as universal political truths expressing the necessary conditions of *any* genuinely democratic aspirations or achievements, then they are surely open to question. To many people in the world today they must seem indeed, not so much questionable as utterly—and in a sense

insultingly–irrelevant to their actual situation. What is the relevance of a Burkian philosophy of political liberties to the great majority of Asians and Africans today?

Chapter 10

1. See *Essay on Metaphysics*, p. 77.
2. See *Essay on Metaphysics*, p. 29.
3. See Professor S. Körner's essay in *Observation and Interpretation* referred to at p. 279 above: cf. also Körner's *Conceptual Thinking*, Chapters 30 ff.
4. As Lord Acton remarked, 'History is not only a particular branch of knowledge, but a particular mode and method of knowledge in other branches. . . . It embraces other sciences, records their progress and the tests by which their truths have been ascertained.' Quoted by Herbert Butterfield, p. 97 of *Man on His Past*.

INDEX

INDEX

INDEX